Euroconstitutionalism and Its Discontents

OXFORD CONSTITUTIONAL THEORY

Series Editors:

Martin Loughlin, John P. McCormick, and Neil Walker

Oxford Constitutional Theory has rapidly established itself as the primary point of reference for theoretical reflections on the growing interest in constitutions and constitutional law in domestic, regional, and global contexts. The majority of the works published in the series are monographs that advance new understandings of their subject. But the series aims to provide a forum for further innovation in the field by also including well-conceived edited collections that bring a variety of perspectives and disciplinary approaches to bear on specific themes in constitutional thought and by publishing English translations of leading monographs in constitutional theory that have originally been written in languages other than English.

ALSO AVAILABLE IN THE SERIES

Beyond the People
Social Imaginary and Constituent Imagination
Zoran Oklopcic

The Metaethics of Constitutional Adjudication
Boško Tripković

Carl Schmitt's State and Constitutional Theory
A Critical Analysis
Benjamin A. Schupmann

Law and Revolution
Legitimacy and Constitutionalism After the Arab Spring
Nimer Sultany

Constitutional and Political Theory
Selected Writings
Ernst-Wolfgang Böckenförde
Edited by Mirjam Künkler and Tine Stein

Constitutionalism
Past, Present, and Future
Dieter Grimm

Europe's Functional Constitution
A Theory of Constitutionalism Beyond the State
Turkuler Isiksel

Post Sovereign Constitution Making
Learning and Legitimacy
Andrew Arato

Popular Sovereignty in Early Modern Constitutional Thought
Daniel Lee

The Cultural Defense of Nations
A Liberal Theory of Majority Rights
Liav Orgad

The Cosmopolitan Constitution
Alexander Somek

The Structure of Pluralism
Victor M. Muniz-Fraticelli

Constitutional Courts and Deliberative Democracy
Conrado Hübner Mendes

Fault Lines of Globalization
Legal Order and the Politics of A-Legality
Hans Lindahl

The Cosmopolitan State
H. Patrick Glenn

After Public Law
Edited by Cormac Mac Amhlaigh, Claudio Michelon, and Neil Walker

Euroconstitutionalism and Its Discontents

Oliver Gerstenberg

OXFORD
UNIVERSITY PRESS

OXFORD
UNIVERSITY PRESS

Great Clarendon Street, Oxford, OX2 6DP,
United Kingdom

Oxford University Press is a department of the University of Oxford.
It furthers the University's objective of excellence in research, scholarship,
and education by publishing worldwide. Oxford is a registered trade mark of
Oxford University Press in the UK and in certain other countries

First Edition published in 2018

Impression: 1

Published in the United States of America by Oxford University Press
198 Madison Avenue, New York, NY 10016, United States of America

British Library Cataloguing in Publication Data

Data available

Library of Congress Control Number: 2018961474

ISBN 978–0–19–883433–5

Printed and bound by
CPI Group (UK) Ltd, Croydon, CR0 4YY

Preface

> *Whether the constitutional essentials covering the basic freedoms are satisfied is more or less visible on the face of constitutional arrangements and how these can be seen to work in practice. But whether the aims of the principles covering social and economic inequalities are realized is far more difficult to ascertain. These matters are nearly always open to wide differences of reasonable opinion; they rest on complicated inferences and intuitive judgments that require us to assess complex social and economic information about topics poorly understood. Thus, [. . .] we can expect more agreement about whether the principles for the basic rights and liberties are realized. This is not a difference about what are the correct principles but simply a difference in the difficulty of seeing whether the principles are achieved.*
>
> John Rawls, Political Liberalism (New York: Columbia University Press 1993), 229–30

The question of the propriety of incorporating 'principles covering social and economic inequalities' in constitutions combines theoretical interest with practical and contemporary political significance. It takes us to the heart of persistent debates about what constitutions can do—the scope of what counts as constitutional questions and who is entitled to participate in deciding them. It invites an exploration and evaluation of the specifically European experience—the jurisprudence of the Court of Justice of the EU (CJEU) and of the European Court of Human Rights (ECtHR)—as representative testcases and illustrations.

As a subject of theoretical concern, the question of what constitutions can do takes us to the heart of constitutional and political theorizing. A longstanding objection to the incorporation of such principles in constitutions focuses on justiciability: courts, it is said, are poorly situated to enforce highly abstract, open-textured, and often costly socioeconomic commitments in the context of particular controversies. Not only would judicial enforcement interfere with the legitimate prerogatives of democratically responsible citizens to decide for themselves through debate and compromise the terms that organize their political association, judicial enforcement would also—given the facts of 'wide differences of reasonable opinion' in ascertaining their actual fulfilment—throw into jeopardy the transparency of a constitution as a shared focus and lodestar of political justification in ideologically deeply divided liberal democracies.

Yet democratic legitimacy also depends on a constitution that deserves recognition in the eyes of the citizens. Citizens in a liberal democracy are expected—and mutually expect one another—to accept and abide by the coercive outcomes of a mutually shared political and legal system even when those outcomes are in conflict with their most deeply held convictions, which set them apart. So the appeal to citizens of a constitution crucially depends on its openness and receptiveness to evolving ideas in society about social justice. The appeal of a constitution rests on its capacity not only to protect the individual against intrusive acts of government, but also to give meaningful expression to a democratic polity's fundamental principles and constitutional value-decisions that permeate the whole legal order, including private law and the law of civil-society relations. These underlying principles must be available for actual critical use and mobilization by the citizens themselves, pushing for ever more inclusive and exhaustive interpretations of the idea of fairness in the basic terms of social co-operation. Yet when it comes to the normative standards associated with egalitarian justice, can courts assist in that process of critical mobilization—or do courts detract from, and distort, democratic self-rule? Can a constitution be simultaneously a higher law of lawmaking and responsive to pluralism and changing social values?

As a question of practical political significance, the question of social constitutionalism, of course, stands in the middle of contemporary debates about the self-understanding of Europe. For reasons of history and democracy, Europeans share a deep commitment to social constitutionalism. But, at the same time, Europe (comprising the EU and the ECtHR) is often excoriated as the epitome of a—from a democratic perspective—disturbing trend towards what is often referred to as a 'judicialization of politics',[1] 'judicial imperialism',[2] or an 'overconstitutionalization'[3]—terms invariably expressing a deep concern with a seemingly self-propagating and unstoppable, if not quasi addictive, reliance by modern polities on courts for addressing their major morally and politically salient

[1] Anne-Marie Slaughter, 'Judicial Globalization', 40 Virginia Journal of International Law 1103 (2000); Ran Hirschl, 'The New Constitution and the Judicialization of Politics Worldwide', 75 Fordham Law Review 721 (2006).

[2] Robert Badinter and Stephen Breyer (eds.), Judges in Contemporary Democracy. An International Conversation (New York: New York University Press 2004).

[3] Dieter Grimm, 'The Democratic Costs of Constitutionalisation: The European Case', 21(4) European Law Journal 460–73 (2015), and more generally idem, 'The Constitution in the Process of Denationalization', 12(4) Constellations 447–63 (2005).

controversies which affect—but increasingly also divide—the citizenry as a whole. It is common ground that, especially over the past fifty years or so, the protection of fundamental rights has become the principal function of courts: a constitution is no longer an instrument that functions in the sphere of politics only. But fundamental rights are often not unqualified or absolute, and they often clash horizontally, meaning that courts must balance between competing values and develop the law. For example, courts, including the CJEU and the ECtHR, must strike a 'fair balance' between economic freedoms and various fundamental social rights; or between economic liberties and fundamental rights to family life or to freedom of conscience; or between free speech and the right to privacy, and so on.

But a first persistent *democratic-minded* worry is that, as a result of judicialization, social rights and protections are thereby weakened as against hegemonic economic liberties or freedoms—'balanced away', as the technique of contemporary proportionality analysis spreads. A second persistent *legalist* worry is that the rule of law itself—in its role of civilizing politics—is thereby thrown into jeopardy. Imposing judicial judgments about justice violates the fundamental constitutional duty of respectful and civil engagement with people with whom one disagrees. The concern is that 'law' is gradually replaced by 'policy' or by transient preferences or opinions of a remote judicial elite, with the dramatic consequence that 'law' no longer stands as a neutral force above, or apart from, politics but itself becomes political throughout, opportunistically exposed to the vagaries of shifting public opinion.

Contemporary Europe therefore seems to be a particularly inhospitable environment for the proposed inquiry. If anything, the specifically European experience seems to demonstrate that courts are not only ill-suited when it comes to redeeming egalitarian principles but even outright detrimental to that project. The deeper suspicion emerging from Europe is that a legal and political culture's entrenched attachment to rights-based legalism-cum-judicial review may render that culture immune against change and unresponsive to changing social values and may stifle the 'constitutional imagination'[4] and thus stand in the way of a 'living constitution' compatible with the claims and dreams of advanced democracy.

In the three chapters of this book, I argue that courts cannot escape the normal political conflicts of pluralistic societies and must enter the

[4] Martin Loughlin, 'The Constitutional Imagination', 78(1) Modern Law Review 1–25 (2015).

real world of politics and its controversies. The various controversies that divide modern societies are political right from the outset, and it is the organization and proceduralization of these controversies that matters. And here courts can nevertheless render an important service to advanced democracy that does not betray but, in fact, vindicates our commitments to both social justice and the rule of law. Courts can channel the discursive evolution of these controversies, ensuring the reaching-out to, and participation of, stakeholders and citizens, including the voices of the hitherto marginalized and despised, and contribute to the gradual emergence and crystallization of an overlapping—but antagonistic—consensus on the applied contextual meaning of constitutional principle.

Indeed, many legal scholars today—especially those who firmly believe that constitutionalism must be responsive to democracy and that democracy necessarily entails respect for social rights—have sought ways to work around and disarm the standard justiciability worry, as I will show in chapter 1, by challenging the doctrine of judicial supremacy which commits constitutional interpretation solely and finally to a constitutional court. Foregoing finality, courts must enter into dialogue with legislatures, administrative agencies, social movements, and other actors in civil society. For its proponents, such dialogic or non court-centric constitutionalism holds the paradoxical promise of being both more democratic and more legitimate by opening a normative and conceptual space for the inclusion of social rights in constitutions.

By engaging with this emergent line of constitutional scholarship, this book argues that, counterintuitively, the retreat from judicial supremacy becomes the most promising and efficient route towards vindicating fundamental and social rights in morally complex and diverse societies. But the proposed retreat can never be a total one—it does not proceed to the very point of a rejection of judicial review altogether as an external, institutionalized supplement on politics, as *political constitutionalists* would have it. Instead, the democratic experimentalist conception of constitutional adjudication—which this book defends—argues that constitutional dialogue occurs around and through processes of judicial interpretation. Without claiming for themselves the final word, courts can exert a more indirect—forum-creative and agenda-setting—role in the process of an ongoing clarification of the meaning of a right. In exerting this role, courts rely less on a *pre-existing consensus*, but a *potential consensus* is sufficient: courts can induce debate and deliberation that leads to consensus. The deliberation-enhancing role of courts depends on their role as 'instigators and non-dictatorial overseers'[5] in a non-hierarchical dialogue in which the conflict parties, state actors, civil society organizations, and the diverse stakeholders themselves develop flexible substantive standards that interpret constitutional requirements, often over repeat litigation.

In other words, the proverbial 'if you don't listen to reason, you will pay a high price' is no empty threat:[6] fundamental rights, in this dialogic process, are no longer merely defensive-negative rights serving as conversation-stopping trump-cards, nor merely 'objective principles' that could be met by any rigid bureaucratic regime, but *destabilization rights*[7] that allow the vulnerable in society to force re-consideration of established—but sometimes thoughtless—routines. On the one hand, judicial judgments never pre-empt or foreclose but provoke and enable deliberation: they are themselves subject to a continuous process of affirmation, resistance, debate, modification, and principled development. But, on the other hand, once authoritative answers begin to crystallize over time, the court will intensify modalities of review and call for substantive compliance with an emergent best-practice consensus on constitutional meaning in particular controversies. The adjudicative process in this way does not undermine but actually deepens and radicalizes democracy by enlarging the repertory of how the various parties, state actors, stakeholders in society, etc. mutually engage with one another.

I will use this democratic-experimentalist conception in chapters 2 and 3 as a foil to evaluate the jurisprudence of the CJEU and of the ECtHR but also to test and develop the conception itself. So, this book is an invitation to search for 'reflective equilibrium', to use John Rawls' familiar concept. Rawls himself noted that this concept has a far wider application beyond political philosophy. It denotes a way of extending and deepening one's understanding of a domain, by searching for an ongoing 'equilibrium' in which framework-principles at a more general level of thought account for the more specific judgments at the level of contextual experience. My aim is to question and ultimately reject the familiar criticism that 'constitutionalization means de-politicization' and closure. Indeed, I will show that both courts—as courts beyond the nation state—in their constitutionalizing jurisprudence are able to constructively *re-open* and

5 Frank Michelman, 'Legitimacy, The Social Turn and Constitutional Review: What Political Liberalism Suggests', in: KritV | CritQ | Rcrit, Jahrgang 98 (2015), Heft 3, pp. 183–205, at p. 199.

6 On this point, cf. Joshua Cohen, Reflections on Deliberative Democracy, in his: Philosophy, Politics, Democracy (Cambridge: Harvard University Press 2009), 341.

7 Charles F. Sabel and William H. Simon, 'Destabilization Rights: How Public Law Litigation Succeeds', in: 117 Harvard Law Review 1016, at 1020 (2003–2004), with reference to Roberto Unger's work.

re-politicize controversies that are blocked at the national level, or which cannot be resolved at the domestic level. In this respect, the emergence of a distinctive form of *Euroconstitutionalism* beyond-the-state is not only the consummation of the political-liberal project but *mutatis mutandis* of the project of radical (or deep) democracy as well.

Acknowledgements

Writing this book has taken me much longer than I thought, although its underlying themes and motives have been with me for a very long time.

Over the years I have accumulated intellectual debts to many individuals, indicated in the footnotes where I could, but—with the usual disclaimer applying—I wish to acknowledge a special debt of personal gratitude, in particular,

to Charles Sabel, for many years of intellectual exchange, collaboration, and of friendship on which I could always count, dating back to 1997: his thinking has deeply inspired my own work and continues to do so, his unwavering encouragement and support throughout the years have also finally enabled me to write and complete this book which reflects, I hope, the spirit of our ongoing discussion;

to Frank Michelman, whom I first met in the early 1990s, whose work initiated me into constitutional theory and showed me the way by setting an (ever unattainable) example, for all the support which he has very generously given me over the years, and also for his immensely helpful comments on the entire first draft of the manuscript;

to Christian Joerges, who introduced me to Europe as a research topic many years ago, when I was still in Germany, and whose work has continued to influence my own to the present day;

to Andy Moravcsik and Anne-Marie Slaughter, at the Center for European Studies at Harvard, then again in the LAPA Program at Princeton, for their generous support and their interest in my project;

to Gráinne de Búrca whom I first met in 1999 in Florence at the EUI where we had offices opposite each other, for her friendship, for our collaboration, and for her encouragement and support;

to Joanne Scott, whom I first met at about the same time, for her friendship, her advice when it mattered, and her crucial support at a critical juncture in my career;

to Takis Tridimas, for our many discussions and our collaboration leading to a joint workshop on dialogic constitutionalism;

to Richard Bellamy, for our many conversations;

to Neil Walker, for his generous support over many years;

to Jonathan Zeitlin, for our ongoing discussion of democratic experimentalism;

to Annabelle Lever, with whom I've shared for many years an interest in the theory of deliberative democracy;

to Jamie Berezin, editor at OUP, for guiding me through the process; and

to Dean Professor Piet Eeckhout for having welcomed me into the UCL Faculty of Laws, and for his kind support.

I owe a debt of a very different kind to my wife Rowshanak Farzaneh-Gerstenberg for her angelic impatience with me over the years.

Oliver Gerstenberg
London
May 2018

Contents

Table of Cases

I. COURT OF JUSTICE OF THE EU (CJEU)

II. EUROPEAN COURT OF HUMAN RIGHTS (ECtHR)

GERMANY

Bundesverfassungsgericht (Federal Constitutional Court)

1

Non-Finality and Dialogue in Constitutional Interpretation

Towards an Analytic Taxonomy of Non-Court Centric Conceptions of Judicial Review

I. BACKGROUND

A. The gap thesis

Any theory of constitutional interpretation must respond to this fundamental dilemma: On the one hand, no one denies interpretive ambiguity. Constitutional texts do not apply themselves: neither text nor history—the circumstances of ratification—alone are decisive of constitutional meaning. But, on the other hand, interpretive ambiguity notwithstanding, a constitution by definition is expected to be determinate enough to legitimate coercive legal ordering, even when citizens will gravely and often reasonably disagree about what justice requires of a coercive state regime.

In principle, coercive enactments by democratic majorities can only be justified to dissenters (or 'losers' in the political process) as legitimate, if those enactments can be shown to be outcomes produced within the procedural framework of a good-enough constitution. But recourse to process and procedure merely displaces the dilemma without resolving it. The meaning of a 'good-enough constitution' is itself open to deep, legitimacy-endangering moral dissensus in the context of particular controversies. The highly abstract framework concepts of a constitution—such as equality or free speech—do not generate uncontroversial answers to particular issues. Call this the *gap-thesis*: there is a gap between normative frameworks and their contextualizing applications. Is, under those circumstances, judicial review a defect in democracy—merely a 'complacent assumption'[1] which is cemented into its dominant position by our contemporary legal and political cultures—or is it plausible that judicial review can actually improve democracy overall by making it more deliberative?

The gap-thesis describes, of course, a generic problem of constitutional interpretation. But this interpretive gap is further widened and aggravated under the contemporary circumstances of modern advanced democracies and the democratic welfare-state. We are witnessing today an expansion of substantive constitutional law beyond the negative basic liberties. Fundamental rights, of course, create, on the one hand, negative obligations for the state—duties not to interfere with what Rawls called the *constitutional essentials*: free speech, freedom of conscience, life, etc. On this defensive-negative role there is general agreement. But far less agreement exists on the question to which extent they also, on the other hand, generate positive obligations of the state to protect and promote fundamental rights. While—in their defensive-negative mode—fundamental rights do create barriers against excessive public intervention for the individual, they also—as expressions of a polity's *shared constitutional value decisions*—increasingly 'permeate'[2] the whole legal order, including private law and the law of civil-society relations, and obligate the state to actively protect and promote liberty also in the social sphere. As a consequence of this *horizontalization of the constitution*, courts must now increasingly, in domain after domain, strike a 'fair balance' between competing values, for example, in the exemplary domain of Euroconstitutionalism, between economic liberties (or freedoms) of traders and fundamental social rights, such as the employees' right to strike; or between contractual freedom of creditors and the right to family life of vulnerable consumers; or between an employer's 'right to conduct a business' and the right of an employee to religious freedom; or between freedom of speech and the right to privacy. In searching for contextualized *fair balance*, courts

[1] Richard H. Fallon, 'The Core of an Uneasy Case for Judicial Review', 121 Harvard Law Review 1693–736 (2008); Richard H. Fallon, Law and Legitimacy in the Supreme Court (Cambridge: Harvard University Press 2018).

[2] This terminology, of course, dates back to the famous *Lüth* decision of the German Federal Constitutional Court ('BVG'), 7 BverfGE 198 (1958), English translation in: English translation in Federal Constitutional Court (ed.) Decisions of the Bundesverfassungsgericht 1, (NOMOS: 1998). As the BVG here reasoned:

> It is equally true, however, that the Basic Law ... has set up an objective value system ... This value system centred round the human personality developing freely in the social community, and its dignity must be regarded as the basic constitutional decision for all spheres of law. Legislation, administration, and the judiciary are given guidelines and inspiration (Richtlinien und Impulse) by it. Accordingly, it also manifestly influences the civil law: no provision of civil law may be in contradiction with it; each one must be interpreted in its spirit.

will necessarily be making consequential value choices for society as a whole and, through interpretation and the use of proportionality analysis, constantly develop constitutional law. But to authoritatively impose judicial judgments on citizens who reasonably disagree with those judgments, critics argue, violates the fundamental duty of civility in a liberal democracy: that of meaningful engagement with those with whom one disagrees.

B. Two strategies of constitutional containment

In response to this dilemma of interpretive ambiguity and legitimizing determinacy, two sceptical strategies of containment have been prominent in traditional constitutional discourse—'sceptical', that is, with regard to their perceived alternatives—judicial moralizing or democratic deliberation. Both seek to contain ambiguity and to reinforce the finality of decisions by constitutional courts within what they see as their proper domain.

The first strategy, which is especially prominent in the US but also has gained some ground in the European context of constitutionalism beyond the state out of a concern with safeguarding state sovereignty, is originalism. Originalism insists that the primary purpose of a constitution is to bind judicial decisionmaking to its expected original public meaning of the constitution, and that the benefits of striving for this outweigh the costs. For to conceptualize the constitution as a 'living instrument' that adapts to changing circumstances inevitably invites judges to opportunistically mould the constitution as they like according to their own preferences and elite perceptions of present-day conditions. On the originalist view, judicial review is consistent with democracy as long as it enforces the original pact or bargain set out in the constitution, but otherwise leaves politics alone. For the future may be tempted to stray from the past's hard-won victories and must be held to the expectations and consensus established by earlier generations. Yet a cogent objection to originalism is that it makes the moral understandings of democracy today hostage to the moral understandings of the founders.[3] But the bare text typically raises more questions than it answers. Contemporary judges necessarily must make principled value choices, often by balancing

[3] Cf. the observation by Jack Balkin, characterizing Scalia's theory of constitutions as 'a narrative of decline: because the future may be tempted to stray from the hard-won victories of the past, later generations must be held to the concrete practices and expectations of earlier generations, who, at least by comparison, are more noble and moral'. In: Jack Balkin, Living Originalism (Cambridge: Harvard University Press 2011), 29.

competing values, especially where they are confronted with conflicts between them. But the challenge—which originalism helps to highlight—remains to understand how constitutionalism can depend on both its democratic responsiveness to public opinion and its legitimacy as law.

The second strategy remains fully committed to a system of judicial supremacy as 'a matter of first principle'[4]—albeit in the narrow domain of economic liberties—out of deep scepticism about deliberative democracy and the modern administrative state and is rooted in the ordoliberal doctrine of market freedom and the libertarian doctrine of limited government. Both these doctrines share a Hayekian presumption in favour of the spontaneous self-organization of social and economic life and a corresponding presumption against extraneous, 'political' intervention—particularly against new legislation, seen as more likely to do harm than good.[5] Hayek's line of argument essentially focused on the self-defeating character of constitutionally unlimited democracy and the need to disempower short-sighted and unprincipled majorities in the name of binding norms. Strong private-law protections of property rights and freedom of contract and economic liberties are seen as both the institutional basis for self-ordering and as checks on political and administrative overreaching. Hayek's chief concern was that it is simply impossible to construct from the knowledge of particulars a desirable social order.[6] We should not 'pretend to be able directly to comprehend social wholes like society, etc., as entities sui generis which exist independently of the individuals which compose them'.[7] Accordingly, judicial departures from those basal private-law notions must be resisted for two reasons: first, because only a well-defined, gapless system of negative (as opposed to positive) rights can reduce incentives for factional intrigue and provide a bulwark against excessive public intervention into society; second, because the private-law baseline provides a bulwark against unprincipled judicial adventurism. Private law notions, on this view, are the essential building blocks of constitutional ordering, and constitutional interpretation should proceed from these notions. For example, Richard Epstein bemoans 'an overexposure to public law and an attention deficit with respect to private law'

[4] Richard A. Epstein, The Classical Liberal Constitution (Cambridge: Harvard University Press 2014), 77–80; but cf. also the German ordoliberal tradition.

[5] Ibid, 78: 'The implicit background assumption is that the initial presumption should be set against new legislation, which is more likely to do harm than good.'

[6] Friedrich Hayek, Law, Legislation, and Liberty (Chicago: University of Chicago Press 1973), vol. 1, Rules and Order, p. 14 ('synoptic delusion').

[7] Friedrich Hayek, Individualism and Economic Order (Chicago: University of Chicago Press 1948), 6.

in contemporary legal discourse and argues that 'the most reliable protections for speech and religion come from the security of a sound basic system of law unrelated to particular issues of either speech or religion'. What is required is that this system 'systematically and unflinchingly protect[s] property rights and economic liberties for its citizens . . .'[8] From this perspective, any attempt to distinguish between 'economic liberties' and 'personal rights' appears as misguided and irrational. What matters is the individual immunity from government. Positive constitutionalism—with its connotation that rights are *interest-sensitive* and have the dimension of 'fair value'[9]—simply undermines that rationale.

C. Negative/positive constitutionalism

Both these strategies of constitutional containment may be contrasted with a longstanding German debate surrounding the understanding of fundamental rights as negative rights and as constitutional principles that radiate into and permeate the whole legal order.

In a highly influential article of 1990,[10] Ernst-Wolfgang Böckenförde diagnosed what he dubbed 'a growth crisis in the development of . . . fundamental rights'.[11] He argued that a constitution could either be a minimally specified liberal framework-order ('Rahmenordnung') of a democratic society; an order that covers the basic relationship between the citizen and the state only and thus exclusively limits itself to protecting the basic negative liberties. Or, in the alternative to a retreat to pure negative constitutionalism, an increasingly judge-made constitution could embrace an understanding of fundamental rights as, in the German terminology, 'objective' constitutional principles that permeate

[8] Richard A. Epstein, The Classical Liberal Constitution (Cambridge: Harvard University Press 2014), 383, 579 . For a somewhat related view, cf. Robert Bork, 'Individual Liberty as the Constitution Understands It', in: Roger Scruton (ed.), Liberty and Civilization. The Western Heritage (New York: Encounter Books 2010), 63–77.

[9] Frank Michelman, 'Liberties, Fair Values, and Constitutional Method, with Reference to Rawls', in: Geoffrey Stone, Richard Epstein, and Cass Sunstein (eds.), The Bill of Rights in the Modern State (Chicago: University of Chicago Press 1992) 91–114, at 97.

[10] Ernst-Wolfgang Böckenförde, 'Grundrechte als Grundsatznormen. Zur gegenwärtigen Lage der Grundrechtsdogmatik', in ibid, Staat, Verfassung, Demokratie (Frankfurt am Main: Suhrkamp 1991) 159–99; reprinted in English as 'Fundamental Rights as Constitutional Principles: On the Current State of Interpreting Fundamental Rights', in: M. Künkler and T. Stein (eds.), Constitutional and Political Theory. Selected Writings by Ernst-Wolfgang Böckenförde (Oxford: Oxford University Press 2017) 235 ff. For an important critical discussion of Böckenförde's article, cf. Jürgen Habermas, Between Facts and Norms (Cambridge: Polity Press 1996) 248 ff.

[11] Ernst-Wolfgang Böckenförde, 'Fundamental Rights as Constitutional Principles: On the Current State of Interpreting Fundamental Rights', in M. Künkler and T. Stein (eds.), Constitutional and Political Theory. Selected Writings by Ernst-Wolfgang Böckenförde (Oxford: Oxford University Press 2017), 235 ff., at 243.

the whole legal order. The constitution would then no longer serve as a mere framework but as a 'foundation of the polity as a whole' ('rechtliche Grundordnung des Gemeinwesens insgesamt')—a comprehensive blueprint for social ordering by constitutional law, increasingly administered by the constitutional court.

Böckenförde saw both these alternatives as deeply disturbing, but abstained from offering a solution to the dilemma one way or the other. The problematic aspect of the first horn of this dilemma—pure negative constitutionalism—lies, as he warned, in its potential normative shortfall: the risk of reducing constitutional value decisions to mere aspirations only and subjecting their redemption to the vagaries and accidents of the legislative process, which might also 'wipe away legal principles and the particular form of a legal field they have shaped'.[12] By contrast, the second horn of the dilemma entails, according to Böckenförde, what he described as the disturbing transition of a modern liberal democracy to a *constitutional-legal jurisdictional state* ['verfassungsgerichtlicher Jurisdiktionsstaat']. The term *jurisdictio* here refers to its pre-modern sense, antedating any modern notion of separation of powers. The judicial 'application of the principle of proportionality, which emerges ever more strongly in the Court's concretization and balancing decisions', Böckenförde argued, 'aims at the one correct solution that gives adequate and proportional consideration to the various constitutional-legal positions and perspectives'.[13] A first consequence of the shift from negative to positive constitutionalism is that the difference between constitutional law and statutory law risks being leveled out: '... what constitutes specifically constitutional law in the hodgepodge ["Gemengelage"] of the radiating effect of fundamental rights into ordinary law and ordinary law itself has tended to remain the mystery ["Arcanum"] of the court'.[14] Constitutional courts become self-programming and engage in judicial legislation. A second dramatic consequence is that the crucial difference between legislation and constitutional adjudication is increasingly being eroded. The judge-made 'web of constitutional guidelines for the legislature becomes more expansive and also increasingly tightly knit',[15] thereby increasing the overall democratic deficit which allegedly inheres the shift to positive constitutionalism.

While Böckenförde referred to the old, pre-modern meaning of *jurisdictio* to illustrate the specific democratic deficit of a transition from negative to positive constitutionalism, he also, with equal emphasis,

[12] Ibid, at 263. [13] Ibid, at 263. [14] Ibid, at 242. [15] Ibid, at 264.

referred to the—distinctly modern—Kantian concept of law, which covers not only the basic citizens-state relation but also the compatibility of each citizen's liberty with an equal liberty for all. As Böckenförde pointed out, it is also the case that, while the borderline between interpreting the law and making law under the guise of interpretation erodes, only the 'additional qualification as objective constitutional principles or value-decisions brings about that fundamental rights fully cover the Kantian definition and thus the sphere of law'.[16] Böckenförde's contribution thus serves to describe, and put centre-stage, the tensions between constitutionalism and democracy.

Accordingly, the task of a theory of constitutional interpretation is to vindicate contemporary constitutionalism against two persistent critiques:

(i) democratic or progressive-minded critiques which object to an expansion of constitutional law beyond the negative basic liberties and to balancing either as a path to an undemocratic judicial control (and possibly, further-down-the-road, a weakening of social rights against negative economic liberties);
(ii) rule-of-law based critiques which object that the basic protections of law are thereby weakened: that 'law' is replaced by 'policy' or by transient preferences or opinions of judges.

In this chapter I propose an analytic taxonomy of contemporary *non-court centric approaches to constitutional interpretation*: those that have concluded that the most promising response to the dilemma of interpretive ambiguity and legitimizing determinacy is to shift the focus from courts as a forum of principle[17] to the dialogue between courts and *other actors*, ranging from (other) courts to legislatures, administrative agencies, private actors, civil society stakeholders, and the wider public, in the jurisgenerative process. In suggesting a taxonomy, my goal is, in part, to make alternative views in this family of positions clearer by spelling out differences and commonalities between them, and thereby to highlight conceptual choices available to those seeking to make a case *for* judicial review against persistent accusations of a democratic deficit.[18] But, more ambitiously, my goal is also, by following the emergent literature on 'weak', proceduralist, and democratic-experimentalist forms of judicial review, to argue the virtues of the latter. Democratic experimentalism

[16] Ibid, at 258.

[17] Ronald Dworkin, 'The Forum of Principle', 56 New York University Law Review 469 (1981).

[18] Robert Post/Reva Siegel, 'Roe Rage', 42 Harvard Civil Rights-Civil Liberties Law Review 373 (2007).

focuses on constitutional frameworks and their ongoing revision through contextualizing application. I will argue that legitimation does not require a pre-existing consensus, but a potential consensus may be sufficient: courts can instigate debate and deliberation that leads to consensus. Democratic experimentalism thus denotes a modality of judicial review that allows judges to enforce avowedly open-ended, fundamental, constitutional commitments in a way that institutionalizes—rather than excludes—continuing, social, and democratic determination, through collaboration with other courts, legislatures, agencies, stakeholders, etc., and progressive clarification of what these commitments can and should come to mean in practice. In this way, judicial review may deepen democracy rather than limit it by providing a focus and reason for public deliberation. The hope is to provide, by setting out contrasting positions, a foil for discussion and to show that the desirability of judicial review is not merely 'complacent assumption'[19] in contemporary constitutional and political thought, but can be supported on democratic grounds as deliberation-enhancing.

II. AN ANALYTIC TAXONOMY OF NON-COURT CENTRIC VIEWS OF CONSTITUTIONAL INTERPRETATION

A. Political liberalism and the experimentalist turn

Against economic liberalism Michelman argues that a constitution is legitimation-worthy only as long as it ensures that no one at any time lacks the means of access to fulfilment of central basic material needs—that is, if it includes positive socioeconomic rights as part of its essentials. Without those assurances, citizens just cannot mutually expect one another to submit their fates to a liberal society's 'freedom-serving structures' such as a largely market-based economy and a mainly democratic-lawmaking system. But the basic dilemma of constitutionalism is only exacerbated by adding the requirement that a legitimation-worthy constitution include socioeconomic rights. Stated very generally the constitution will be legitimation-worthy even under these conditions provided that there is, as Frank Michelman says,

> in operation a dedicated institutional service whose considered judgments [regarding constitutionality] were in fact widely trusted to fall within the

[19] Richard H. Fallon, 'The Core of an Uneasy Case for Judicial Review', 121 Harvard Law Review 1693–736 (2008).

> bounds of honest, discursive defensibility [...] with a frequency sufficient to qualify those judgments as publicly authoritative for legitimacy-sustaining purposes. [...]. It is, I believe, precisely with a view to this crucial function [...] that many liberals [...] defend the use of courts as authoritative public arbiters of the fulfillment of constitutional essentials.

But the key institutional question is how this condition of deliberative trust can be met given the well-known limitations of courts.[20] If judicialization of socioeconomic rights is deemed intolerable, according to this worry, then socioeconomic rights cannot be allowed to be constitutional essentials after all.[21] Hence, it becomes necessary to find a way to disarm or evade the standard worry about judicial review by retreating from judicial supremacy in order to meet the categorical requirements of legitimation-worthiness.

1. Reasonable disagreements about justice

Michelman has explored this apparent dilemma in depth, framed by close reference to Rawlsian categories. Rawls saw the concept of *justice* as a functional (but also as a moral) one: the function of a shared conception of justice was to provide an accepted touchstone to which members of what he called a well-ordered society, divided by economic and cultural differences, could refer so as to assess, justify, denounce, and reform their societies' basic institutions and interpretive practices and push for an ever more exhaustive interpretation of equal rights—towards the elimination or reduction of arbitrary inequalities in people's life prospects. Rawls believed in reasonable pluralism and was concerned that lack of consensus because of society-wide, often reasonable, disagreement on questions of fundamental value would unseat agreement on a conception of justice and prevent society from being 'well-ordered'.

Justice is the category of the right and the morally mandatory in political relations and arrangements. Central is a—political—conception of co-operation which, crucially, 'involves the idea of fair terms of cooperation'.[22] Embedded from the start in that notion are ideas of reciprocity

[20] As Michelman himself describes the 'standard worry', a constitutionalized commitment to socioeconomic rights would force courts 'into a hapless choice between usurpation and abdication'—either by fully dictating 'the most basic resource-management priorities of the public household against the prevailing political will'; or by 'debas[ing] dangerously the entire currency of rights and the rule of law ... [by] openly ceding to executive and legislative bodies a nonreviewable privilege of indefinite postponement of a declared constitutional right.' From this dilemma, there would be 'no escape without either embarrassment or discreditation'. Frank Michelman, ibid, at 188.

[21] Frank Michelman, 'Legitimacy, The Social Turn and Constitutional Review: What Political Liberalism Suggests', in: KritV | CritQ | Rcrit, Jahrgang 98 (2015), Heft 3, pp. 183–205, at p. 11.

[22] Rawls, Political Liberalism 16 (1993).

and reasonableness.[23] In order for terms of co-operation to count as fair, 'citizens offering them must reasonably think that citizens offered them might also reasonably accept them'.[24] Rawls emphasizes that in this formulation the term *reasonably* 'occurs at both ends':[25] citizens become deliberators. As deliberators, citizens ascribe to each other certain 'moral powers' and 'higher-order interests' in the development and exercise of these powers. These moral powers are not only the capacity 'to form, follow, and revise' their own individual conceptions of the good,[26] but also 'to understand, ... to propose, or to endorse, and then to be moved to act from fair terms of cooperation for their own sake'.[27]

To underscore the role of citizens as deliberators, contrast Rawls' political-liberal conception of social co-operation with Hayek's economic-liberal conception. Again, abstract and general rules are necessary for co-operation. But these rules are not themselves subject to explicit discursive elaboration by the individuals themselves as co-operators: they simply emerge exogeneously to the co-operators as 'adaptations to the impossibility of anyone taking conscious account of all the particular facts which enter into the order of society'.[28] Co-operation under common rules, Hayek argued, rests on 'a sort of division of knowledge', according to which 'the individual must take account of particular circumstances but the law ensures that their action will be adapted to certain general or permanent characteristics of their society'.[29] But this division of knowledge implies an important limitation—co-operation 'under common rules' is not itself jurisgenerative with regard to those rules of conduct themselves in the sense of deliberative democracy. Those rules owe their authority not to an explicit shared public commitment among democratic citizens to public reasoning, for example through participatory discussions and public decisionmaking, but instead to gradual *tacit evolution* and adaptation-of-society-to-circumstances.[30]

According to Rawls, in contrast, the political and legal system must in its institutions always reflect these fair terms of co-operation. But the

[23] Rawls, Political Liberalism 17 (1993).

[24] Rawls, Political Liberalism xliv (1993).

[25] Rawls, Political Liberalism xliv (1993).

[26] Rawls, Political Liberalism xlvi (1993).

[27] Rawls, Political Liberalism 19, 54 (1993).

[28] Friedrich Hayek, Law, Legislation, and Liberty (Chicago: University of Chicago Press 1973), vol. 1, Rules and Order, p. 13.

[29] Friedrich Hayek, The Constitution of Liberty (Chicago: University of Chicago Press 1960) 157.

[30] Ibid, 157: 'Most of these rules have never been deliberately invented, but have grown through a gradual process of trial and error in which the experience of successive generations has helped to make them what they are.'

political and legal system must at the same time also actively sustain and support the deliberative process in which citizens can actually offer each other fair terms: 'the definite idea for deliberative democracy is the idea of deliberation itself'.[31] Citizens must be able to deliberate, 'as free and equal, and not as dominated or manipulated, or under the pressure of an inferior political or social position'.[32] As Rawls observed, '[i]n a democratic culture, we expect, and indeed want, citizens to care about their basic liberties and opportunities in order to develop and exercise their moral powers and to pursue their conceptions of the good. We think they show a lack of self-respect and weakness of character in not doing so'.[33] Accordingly, the legal and political system must 'support their self-respect as citizens' by providing 'equal basic rights and liberties, the fair value of political liberties and fair equality of opportunity, as the social bases of self-respect'.[34] In this way, 'fair terms' are both the precondition and the outcome of an ongoing deliberative process between and among free and equal citizens. Herein lies the normative essence of political liberalism. As Thomas Nagel has explained, Rawls' liberalism is motivated by 'the recognition of the importance of social and economic structures [and] political and legal institutions in shaping people's lives' and, concomitantly, by 'a gradual acceptance of social responsibility for their effects'.[35] Economic liberties are not seen as an essential part of personal rights.[36] Rawls' political liberalism in this way takes society as a whole, and all its institutions that form part of the 'basic structure'[37] have to be continuously assessed by a common standard.

But, as Michelman and others, following him, have argued, the hope for an 'overlapping consensus' on a conception of justice may appear 'surprising and unrealistic',[38] not only because shortfalls from justice are inevitable, but also because citizens fail to share a common conception of justice at all and are likely to persistently and sharply disagree about what counts as a shortfall from justice. Michelman—arguing with Rawls

[31] John Rawls, Collected Papers (Cambridge: Harvard University Press 1999) 579–80.

[32] Rawls, Political Liberalism xliv (1993).

[33] Rawls, Political Liberalism 76 (1993).

[34] Rawls, Political Liberalism 82 (1993).

[35] Thomas Nagel, 'Rawls and Liberalism', in Samuel Freeman (ed.), The Cambridge Companion to Rawls (2003) 62–85, at 63.

[36] Cf. Thomas Nagel's observation: 'In Rawls' theory individual property rights are the consequence, and not the foundation, of the justice of economic institutions. In theories of libertarian tendency, the reverse is the case.' In: ibid, at 68.

[37] Rawls, Political Liberalism (1993).

[38] Thomas Michael Scanlon, 'Provocation: Everyone is a Philosopher!', 125 Harvard Law Review Forum 228, at 230 (2012), commenting on, and following, Frank Michelman.

against Rawls—turns what, following Rawls, he calls the 'burdens of judgment'—which refer to the ways in which our differing experiences cause us in perfect good faith to see the world differently—against Rawls himself. Reasonable disagreement, as Michelman explains, 'cuts deeper'—it refers to 'the fact of irresolvable uncertainty and, in real political time, irreparable reasonable disagreement among inhabitants in a modern country about the set of entrenchments and interpretations of human rights [. . .] that would truly satisfy justice in the country's historical circumstances'.[39] The lack of consensus, then, is driven 'just as much by disagreements about questions of socioeconomic justice (welfare rights, for example) as by disagreements over matters of religion and basic cultural values';[40] and 'one might have said instead that in a free society there are bound to be deep disagreements among libertarians, liberals, and others about economic justice, independent of disagreements about religious and cultural values'.[41]

2. The distinction between justice and legitimacy

Reasonable disagreement about justice forces a distinction between justice and legitimacy. In modern, complex, and pluralistic societies, we need the medium of coercive law to partake of what Michelman calls (following Rawls) the 'goods of the political'—the goods of solidarity and co-operation.[42] Without legal ordering, in complex societies there would simply be no hope of achieving the co-ordination of large numbers of people necessary for these goods. Even if we attribute to individuals non-self-interested *other-regarding* motives that lead them to want to live on fair terms with other people, we still need ordering by law, not only for motivational and cognitive but also moral reasons. For each citizen needs the reciprocal assurance that, if he or she abides by these terms of co-operation, the others—at least 'most of them, most of the time'—will abide by the same terms as well.[43] Only a legal system—with its centralized authority to determine those terms and with its monopoly in enforcing them—can provide these reciprocal assurances to its addressees, for it doesn't take many defectors—as both Michelman and Nagel have pointed out—for an ongoing system of social co-operation to unravel. 'Visible guarantees of institutional backup' are therefore necessary to confer stability

[39] Ibid, at 70. [40] Scanlon, ibid. [41] Scanlon, ibid.

[42] Frank Michelman's, 'Ida's Way', 72 Fordham Law Review 345, 352 (2003).

[43] On this aspect, cf. also Thomas Nagel, 'The Problem of Global Justice', in: Secular Philosophy and the Religious Temperament. Essays 2002–2008, (2010) 63. But see also Jürgen Habermas' concept of 'Rechtsform' to which the 'discourse principle' must be applied, in: Between Facts and Norms, Contributions to a Discourse Theory of Law and Democracy (Polity Press: 1997), drawing on Max Weber.

on a reliable and effective system of co-operation. Michelman calls this 'Hobbes' thesis'.[44]

So, for egalitarian, reciprocity-minded citizens, the pursuit of effective social ordering by law therefore itself becomes a moral imperative. The problem, however, is that citizens disagree about which laws can justifiably be made binding. Ethical diversity and moral dissensus invariably give rise to frequent, sincere, and intractable disagreements over what the laws for a society of notionally free and equal persons ought in all reason and justice to provide.[45] Yet it remains the case that 'every concrete instance of a liberal rule-of-law regime presents unremittingly a question of moral justification'.[46] But how can the laws be justifiable to all when there is persistent, obdurate disagreement about political goods?

The fact that persistent reasonable disagreements among citizens about the values of justice must be expected, opens a gap—and implies the crucial distinction—between justice and political legitimacy. Of the two, legitimacy is the weaker—less demanding—notion. A *legitimate* regime is one whose requirements the citizens *generally* have reason to comply with because they are its 'framework'-requirements. The intuitive idea is that, because of the fact of coercion, questions of legitimacy attain a particular urgency, which transcends the urgency that surrounds considerations of justice generally.[47] *Legitimacy* thus provides an answer to the problem of overall moral-political justification, which—as Michelman explains—the 'irreducible element of coerciveness [of any legal and political order] vis-à-vis […] ideally and primordially free and equal citizens'[48] in modern, morally diverse, and complex societies always invites. The gap between justice and legitimacy 'allow[s] for human imperfection and for honest political disagreement' which includes disagreement about what counts as a shortfall from justice. A legitimacy standard 'must be more accommodating of real-world political imperfection and disagreement than any corresponding ideal standard of justice conceivably could be'. If

[44] Ibid, 346. [45] Ibid, 352.

[46] Frank Michelman, 'Legitimacy, The Social Turn and Constitutional Review: What Political Liberalism Suggests', in: KritV | CritQ | Rcrit, Jahrgang 98 (2015), Heft 3, pp. 183–205, at p. 190. And in 'Ida's Way', 72 Fordham Law Review 345, 352 (2003) he says: ' "Political" liberals … shy away from coercion … We want to feel that we always, when called upon, can give to others "public" reasons sufficient to justify the actual processes and practices of legal coercion in which we connive. Very roughly, public reasons are reasons that the giver sincerely believes ought to count as such for any rightminded (a/k/a "reasonable") political associate.'

[47] For a related point on human rights, cf. Joshua Cohen, 'Is There a Human Right to Democracy?' in: J. Cohen, The Arc of the Moral Universe (Cambridge: Harvard University Press 2010), 349–72, at 357.

[48] Frank Michelman, 'Human Rights and the Limits of Constitutional Theory', in: 13(1) Ratio Juris 63–76 at 70 f (2000).

consonance with justice were to provide a standard for legitimacy, then, as Michelman writes, 'no modern real-world, concrete legal order could ever be deemed truly deserving of support by any fraction of the citizens remotely approaching a totality'.

Michelman calls the step from justice to legitimacy 'proceduralist' in the following sense. The strategy relies on the hope or expectation that individuals with persistently differing (but often reasonable) understandings of justice and fairness nonetheless can come together and agree on a background institutional framework of political legitimacy, to be used in deciding how agreements over substance (that is to say, socioeconomic justice) are to be dealt with. Michelman frequently refers to what Rawls called the 'liberal principle of legitimacy',[49] according to which the exercise of political power is legitimate only when it is in accordance with a constitution the essentials of which all citizens may reasonably be expected to endorse in the light of principles and ideals acceptable to them as reasonable and rational. Hence, the proceduralist solution is also inevitably a *substantive* one, because citizens express to one another a firm commitment about their common status as citizens: '[w]ithout tying ourselves to naïve claims about a clean separability of substance from procedure, it seems we can sometimes reasonably hope that parties caught in profound disagreement about matters of great importance to them—those being what we call the "substance" of their debate—can nevertheless be brought to agree on an institutional framework (call it "procedure") to be used in deciding how those matters are to be dealt with'.[50] If individuals can agree to this law of lawmaking, then—according to the proceduralist strategy—they would have in some relevant sense also agreed to the laws which the procedure produces, and hence those laws will be justified.

Michelman calls Rawls' proceduralist strategy 'legitimation-by-constitution'. But this 'proceduralization' must be accompanied by another—second—proceduralization involving a constitutional review mechanism. Michelman insists that securing legitimacy for a political system requires the existence of some institution that is apart from the rest of the system and whose function is to offer regular assessments of the extent to which those other parts are working in ways that conform constitutional and democratic self-governance. For the 'idea of verification-as-right', Michelman says, 'cannot be fully represented in a set of abstract statements, the rightness of which is apparent to all but only because the abstractions paper over the persisting disagreements that inevitably

[49] Rawls, op. cit., at 137 (*et passim*).

[50] Cf. Frank Michelman [2012].

will surface at the point of application of them to live political issues'.[51] Those constitutional-interpretive disagreements among citizens 'will be nothing less than comings apart over the legitimacy of the regime' itself. Hence, the '[c]ompletion of the idea of legitimation by constitution, requires ... a special institutional service' in order to meet the requirement for 'authoritative resolutions, from time to time, of questions of constitutional meaning'[52] and for official 'institutional settlement'. This 'second proceduralization'—without which '[p]olitical-liberal constitutionalism cannot make do'—is 'a distinct and dedicated institutional site for pronouncements on disputed questions of constitutionality'. Such an institution or site might be a parliamentary committee or even the Parliament sitting from time to time in committee of the whole; its 'speech could be more common than technical',[53] but '[t]he fact is ... that courts and adjudication are the site and the process that are cemented into those positions by our currently dominant political cultures'.

Rawls' proceduralizing strategy of 'legitimation-by-constitution' thus relied on the expectation of an intuitive, wide agreement or consensus within contemporary constitutional-democratic societies over when there has been a violation of the 'central ranges' of the basic negative liberties. But notice that the Rawlsian strategy poses two severe, interrelated problems.

First, while constitutionalism must avoid overextending itself beyond what are reasonable aspirations, it must also avoid *minimalism*—a conception of the 'framework' of constitutional essentials so sparing and narrow that it would leave the most vulnerable citizens without what it takes to protect and sustain their role as political associates: the constitution would otherwise no longer be 'legitimation-worthy'. We are pushed towards minimalism by the standard justiciability-worry.[54] But shortfalls from justice—an overall justice-deficit of a legal order, even if as a result not of (a, say, ordoliberal) hostility to socioeconomic rights per se but merely of the standard justiciability-worry of lawyers—may detract

[51] Frank Michelman, 'Why Not Just Say So? An Essay on the Obduracy of Constitutional Fixation', 94 Boston University Law Review 1141–58, at 1156 (2016).

[52] Ibid, at 1157. [53] Michelman, 'Why Not Just Say So?', at 1157.

[54] As Michelman restates this concern:

> [d]own one path [...] lies the judicial choice to issue concrete, positive enforcement orders in apretentious, inexpert, probably vain but nevertheless resented attempt to reshuffle the most basic resource-management priorities of the public household against prevailing political will. Down the other lies the judicial choice to debase dangerously the entire currency of rights and the rule of law—the spectacle of courts openly ceding to executive and legislative bodies a nonreviewable privilege of indefinite postponement of a declared constitutional right.

from, subvert, and compromise its overall legitimacy. The bad currency of persistent structural social injustice—the various, manifold denials of fair equality of opportunity in a modern capitalist economy—would then begin to affect, contaminate, gradually erode, and ultimately drive out the good currency of political legitimacy. The proceduralist strategy leaves the substantive egalitarian considerations which underlie and animate the 'political conception of justice' pending in an uncertain state of institutional limbo, that is, without any institutional counterpart or 'contextualization regime', moral aspiration aside.

Second, the Rawlsian liberal principle of legitimacy comes to something too strong. For the problems of agreement, interpretation, and enforcement inhere even a more minimalist-liberal conception of constitutional essentials. At the point of application, justice-related moral disagreement translates *all-the-way-up* into moral dissensus about the true meaning of the legitimacy-conferring framework of 'principles and ideals' enshrined in the constitution itself. Common ground might just dwindle. A purely 'substantive' resolution will not be possible: citizens, Michelman argues, cannot simply put aside those differences of comprehensive and justice-related outlook that make for reasonable interpretive pluralism when they turn to matters of constitutional interpretation. Indeed, suppose citizens could somehow put their reasonable differences aside and agree on uncontroversial constitutional essentials, on the contents of 'the really high law':[55] application of those—inevitably abstract and broad—constitutional essentials to any particular problem would themselves require interpretation and further specification; this process, however, opens the constitution to divisive, eventually destructive and legitimacy-endangering, conflict.

There is, then, a serious and obvious conflict between the requirements of liberal-proceduralist legitimacy and the kind of decisions conscientious judges must make in a contemporary constitutional regime—and this conflict will be aggravated, once this regime opens itself to a recognition of socioeconomic rights. While constitutionalism must avoid overextending itself beyond what are reasonable aspirations, it must also avoid a conception of the constitutional essentials so sparing and narrow that it would leave the most vulnerable citizens without what it takes to protect and sustain their role as political associates. But the problems of agreement, interpretation, and enforcement inhere any conception of constitutional essentials, however narrow or minimalist.

[55] Frank Michelman, Brennan and Democracy (Princeton: Princeton University Press 1999), at 50.

Constitutional-liberal discourse seems to stand at the 'edge of a cliff' here, on the 'verge of a potentially infinite regression', as Robert Post comments, with moral dissensus percolating all the way up and down, potentially undermining *just any* strategy for salvaging judicial review in a morally complex contemporary world, marked by pervasive uncertainty—less about the principles or 'essentials' themselves than about their applied meaning when it comes to applying them to any particular problem, that is, to contextualizing them. The lingering de-facto public commitment to judicial-supremacist strong-form judicial review would amount, as Mark Tushnet has suggested, to 'a sign of resignation to the fact that democratic majorities have been unable to eliminate a practice favored by political elites than of positive support for the practice'.[56]

3. The experimentalist turn

Democratic experimentalism comes to the aid of the political-liberal project. Michelman has, in earlier writings, suggested an idea of constitutional tolerance and later suggested the possibility of an 'experimentalist response'.[57] Radical moral dissensus, he argues, can help render citizens aware of a required background that is supposed to be shared, at least implicitly, in terms of a historically situated discursive practice. And this background does not remain merely tacit but might itself be transformative as the practice moves along. In contradistinction from Dworkin's imaginary judge 'Hercules', he invites us to imagine a non-judicial, 'non-official personage' called 'Ida'[58] who, faced with uncertainty about constitutional meaning, interprets or rationally reconstructs the constitution. On the one hand, every 'Ida'—each with different moral priors, but at the same time motivated by 'the very great public good'[59] of the political and of political union—anticipates reasonable disagreement at the level of major public policy choices: 'reasonable disagreement is going to reach its tentacles into the system-constructions arrived at by [other discourse-participants] all acting in the best of faith'.[60] Yet, on the other hand,

> [e]very Ida ... who attaches great moral importance to the general goods of union has strong, moral reasons to wish for a favorable judgment

[56] Mark Tushnet, Against Judicial Review, Harvard Law School Public Law & Legal Theory Working Paper Series, Paper 09–20, at 16.

[57] Frank Michelman, 'Legitimacy, The Social Turn and Constitutional Review: What Political Liberalism Suggests', in: KritV | CritQ | Rcrit, Jahrgang 98 (2015), Heft 3, pp. 183–205, at 197 ff.

[58] Frank Michelman, 'Ida's Way', 72 Fordham Law Review 345, 348 (2003).

[59] John Rawls, Political Liberalism 139, 157 (1993).

[60] Frank Michelman, 'Ida's Way', 72 Fordham Law Review 345, 353 (2003).

> regarding the respect-worthiness of the system-in-place as she reconstructs it. All reasonable Ida, therefore, have reasons to be tolerant of what they see as moral mishaps in the systemic history—specifically, by writing off those mishaps as 'mistakes'. In short, the Idas all may tend to construe the system ... in ways that are morally optimistic. Since their moral priors differ, so will the systemic reconstructions they arrive at. And this is a political-moral advantage, not a disadvantage! The plurality of the reconstructions ... will be precisely geared to a convergence across their number of favorable judgments of respect-worthiness of their country's political 'procedure'—which is exactly what political liberals are driving at.[61]

Moral disagreement, then, when legally framed by, and conducted according to, the two proceduralizations, might paradoxically sustain and reinforce the constitution. Consensus is no longer taken as given or pre-existing. Consensus can be induced by deliberation over time and public debate can legitimize retroactively.

Consider the emergent conception of dialogic constitutionalism in more detail:

As participants to the—dialogic—'political "procedure"', the egalitarian liberal-minded citizens all have an overriding moral interest simultaneously

(1) in the pursuit of effective social ordering by law ('Hobbes' thesis') and
(2) in the pursuit of legitimacy as the condition under which laws enacted by majorities can justifiably be made binding on dissenters.

The concept of 'legitimacy', in turn, has both a normative and an empirical or sociological dimension—but both remain closely interconnected. In its

(a) normative dimension, legitimacy denotes the only condition under which the citizens' mutual expectation of a general disposition of law-abidingness can morally be justified (moral legitimacy). By contrast, in its
(b) sociological dimension, legitimacy refers to the citizens' acceptance in fact of a legal system's claim to merited political authority by way of a sufficiently wide and inclusive overlapping consensus.

But, importantly, in Michelman's transformation, the overlapping consensus is no longer presumed to be pre-existing and limited to the 'central ranges' of the basic negative liberties (as in the case of Rawls' 'legitimation-by-constitution'), but is focused on the *deliberative procedure*

[61] Ibid, 364.

itself of *meaningful engagement* between citizens (that is, Michelman's 'Idas') themselves as participants, each with different contextual readings or rational reconstructions of a shared constitutional project. The argument recognizes that there are plural judgments about legitimacy by plural citizens. Michelman has accordingly emphasized the *dialogical* and *intersubjective dimension* of this procedure: 'My experience of E is in part a reflection of my experience of your experience, and vice versa, and so on.'[62] As participants, the citizens—each with different rational reconstructions—thus have a moral reason to reconstruct their shared constitutional practice in ways that are conducive to success as regards the achievement of its moral legitimacy. Moral legitimacy is a regulative ideal, a practice-constitutive presupposition we, *as discourse-participants*, unavoidably make, for otherwise our shared constitutional practice would become unintelligible and pointless.

In Rawls' proceduralizing scheme of legitimation-by-constitution, the constitutional court was 'an exemplar of public reason', but its role and remit remained confined to administering the central ranges of negative liberties which—so the assumption on which the proceduralist strategy relies—are less controversial and more amenable to producing and sustaining a society-wide agreement. Dialogic constitutionalism, in contrast, *decentres* and *horizontalizes* the constitution. The court's role is forum-creative, and the court *deepens* (rather than forecloses) *democracy* by multiplying the sites of contextual deliberation. The court, as Michelman characterizes the democratic-experimentalist approach,

> ... acts in the first instance as instigator and non-dictatorial overseer of engagements among stakeholders very broadly defined, among whom state actors hold no privileged position, in an ongoing process of interpretive clarification of what a constitutionally declared right [...] consists of in substance and, simultaneously and reciprocally, of what sorts of steps by what classes of actors are concretely—in the current conditions of society, economy, and so on—now in order toward the achievement of due and adequate service to everyone's core interest, a process of successively clarified 'benchmarking' as it is sometimes called. As the discursive benchmarking moves along and the emerging answers gain public recognition and authorization, the court might turn up the heat on deployment of its powers of review. At a relatively early stage, what the court presumes to dictate will be agendas of questions to be addressed and answered by

[62] Frank Michelman, 'Legitimacy, Strict Scrutiny, and the Case Against the Supreme Court', in: Robert C. Post (ed.), Citizens Divided. Campaign Finance Reform and the Constitution (Cambridge: Harvard University Press 2014) 106–24, at 118.

> one or another stakeholder group or class. At later stages, the court starts calling for substantive compliance with an emergent best practice consensus, in the name of the constitutional right […]. The screws tighten on what can count as a reasonable, sincere governmental response. The court serves as arbiter but it never has or claims a door-closing last word.[63]

This dialogic-constitutionalist argument, if successful, would show that courts can act in the service of radical democracy—rather than undermining it. The proposition is that experimentalist forms of judicial review can go a long way in allaying justiciability-related concerns about the contextualization of open-textured rights in general, and social rights in particular, and can serve as a creative device for securing an important role for courts even in domains where they work under obvious institutional constraints.

B. Political constitutionalism and weak-form review

Popular or political constitutionalism exalts public discourse as embodied in parliamentary systems 'in good working order' to the point of making courts redundant or illegitimate as a check on democratic decision making[64] or to the point of allowing courts merely to raise constitutional objections to legislation that can be overridden through the exercise of a final legislative word.[65]

Of course, if constitutional judicial review could be limited to protecting 'the fundamental rights that are necessary to the existence of a democratic political system' and be made to firmly operate 'within this sphere of fundamental democratic rights', then—as Robert Dahl and JH Ely have influentially argued—judicial review can hardly be faulted as undemocratic but should be recommended as actually democracy-reinforcing.[66] But it's easy to see why many political constitutionalists are wary of this kind of *democratarian*[67] argument: however sophisticated they may be, democracy-related justifications of judicial review themselves rest on contestable substantive judgments about democracy and its

[63] Frank Michelman, 'Legitimacy, The Social Turn and Constitutional Review: What Political Liberalism Suggests', in: KritV | CritQ | Rcrit, Jahrgang 98 (2015), Heft 3, pp. 183–205, at 199 (footnotes omitted).

[64] Waldron; Bellamy.

[65] Stephen Gardbaum, The New Commonwealth Model of Constitutionalism. Theory and Practice (Cambridge: Cambridge University Press 2013).

[66] Robert A. Dahl, How Democratic Is the American Constitution? (New Haven and London: Yale University Press, 2nd edition: 2003) 153 f.

[67] For the term and its elaboration, cf. Lawrence Sager, Justice in Plainclothes, a Theory of American Constitutional Practice (New Haven: Yale University Press 2004).

proper scope or 'sphere'. In this sense, those justifications simply become indistinguishable from contested direct judgments about justice. The constitutionalization of social rights may even appear as a sinister culturally hegemonic move—an 'appropriation of the rhetoric of social justice by threatened elites to bolster their own position in the ongoing political struggles of a specific polity'.[68] Accordingly, radical (or deep) democrats have concluded that the task of rights-based review must rightly fall to the citizens themselves whose politics and self-government are at stake, in part, out of a mistrust of the capacity of judicial elites to give a fair shake to socioeconomic rights, in part out of a concern that judicialization may fatefully bias modern democracies against innovation and openness.

Jeremy Waldron opposes strong-form judicial review on grounds, among others, of its non-compatibility with liberal conceptions of dignity and political equality.[69] Strong-form rights-based judicial review withdraws too much decision space from open political contestation in ways that undermine 'the dignity of citizenship'[70] and 'the public as actors themselves'.[71] If legitimacy-endangering dissensus extends even into the core-range of civil and political liberties, then there can only be the liberal-dignitarian master-right to participate as an equal in an undominated conversation in civil society, in which the nation itself develops—not imposed from above, but generated from the bottom—its own value-judgments on controversial questions of rights-interpretation. The parliament is the catalyst of that conversation and therefore the adequate and final custodian of individual rights. Majority decision ('MD'), Waldron contends, 'is neutral between the contested outcomes, treats participants equally, and gives each expressed opinion the greatest weight possible compatible with giving equal weight to all opinions'.[72] To suggest that constitutional judges resemble Ulysses' shipmates, because they are merely enforcing society's own precommitments impermissibly begs the question in favour of judicial review and against ordinary legislative procedures, whenever citizens reasonably disagree about the meaning of those precommitments.[73]

[68] Ran Hirshl, Towards Juristocracy. The Origins and Consequences of the New Constitutionalism (Cambridge: Harvard University Press 2004), 49.

[69] Waldron, 'The Core Case Against Judicial Review', in: 115 The Yale Law Journal, 1346–405, 1353 (2006). Judicial review 'disenfranchises ordinary citizens and brushes aside cherished principles of representation and political equality in the final resolution of issues about rights'.

[70] Jeremy Waldron, Citizenship and Dignity (ms. 2013).

[71] Richard Bellamy, 'Public Law as Democracy: The Case of Constitutional Rights', in: Cormac MacAmblaigh, Claudio Michelon, and Neil Walker (eds.), After Public Law (Oxford: OUP 2013).

[72] Ibid, at 1388. [73] Ibid, at 1393 f.

But there is a cost: why should persistent, 'discrete and insular minorities'—consistent losers with little hope or chance of ever getting their way in the majoritarian process—ever accept this way of looking at it?[74] Strong democrats might face a considerable cost, if outright rejection of judicial review were to imply a total absence of subjection of procedural democracy to any form or sense of constitutional-moral 'bindingness'—the subjugation of the actual, living popular will to the considered judgments of higher law. There is a slippery slope away from constitutional bindingness and towards antinomianism.

In response, to avoid political antinomianism, Waldron insists on an important qualifying assumption pointing beyond a pluralist (aggregative) conception towards a deliberative conception of democracy—by stipulating that a polity's democratic institutions must be in a 'reasonably good working order'. The 'good working order' condition is rather strongly defined to include an adequate respect for the liberal idea of rights. On the parliamentary side, 'debates must be informed by a culture of democracy, valuing responsible deliberation and political equality' and members, both of the majority and of minorities, must actually care about rights and disagree in good faith. With these assumptions in place, 'if there are perceived inequities of representation that derogate seriously from the ideal of political equality, it is understood among all the members of the society that this is an appropriate criticism to make and that, if need be, the legislature and the political system be changed to remedy it'—either by parliamentary initiative or by referendum,[75] and with the legislative process being 'open to consideration of individual cases'.[76]

Richard Bellamy presents an analogous case for a form of 'political constitutionalism'—a case more closely tailored to the British system with the Human Rights Act 1998 and its exposure to Europe (the EU and the ECHR). Again, MD is the final decider; and its special role is thought to follow directly from rights disagreements. 'Part of the political constitutionalist move', as Bellamy explains, 'is to point out that the political process itself—including majority rule—is a constitutional constraint on how politics is done'.[77] Liberal constraints on politics are wholly internalized into the political process itself, correctly understood. Bellamy rejects the 'liberal conception' of rights as

[74] Stephen Macedo, 'Against Majoritarianism: Democratic Values and Institutional Design', 90 Boston University Law Review 1029–42, at 1038 (2010), with reference to Ely.

[75] Ibid, at 1362. [76] Ibid, at 1380.

[77] In correspondence with author [email of 24 January 2013].

non-interference and endorses a republican conception of liberty as discursive non-domination. Constitutional rights 'need to be themselves constituted through, maintained, and regulated via a democratic process';[78] and the 'best available way of mediating between rival [rights-] claims is a fair process in which each person's views are treated on par with everyone else's'—a process reflecting 'the democratic spirit that lies at the heart of any reasonable rights claim'.

But Bellamy, too, in order to avoid infinite regression—permanent disregard for the rights and interests of the vulnerable—insists on an all-important qualifying assumption similar to Waldron's 'good-working-order' condition. He identifies three constraints on good politics: first, participants must show an 'equal respect for the different views of individuals as rights bearers', secondly, they must also demonstrate an 'equal concern for [the individuals'] capacity to employ their rights on the same terms as others'; and thirdly, collective decisionmaking 'will have to answer the "traditional purpose" of rights as a means of holding power to account and marking its limits'. Hence, not everything is construed, rather these three requirements must be met: they are constraints on good politics. The three constraints of course closely mirror, in reverse order, TH Marshall's triad of rights in the modern welfare state—liberal, social, and political.

So: the inclusion in politics of an adequate respect for the idea of liberal rights depends, according to both Waldron's and Bellamy's political constitutionalist analysis, entirely on whether the conditions set out by the qualifying assumptions are satisfied: the country's political and practical life *is* in a 'good working order' and politics *is* imbued with the right 'democratic spirit' and pursued with the right ethos. But, again, it is not clear why 'discrete and insular minorities'—consistent losers with little hope or chance of ever getting their way in the majoritarian process—should ever accept this way of looking at it. If reasonable interpretive disagreement is pervasive, then the fulfilment of these conditions—the answer to the question whether the 'good-working-order' requirement *is* satisfied *in particular controversies about rights-application*—will of course also be subject to interminable reasonable disagreement among citizens, according to the very premise of reasonable interpretive pluralism on which turns the entire argument. Persistent minorities will simply disagree and argue that the choice of a majoritarian procedure itself is question-begging: there is

[78] Bellamy, op cit.

no conceptual 'escalator' which would straightaway take us from the premise of rights disagreements directly to parliamentary supremacy and legislative finality. In other words, we should acknowledge, as Macedo has pointed out in his trenchant critique of Waldron's majoritarianism, the existence of an 'interpretive gap' between the principle of political equality and the more concrete rules and norms that structure decisionmaking in particular institutional settings and accordingly accept that 'other decision rules are also consistent with political equality and may be fairer and more inclusive'.

Both Waldron and Bellamy are aware of this concern. Both distinguish between 'strong' and 'weak' review and declare only the former to be their target. An argument for—weak—judicial review which Waldron says he does 'respect' is that it may not always be easy for legislatures to see what issues of rights are embedded in a legislative proposal brought before them; it might not always be easy for them to envisage what issues of rights might arise from its subsequent application. So it is useful to have a mechanism that allows citizens to bring these issues to everyone's attention as they arise. But this is an argument for weak judicial review only, not for a strong form of the practice in which the abstract question of right that has been identified is settled in the way that the court deems appropriate.[79] Weak-form judicial review, Waldron says, operates as 'a kind of institutionalization of [. . .] alertness to issues of rights'.

But introducing an alertness mechanism does nothing to assuage the concern mentioned above about constitutional bindingness. The legislature retains the final word about constitutional compliance. Waldron's and Bellamy's political constitutionalism thus can be seen as an application of a principal/agent conception of democracy. The people (the Principal) instruct the parliament; the courts (as agents) are instruction-takers. But the principal/agent model resolves the problem of constitutional bindingness only by defining it away. In major, water-shed cases about constitutional meaning, judicial intervention will lead to a prolonged process of deliberation and contestation. In the course of that deliberative process, the preferences and identities on all sides—of citizens, parliaments, stakeholders, courts—and the sense of what counts as a valid reason and what doesn't will be transformed. Once deliberation moves centre-stage, it is no longer evident who is the Principal and who the agent.

[79] J. Waldron, 'The Core Case Against Judicial Review', in: 115 The Yale Law Journal 1346–405, 1370 (2006).

C. Political constitutionalism, weak-form review, and the experimentalist turn

Prompted by these concerns, Mark Tushnet has developed a more nuanced account of how judicial review can improve democracy over time. Tushnet broadly agrees with Michelman's 'second proceduralization' but still defends political constitutionalism as 'one front in the on-going effort to change cultural understandings', according to which courts are the culturally privileged sites of constitutional contestation.[80]

Tushnet re-interprets the familiar countermajoritarian difficulty as an institutional version of reasonable disagreement over the proper specification of abstractly defined values. Neither legislators nor courts *ex ante* understand how best to vindicate those values. The obvious problem with strong-form review accordingly is that 'the court's position on the question of specification, while reasonable, prevails over the legislature's also-reasonable position on that question';[81] but it is 'hardly clear that constitutionalism requires that the reasonable views of the courts or other reviewing institutions prevail over the reasonable views of the enacting legislature'.[82]

'Weak-form review', as Tushnet uses the term, is the idea that the specification of constitutional values no longer depends on courts alone but on the outcome of a judicial-legislative dialogue, conducted over time. Responding to lawsuits that have been brought, courts assess legislation against constitutional norms, but 'do not have the final word on whether statutes comply with those norms'.[83] The legislature reassesses its position in the light of what the court has said; and if the legislature concludes that its initial position was reasonable enough, its interpretation prevails, without the need for recourse to the intentionally burdensome process of constitutional amendment.[84] The iterative features of weak-form review improve the legislative process overall by making it more attentive to reasons and thus by making the democratic Principal more true to herself. Tushnet describes the advantages of dialogic review systems with regard to three scenarios that may arise in two-party political systems: first, as a device for overcoming legislative inertia (for example

[80] Mark Tushnet, Questions about Michelman's Second Proceduralization, op. cit., at 220 f.

[81] Mark Tushnet, Comparative Constitutional Law . . ., at 58.

[82] Mark Tushnet, 'The Rise of Weak-Form Judicial Review', in: Tom Ginsburg and Rosalind Dixon (eds.), Comparative Constitutional Law (Cheltenham: Edward Elgar Publishing 2011) 326–7, at 323.

[83] Mark Tushnet, Weak Courts, Strong Rights. Judicial Review and Social Welfare Rights in Comparative Constitutional Law (Princeton: Princeton University Press 2008), at IX.

[84] Ibid, at 57.

when a statute is found to be outdated); second, with regard to unconstitutional details of a complex statutory scheme (details which the legislature has overlooked and which could be altered without impairing the statute's overall effectiveness); and third with regard to overcoming the legislative blockade by intense, well-organized minority factions (e.g. when judicial invalidation of a contested statute has strong public support and the intense minority faction no longer has the bargaining power to insist on its re-enactment).[85]

Tushnet argues that these iterative features of weak-form review make it particularly well-suited for the enforcement of socioeconomic rights. To enforce those rights courts will typically issue systemic remedies rather than individual-level remedies which, due to their costliness and random nature, are seen as too intrusive on legislative prerogatives. Systemic remedies involve a dialogue between complex bureaucracies, local elected officials, and various civil society stakeholders in addition to the legislature. The judge makes an initial effort to intervene in the bureaucracy's operation and observes how the initial intervention works in practice, and then alters the remedy in the light of the information that is revealed. This iterative process can recur many times until a best-practice consensus emerges.[86] Notice that here the focus shifts from 'weak-form' review, which is focused on the binary judicial-political dialogue, to experimentalist review, which is focused on a multipolar discursive process involving multiple stakeholders.

In his more recent work, Tushnet has begun to endorse experimentalist review and has argued that experimentalist review is not confined to socioeconomic rights but may even be invoked in connection with classic negative liberties.

In a comment on Michelman, Tushnet has offered two illustrations, drawn from the US constitutional experience, of where the experimentalist model might be appropriate even in the domain of freedom of expression.[87] The first example concerns the system of regulating the financing of political campaigns. The moral dissensus here is between those who defend extensive regulation of campaign finance in an effort to neutralize or minimize the influence of money accumulated in the private market on *deliberative democracy*, and those opposing regulation on the basis of a view of democracy as a *pluralist marketplace of ideas* where adherents of specific views are free to advertise their views as extensively

[85] Ibid, at 58. [86] Mark Tushnet, Comparative Constitutional Law ..., at 65 f.

[87] Mark Tushnet, Questions about Michelman's Second Proceduralization, op. cit., at 222.

as they can. The second illustration is drawn from the Supreme Court's case law starting with the 1971 decision in *Cohen v California*[88] where the Supreme Court held unconstitutional a criminal prosecution of a young man wearing a jacket with 'Fuck the Draft' emblazoned on its back. As Tushnet reports, the Supreme Court in *Cohen v California* noted that the only arguably defensible ground for the prosecution was a government interest in elevating the level of public discourse and in counteracting an implicit risk of incitements to lawbreaking but concluded that freedom of expression precluded the government from pursuing that interest by means of suppressing expression, in part because of the high risk that prosecutors might move selectively against disfavoured groups. Yet, as Tushnet points out, the legislature might wish to strike the balance differently, and the question arises why the Supreme Court should have the ultimate power to usurp the legislature's also-reasonable choice.

As Tushnet explains, one might read both these examples as the Court signalling to the legislatures that the principles they are seeking to implement are defensible, but that the means were flawed in identifiable ways:

> We might even draw one immediate doctrinal implication from the thought that experimentalist review is suitable for freedom of expression problems … [M]ost of the law of freedom of expression in the *United States* is substantive, specifying that some rules are constitutionally impermissible because of their content. Experimentalist review would replace most substantive rules with a much-expanded role for doctrines like vagueness and overbreadth. Invoking vagueness, a court would tell the legislature that it should try again to identify more clearly the expressive activity that it seeks to regulate; invoking overbreadth, a court would tell the legislature to reconsider the scope of its regulation, to see whether it could be rewritten in a way that targeted more precisely the expressive concern.[89]

As Tushnet explains with regard to the second illustration, the Supreme Court initially allowed persecutions only when they agreed that a risk of lawbreaking existed, without asking serious questions about likelihood and causality between expression and unlawful activity. But experience showed that this approach led to prosecutions that seemed to exaggerate the risk of harm and to underestimate the contribution the regulated speech could make to political discussion. Hence, '[o]ver time', as Tushnet explains, the Supreme Court began to require a tighter causal connection between speech critical of government policy and ensuing law-breaking, 'with an "emergent best-practice consensus" eventually

[88] *Cohen v California*, 403 U.S. 15 (1971). [89] Ibid, at 223.

arising'.[90] The new consensus was that the causal connection had to be extremely close and expression had to take the form of incitement to lawbreaking. As Tushnet concludes, these requirements 'are not founded in deep principles about free speech, but rather in concerns about how real world institutions actually go about implementing rules dealing with speech that is (reasonably) believed to have some causal connection to law-breaking. Such concerns, in my view, are at the heart of experimentalist review'.[91]

By emphasizing the temporal or evolutive dimension of judicial review, Tushnet's view moves beyond Waldron's and Bellamy's conception of judicial review as a mere alerting mechanism. Importantly, Tushnet emphasizes that the progressive clarification of the meaning of a right may transform disputes themselves: as constitutional disputes mature over repeat litigation, a deeper understanding of the importance and weight of the principle involved—here freedom of expression—crystallizes. Call this the dimension of justificatory ascent: the requirement (in Tushnet's example) of an 'extremely close' connection between expression and harm (the risk of incitement to lawbreaking) makes sense only against the backdrop of a principled and deeper understanding of why free expression deserves a very high degree of protection in a particular context. Tushnet envisages a recursive constitutional learning process: in time, 'strong-form review may emerge out of weak-form review with respect to particular topics'; and this involves 'the possibility that strong-form review can be chosen by a nations' people as the result of the self-understanding they reach over time'.[92] Enough experience may have accumulated 'to give us—judges, legislators, and the people alike—confidence that giving judges the final word will not interfere with our ability to govern ourselves in any significant way'.[93]

An important consequence of the experimentalist turn is that the relationship between courts and democracy can no longer adequately be captured by the traditional principal-agent model of democratic accountability. According to that model, there is a sequence from the exercise of legislative power that lays down a general rule applying to everyone to judicial proceedings that make a determination that a specific problem falls within the ambit of that rule. But the principal (the people) is typically

[90] Ibid, at 223, with reference to Frank Michelman's concept of best-practice consensus.

[91] Ibid, at 223.

[92] Mark Tushnet, Weak Courts, Strong Rights. Judicial Review and Social Welfare Rights in Comparative Constitutional Law (Princeton: Princeton University Press 2008), at 75 and 263.

[93] Ibid, at 263 f.

divided and ambiguous on nearly any normative dispute concerning society as a whole. Even when the principal has spoken it may not know what it has said. In the course of an extended process of deliberation and contestation the principal and the agent will both be transformed, and one cannot determine with certainty at any point in time who is the principal and who the agent. Unlike traditional weak-form review, experimentalist review does not primarily focus on a binary judicial-political dialogue. Instead, it focuses on the process in which the various stakeholders themselves develop substantive standards that interpret constitutional requirements.

As I will argue in the next step, the move beyond principal-agent analysis also involves a more general shift of attention on the relation between courts and the process of public-opinion formation.

D. From 'dualist democracy' to 'democratic constitutionalism'

1. 'Dualist democracy'

Bruce Ackerman conceives of constitutional democracy as *dualist*, where the 'higher law', enacted by a democratic constituent power through cycles of popular sovereignty and enforced by judicial review, is held distinct and apart from subordinate ordinary law made by the legislative bodies.[94] Whereas 'the monist treats *every* act of judicial review as presumptively anti-democratic', constitutional dualists, as Ackerman suggests, are able to argue that constitutional courts can '*serve* democracy by protecting the hard-won judgments of a mobilized citizenry against fundamental change by political elites who have failed to establish the requisite kind of mobilized support from the citizenry at large'.[95] Accordingly, the court's role is to protect and preserve the integrity of those past 'constitutional moments' when a refounding occurred. As John Rawls has remarked, endorsing Ackerman's dualism, '[i]f the court assumes this role and effectively carries it out, it is incorrect to say that it is straightforwardly antidemocratic'.[96]

Ackerman's 'dualist democracy' can be seen as a version of a principal/agent conception of democracy. The Principal (the mobilized citizenry), from time to time,—in a process analogous to Thomas Kuhn's model of scientific discovery and innovation—enacts transformative, paradigm-changing framework understandings of constitutional law

[94] Bruce Ackerman, 'Constitutional Politics/Constitutional Law', 99 Yale Law Journal 453–547 (1989); and, recently, Bruce Ackerman, We the People (3): The Civil Rights Revolution (Cambridge: Harvard University Press 2014).

[95] Ibid, at 465.

[96] John Rawls, Political Liberalism, op. cit., at 233 f.

through periodic citizenship and the Court (the agent) exercises the citizens' right to self-government *vicariously* in times of 'normal politics' when the broad popular movement for constitutional change has become a distant memory. Ackerman's aim is to defend a conception of the 'living constitution' as consistent with the foundational 'historical commitments . . . [made] by the American people'.[97] To that end, he reconstructs the 'lost logics of *Brown v Board of Education*'. *Brown*, he suggests, was doubly innovative. First, in *Brown* the Supreme Court established a conception of 'spherical justice'. In the past, 'for Reconstruction Republicans, only three spheres of life were worth distinguishing: the political sphere, which involved voting and the like; the civil sphere, which involved the legal protection of life and liberty, including rights of property and contract; and the social sphere, which involved everything else'.[98] But the innovation by Justice Warren in *Brown* was 'to pluralize the social realm into a series of more discrete spheres'[99] and to recognize that *institutionalized, systemic humiliation*—the denial of human agency as a minimally competent actor[100]—can occur in any of the sundry spheres of modern life, ranging from schools to employment, housing etc.[101] Judges, accordingly, are to rely on their contextual 'judicial situation-sense'[102] and 'make commonsense judgments about the prevailing meaning of social practices'[103] by identifying 'the dominant norms that prevail in particular spheres of life'[104] in order to faithfully carry out the People's instructions.

Second, *Brown* was innovative insofar as it lay the ground for subsequent inter-branch engagement and an emergent system of 'coordinate constitutionalism'.[105] Thus, Congress responded to *Brown* with the 'landmark statutes of the civil rights revolution',[106] including two 'quasi-constitutional . . . super statutes':[107] the Civil Rights Act of 1964 and the Voting Rights Act of 1965, creating new opportunities for private enforcement and empowering the executive branch to enforce them in new ways. While the Court still took the lead during the first decade after *Brown*, its new role became 'to participate constructively in a joint project with the political branches and executive agencies to redeem the egalitarian objectives defined by the president and Congress in the name of the American people'.[108]

[97] Ibid, at 34 f. [98] Ibid, at 130. [99] Ibid.

[100] Bruce Ackerman, We the People (3): The Civil Rights Revolution (Cambridge: Harvard University Press 2014), at 138.

[101] Ibid, at 13. [102] Ibid, at 131, with reference to Karl Llewellyn. [103] Ibid, at 132.

[104] Ibid, at 132. [105] Ibid, at 162. [106] Ibid, at 34. [107] Ibid, at 34. [108] Ibid, at 229.

Commenting on Ackerman's seminal 1989 article, Michelman critically observed that, in Ackerman's project, 'judicial power cannot be legitimate unless its exercise consists, in the final analysis, of the translation of directions uttered in the past by someone else—the people acting in a suitably organized and galvanized jurisgenerative political modality'.[109] But, as Michelman objects, 'the *Brown* Court spoke in the accents of invention, not of convention; it spoke for the future, criticizing the past; it spoke for law, creating authority; it engaged in political argument'.[110] In other words, in Ackerman's account *legitimacy* is historical-authorial, not moral-theoretical (in the sense of Rawls' liberal principle of legitimacy). In contrast to Ackerman, the democratic-experimentalist view does not reserve deliberation to self-validating *exceptional* constitutional moments. Instead, democratic experimentalism is proceduralist and envisages a recursive constitutional learning process in which the framework understandings are subject to *ongoing revision* in the course of their application to live political issues as they arise. 'Spherical equality'—the intrinsic norms and mutual boundaries of social spheres—is never naturally given but in flux and deeply contested in particular controversies. As Rawls explained,

> A domain so-called, or a sphere of life, is not [. . .] something already given apart from political conceptions of justice. A domain [. . .] rather is simply the result [. . .] of how the principles of political justice are applied, directly to the basic structure and indirectly to the associations within it. The principles defining the equal basic liberties and opportunities of citizens always hold in and through all so-called domains.[111]

In other words, we need procedures to define the proper meaning and scope of spheres.

2. 'Democratic constitutionalism'

'Democratic constitutionalism', as advanced by Robert Post and Reva Siegel, does not take a consensus on constitutional meaning for granted.[112] Post and Siegel argue that, in the context of US constitutionalism, nationwide understandings of constitutional meaning on matters such as gender equality, abortion, and same-sex marriage have been, and continue to be,

[109] Frank Michelman, 'Law's Republic', 97 Yale Law Journal 1493–537, at 1522 (1988).

[110] Ibid, at 1524.

[111] John Rawls, 'The Idea of Public Reason Revisited', in: Samuel Freeman (ed.), Collected Papers (Cambridge: Harvard University Press 1999), 573–615, at 598–99.

[112] Robert Post and Reva Siegel, 'Democratic Constitutionalism', in: ibid (eds.), The Constitution in 2020 (Oxford: OUP 2009), 25–34, at 27.

transformed as a consequence of social and political mobilization within a shared constitutional framework. Ongoing struggles about constitutional meaning, often triggered by social movements, in this way continuously shape the content of constitutional law.

But while the constitution must be responsive to public opinion and changing social values, the constitution must also continue to function as a fundamental law, as a limit and foundation of politics. The constitution's legitimacy as law, in part, depends on its being a living constitution, but, in part, it also, as Post and Siegel insist, depends on the constitution being distinct from popular politics.

In order to address this dilemma, Post and Siegel develop a concept of agonistic consensus which is reminiscent of Michelman's concept of constitutional tolerance. They argue that, although interpretive disagreement might pose a threat to the constitution's legitimacy, disagreement about constitutional meaning can, under suitable conditions and over time, paradoxically actually sustain, rather than undermine, the constitution.[113]

For that to be the case, the constitution must provide citizens with the possibility of influencing the shape of constitutional law which they are supposed to share. Citizens can share a constitution—that is, continue to regard the constitution as their fundamental law, even when their own respective constitutional views do not prevail—as long as they can plausibly 'believe in the possibility of persuading others—and therefore ultimately the Court—to embrace their views about constitutional meaning'.[114] Legitimacy, in this sense, can come from *potential*—more so than actual or pre-existing—consensus. As long as the citizens are able to formulate their most passionately held commitments in the language of an ongoing, shared constitutional tradition, DC argues, they will in fact invigorate and reconfirm that intersubjectively shared background.

Courts play a crucial role in preventing constitutional agonism from degenerating into destructive social antagonism. Post and Siegel emphasize the 'constructive effects of backlash'.[115] For example, courts may articulate what they believe to be a constitutional value, and social movements may then use the courts' interpretations to mobilize a political backlash that rebounds to affect judicial interpretations of a constitutional right. As Post and Siegel write, '[i]f courts interpret the Constitution in

[113] Ibid, at 27; ibid, 'Roe Rage: Democratic Constitutionalism and Backlash', 42 Harvard Civil Rights and Civil Liberties Law Review 373–433 (2007).

[114] Ibid, at 27.

[115] Post/Siegel, 'Roe Rage: Democratic Constitutionalism and Backlash', 42 Harvard Civil Rights and Civil Liberties Law Review 373–433 (2007), at 375.

terms that diverge from the deeply held convictions of the American people, Americans will find ways to communicate their objections and resist judicial judgments'.[116] Or social movements may take the initiative in proposing that certain constitutional values do exist and courts may subsequently give these values legal form in the context of constitutional adjudication.[117] Political backlash, then, is 'constructive', when it promotes constitutional solidarity: '[d]emocratic constitutionalism suggests that it is neither feasible nor desirable for courts to elevate conflict avoidance into a fundamental principle of constitutional adjudication'.[118]

Post and Siegel's discussion of the US Supreme Court abortion-law decision *Planned Parenthood v. Casey*[119]—decided nineteen years after *Roe*—offers one illustration of how, in their view, judicial authority can be deployed 'to channel dispute rather than to end it'.[120] *Casey* demonstrates, Post and Siegel argue, that judicial review and deep disagreement in society are not incompatible and that constitutional law can emerge from political controversy.[121] In *Casey*, the Court responded to both sides of the dispute by fashioning a form of constitutional law 'in which each side can find recognition'[122] and respect to both sides of the abortion controversy is accorded. The Court 'articulate[d] with great eloquence the ideals of both proponents and opponents of abortion' in an effort to 'to draw those engaged in the abortion controversy into a common discussion about the meaning of the Constitution'. Thus, on the one hand, the Court proclaimed that a woman's 'suffering is too intimate and personal for the State to insist, without more, upon its own vision of the woman's role', however culturally dominant that vision may have been.[123] But, on the other hand, the Court also acknowledged that the State remains free to encourage women, through its rules and regulations, 'to know that there are philosophic and social arguments of great weight that can be brought to bear in favor of continuing the pregnancy to full term and that there are procedures and institutions to allow adoption of unwanted children as well as a certain degree of state assistance if the mother chooses to

[116] Ibid, at 374.

[117] Robert Post, 'Theorizing Disagreement: Reconceiving the Relationship Between Law and Politics', 98 California Law Review 1319–50, at 1344 (2010).

[118] Post/Siegel, Roe Rage, at 376.

[119] *Planned Parenthood of Southeastern Pennsylvania v. Casey*, 505 U.S. 833 (1992).

[120] Post/Siegel, 'Roe Rage: Democratic Constitutionalism and Backlash', 42 Harvard Civil Rights and Civil Liberties Law Review 373–433 (2007), at 428. Notice, however, Mark Tushnet's contrasting view according to which *Casey* forms part of a '*jurisprudence of "wrong the day it was decided"*' for its 'undue burden' test, cf. M. Tushnet at http://balkin.blogspot.co.uk/2016/05/abandoning-defensive-crouch-liberal.html.

[121] Ibid, at 430.

[122] Ibid, at 439.

[123] *Casey*, 505 U.S. at 852; Post/Siegel, at 428.

raise the child herself'.[124] By dismantling the trimester system of *Roe*, the 'Janus-faced holding'[125] in *Casey* 'insists on the independence of law even as it subjects law to democratic pressure'[126] and offers an illustration of how the requirements of political responsiveness and democratic legitimacy, on the one hand, and a commitment to the law/politics distinction and to judicial independence, on the other, can go hand in hand and support one another as part of a new 'jurisprudential model' that does not avoid but constructively harnesses interpretive conflict.[127]

So: the legitimacy of judicial judgments depends in part on the contribution these judgments can make to the *ongoing formation* of consensus by *creating fora* in which contending claimants to rights can enter dialogue, with each other and the judiciary. Judicial judgments '[i]n point of fact' never foreclose or pre-empt politics,[128] but meaningful engagement becomes possible and each side of the conflict can eventually find recognition as a participant to a shared deliberative process.

But there is a tension between this *forum-creative role of courts*, on the one hand, and democratic constitutionalism's *exceptionalistic* conception of constitutional courts as prudential guardians of the 'values that from the perspective of the legal system underlie the identity and nature of the polity itself',[129] on the other. In order to render the constitution responsive to changing (but contested) social values while at the same time preserving public confidence in its legitimacy as a shared fundamental law of the polity, judges must exercise prudent 'judicial statesmanship'[130] and 'bear an ethic of responsibility for their decisionmaking'.[131] In exerting this role, the Court 'imagines itself as conserving the shared social values that make the nation possible and that are therefore essential to the preservation of the polity'.[132] In the Court's framework-setting decisions, such as *Marbury* or on freedom of expression, 'an ethic of responsibility may vindicate such judges if their decisions are deemed necessary to secure overmatching benefit to the legal system or to the polity, or if their decisions are perceived as necessary to avert greater harm to the legal system or to the polity'.[133]

[124] Casey, at 872; Post/Siegel, 'Roe Rage: Democratic Constitutionalism and Backlash', 42 Harvard Civil Rights and Civil Liberties Law Review 373–433 (2007), at 429.

[125] Post/Siegel, at 429. [126] Post/Siegel, at 430. [127] Post/Siegel, at 433.

[128] Robert Post, 'Theorizing Disagreement: Reconceiving the Relationship Between Law and Politics', 98 California Law Review 1319–50, at 1347 (2010).

[129] Ibid, at 1345. [130] Ibid, at 1346 ff. [131] Ibid, at 1348. [132] Ibid, at 1346.

[133] Ibid, at 1349.

The Post/Siegel approach seems most relevant to the formative stages of conflict resolution where a clear sense of direction has yet to emerge. In those primordial formative stages, the emphasis must lie on everyone's inclusion in public discourse, as Post/Siegel argue. But even if we assume that it is possible to clearly distinguish between progressive and non-progressive causes, democratic constitutionalism still retains an element of judicial finality, if only in ensuring the non-finality of public discourse. Democratic constitutionalism seems to have less traction when foundational public debates have cooled down but deeply divisive questions of constitutional application still persist. These may be questions which, despite the questions of justice they clearly pose, may fail to reach sufficient public political salience or questions of justice that fail to mobilize a broad social movement, given the deeply unpopular nature of the cause in a current political climate.

Democratic experimentalism, by contrast, does not reserve deliberation to exceptional conditions—defined either as episodic 'constitutional moments' (Ackerman) or by the ongoing struggles about constitutional meaning catalysed by progressive social movements where they arise (Post/Siegel). Robert Post himself has pointed out that, while the internal legal presumption of agreement must never blind actors to the ongoing social fact of disagreement, '[t]he professional and institutional structure of judicial decision making requires actors to argue cases *as though* they could be subject to definite resolution'.[134] It is precisely on this dialogic aspect of mutual engagement that experimentalism builds.

From a *non-state* European perspective what seems important in Post/Siegel's reconstruction of the US constitutional experience is the both normative and sociological insight that exercises of judicial authority never foreclose politics but, due to their iterative and recursive nature, can constructively channel disputes and thereby provide a *forum* in which each side can eventually find recognition as a participant to a discourse in the ongoing struggle about constitutional meaning. But while EU law has its own obvious examples of judicial statesmanship—*van Gend en Loos* comes to mind—the idea of judicial statesmanship (undergirded by an ethic of responsibility) overtaxes the 'deep forms of agreement'[135] (as a shared 'realm of meaning'[136]) on which a (national) polity is thought to depend: a consensus which seems less available as a resource in the European experience of constitutionalism beyond the state. Here, in

[134] Ibid, at 1347. [135] Ibid, at 1339.

[136] Robert Post and Reva Siegel, 'Democratic Constitutionalism', in: ibid (eds.), The Constitution in 2020 (Oxford: OUP 2009), 25–34, at 27 (with reference to Robert Cover's concept of 'nomos').

the more legally pluralist and heterarchical European context—where questions of application and entrenchment of a principle remain deeply intertwined—the proceduralist dimension of adjudication radically moves to the foreground.

E. Democratic experimentalism as a legal and constitutional theory

Vis-à-vis liberal constitutionalism's reliance on a negative consensus on the 'central ranges' of the basic negative liberties, on the one hand, and political constitutionalism's reliance on a consensus on majoritarian democracy 'in good working order', democratic experimentalism occupies a third position by virtue of its relentless proceduralism. As participants to constitutional discourse, we as (non-official) citizens invariably attempt to deliberate and argue in good faith in ideologically divisive cases and also perceive and recognize others who disagree with us as proceeding on the same basis from their different, if not antagonistic, perspectives, not as cynical manipulators. In doing so, we ascribe a moral point and purpose not only to our shared deliberative practice but also to the constitution itself: this is what the shared underlying commitment to interpretive charity means. The recognition of others as equally legitimate interlocutors and the ascription of value to the shared deliberative practice we jointly engage in are what transforms stakeholders from antagonists into *participants* in a deliberative procedure. Accordingly, as participants we are able to experience novel conflict constellations, where they arise, less as threats to an existing compromise or modus vivendi than as invitations to reconsider, and successively deepen and broaden, our shared understanding of the constitution and its moral point and purpose: its telos of achieving principled fair balance. But, of course, ascriptions of good-faith plausible value—of what fair balance means both at the level of application and in theory means—remain agent-relative and will sharply and persistently differ among participants.

In contested cases, where there is no right answer that satisfies everyone, that is, under contemporary conditions of uncertainty and moral dissensus, courts can nevertheless exert an important forum-creative and agenda-setting role as initiators and, over continuous political time, as referees of reasonable debate: courts can induce a non-hierarchical dialogue in which the conflict parties themselves, state actors, civil society organizations, and the diverse stakeholders in the public sphere develop flexible substantive standards of what *fair balance* must mean that meet and interpret constitutional requirements. The distinct feature of the model, then, lies in the shift it proposes towards a *more indirect form of judicial intervention* that relies on the role of stakeholders themselves in progressively clarifying constitutional meaning but always subject to recursive court supervision.

What are the normative and institutional prerequisites of this dialogue? What principles can guide recursive court-supervision and the choice between more experimentalist and more strong-form modalities of judicial intervention? Recall two standard concerns about democratic-experimentalist modalities of adjudication.

First, there is the democratic-minded concern that experimentalism will outrun the political legitimacy of the judiciary and exhaust its practical and cognitive resources. It is undemocratic for judges to make the kind of fundamental moral judgments that fidelity to the true spirit (not just the letter) of the constitution requires, because democratically responsible citizens ought to decide those fundamental, but morally controversial, issues which concern (but divide) society as a whole, for and by themselves through a process of meaningful reciprocal engagement. But critics allege that democratic experimentalism offers to the vulnerable in society only procedure and endless postponement in lieu of closure and of a more robust substantive social right to demand a specific outcome or resolution.[137] As a consequence of the deliberative turn, social protections are weakened against economic liberties; those protections are constantly put at risk of being 'balanced away'. Experimentalist modalities of review would only cement an institutional asymmetry between law and politics which cuts deeply into the substance of socioeconomic rights in modern social market economies. But judicial elites are unlikely to give a fair shake to socioeconomic rights: those rights might forever remain *under-constitutionalized*.

Second, and coming from the opposite direction, there is a concern relating to the rule of law, to legalism, and to the constitutional framework itself as a consequence of *over-constitutionalization*. Critics argue that the retreat from judicial supremacy which democratic experimentalism proposes may amount to a decline of rights generally as judicially enforceable rights.[138] If ever more social interests could be claimed as rights, then the very idea of the constitution as a shared framework and higher law of

[137] For representative statements: Fritz Scharpf (in the EU context); Sandra Liebenberg and Katharine G. Young, 'Adjudicating Social and Economic Rights: Can Democratic Experimentalism Help?', in: Helena Alviar García et al. (eds.), Social and Economic Rights in Theory and Practice: Critical Inquiries (London and New York: Routledge 2015), 237, 251–53, at 219.

[138] Cf. Richard A. Epstein, The Classical Liberal Constitution (Cambridge: Harvard University Press 2014), 77–80 ; but also Martin Loughlin, 'Political Liberalism or Political Right? A Commentary on Michelman's

lawmaking would quickly lose its purchase. There is, if you will, a risk of hypertrophy. The constitution would no longer serve as a shared framework in morally divided societies, because imposing essentially contested judgments about justice *through the constitution* would violate the fundamental moral obligation of civility we, as citizens, owe to one another of respectful engagement with disagreeing fellow citizens as presumptively reasonable and equally arguing in good-faith, albeit with different moral priors. Those at the losing end of debate will object that democratic experimentalism replaces 'law' by 'policy' or by transient preferences or opinions of contemporary judges, thereby throwing into jeopardy the hard-won separation between law and politics—the sense that law and politics must be kept apart as much as possible in theory no less than in practice.

The engagement with these two concerns must be both at the theoretical and at the level of practice. Here, in the remainder of this section, I will spell out the substantive-normative and institutional elements of the democratic-experimentalist conception of adjudication by focusing on two aspects: democracy and legitimacy.

1. Deep (or radical) democracy

There are two different conceptions of democracy, one much narrower than the other. The differences between both have important implications for our understanding of the role and practice of judicial review.

The narrow view sees democracy as the rule of the majority, limited by the rights of political and social minorities, and as interpreted essentially in terms of voting.

A brief excursion may illustrate the point: in an important 1955 article on the *Foundations of Democracy*, Hans Kelsen described and defended—as against autocratic rule which maximizes domination and the will to power[139]—'liberal democracy [as] in the first place a specific procedure'[140]—procedure of guaranteeing the participation of the governed in government. But the transformation of the initial idea of natural freedom—the absence of government—into the idea of political freedom—participation in government—must never imply, as Kelsen went on to insist, the complete abandonment of the former, for '[w]hat remains is the principle of

Legitimacy, The Social Turn and Constitutional Review', in: KritV | CritQ | Rcrit, Jahrgang 98 (2015), Heft 3, pp. 212–19, at p. 217.

[139] Kelsen here explicitly argued against Carl Schmitt, cf. ibid, at footnote 49.

[140] Hans Kelsen, 'Foundations of Democracy', in 66(1) Ethics, Part 2: Foundations of Democracy 1–101, at 4 (1955).

a certain restriction of the power of government [...] which must not interfere with certain spheres of interest of the individual'[141] in the interest of the protection of minorities against arbitrary rule by majorities. Kelsen insisted that what he called the intellectual freedoms—the negative freedoms such as freedom of religion, opinion, and press—'belong to the essence of democracy'.[142] Hence, '[m]odern democracy cannot be separated from political liberalism',[143] while simultaneously 'there exists even a certain antagonism between them'.[144] So as to guarantee 'internal peace', this antagonism was to be eased through 'the permanent tension between majority and minority, government and opposition', which 'results in the dialectical process so characteristic of the democratic formation of the will of the state, that one rightly may say: democracy is discussion'.[145] The corresponding type of *psychological* attitude in a democracy is one of *tolerance* where—because the animating principle of democracy is not merely compromise but freedom combined with equality[146]—'the individual, the ego, wants freedom not only for himself but also for the others, for the *tu*'[147] and where the individual 'recognizes himself [or herself] in the other' and where the 'tendency toward aggression is diverted from its original direction against others to himself and thus is manifested in the tendency toward self-criticism ...'[148] In safeguarding the procedural (or 'rationalistic') character of democracy, legality plays a decisive role. Legality must aim at providing 'legal security',[149] allowing the individual 'to foresee, to a certain extent, the activities of the law-applying [by the administrative and judicial organs of the state]'.[150] In order to avoid arbitrary government, the rule of law must tie the exercise of the administrative and judicial functions 'as far as possible' to 'preestablished general norms'.[151] The provisos are important since they highlight that 'the application of the law ... is necessarily also a creation of law'[152] because the former 'implies an interpretation of the law' and because the ambiguity of human language allows 'almost always [for] different, sometimes contradictory interpretations of a general norm', meaning that '[t]here is practically no possibility of limiting the discretionary power of a supreme administrative or judicial organ'.[153]

141 Kelsen, ibid, at 27.
142 Kelsen, ibid, at 28.
143 Kelsen, ibid, at 27.
144 Kelsen, ibid, at 3 f.
145 Kelsen, ibid, at 28.
146 Kelsen, ibid, at footnote 48.
147 Kelsen, ibid, at 25 f.
148 Kelsen, ibid, at 26.
149 Kelsen, ibid, at 29.
150 Kelsen, ibid, at 77.
151 Kelsen, ibid, at 77.
152 Kelsen, ibid, at 78.
153 Kelsen, ibid, at 79.

Kelsen's *irenic* conception of democracy thus is inherently dialogical in its focus on mutual-perspective taking and, concomitantly, rejection of autocracy, authoritarianism, and non-discursive domination. But the conception also is a narrow or negative one which assigns to legality the role of ensuring legal security ('Rechtssicherheit'[154]) but not of *enhancing democracy*.

By contrast, the second—both broader and deeper, *deliberative*—conception interprets democracy in terms of public reasoning, through participatory discussions and public decision-making and by giving voice to hitherto despised and marginalized groups. The 'deliberative view ... requires that we offer considerations that others, despite fundamental differences of outlook, can reasonably be accepted to accept, not simply that we count their interests ...', as Joshua Cohen explains, and this requirement 'will ... impose some desirable constraint on the proposals that I can advance and defend'.[155] By the same token, this requirement also highlights the importance of bringing diverse (and adverse) perspectives to bear in addressing a common problem. Richard Rorty's insight that moral progress involves 'an increase in our ability to see more and more differences among people as morally irrelevant'[156] here comes to mind.

But, as the literature on democratic experimentalism points out, deliberative democracy becomes *deep* or *radical democracy*, if—as Roberto Unger has argued—the constitutional regime as a whole opens itself up, sphere-by-sphere, 'to a broad range of experiments in individual and social life and [is] maximally susceptible to correction in the light of experience'[157] and thus is no longer focused on parliamentary legislation exclusively. A constitutional regime can ensure its own corrigibility by extending what Unger calls a 'prerogative of apostasy'[158] to the vulnerable and excluded: a right to throw into doubt, and to force reconsideration of, existing legal and political routines and institutional settlements when they lack inclusiveness. Experimentalism in this way aims at attenuating the contrast 'between both inside a context and being outside it' by making society and culture more open to criticism and revision.[159]

154 Kelsen occasionally uses the German term.

155 Joshua Cohen, Reflections on Deliberative Democracy, in: Joshua Cohen, Philosophy, Politics, and Democracy (Cambridge: Harvard University Press 2009) 334–35.

156 Richard Rorty, Truth and Moral Progress: Philosophical Papers (Cambridge: Cambridge University Press 1998), 11.

157 Roberto M. Unger, The Religion of the Future (Cambridge: Harvard University Press 2014), 290.

158 Ibid.

159 Roberto M. Unger, Free Trade Reimagined (Princeton: Princeton University Press 2007), 102.

For sure, the idea of 'immanent criticism' strongly figured also in Hayek's conception of the exigencies of spontaneous social order and of the function of the judge as an organ—not creator, but servant—of an existing spontaneous order, acting 'to make the whole more consistent both internally as with the facts to which the rules are applied'.[160] But by emphasizing self-revision and *public deliberation and reason-giving*, democratic experimentalism is fundamentally different in its normative outlook from Hayek's view of a supposedly neutral market order, with a pre-ordained system of private law as the necessary and natural expression of spontaneous order in economic life.

In a similar vein, Charles Sabel and Bill Simon have emphasized democratic experimentalism's deep roots in American pragmatist philosophy, notably in John Dewey's work, in an effort to spell out the conceptual link between democracy and problem-solving under uncertainty and, concomitantly, 'to seek a kind of accountability we associate with law'.[161] Far from being paralysing, 'a persistent increase in uncertainty', Sabel argues, 'favors the emergence of a world ... in which mutual learning and joint problem solving give rise to a democratic community'.[162] Hence, the need for problem-solving under conditions of deep uncertainty strengthens, rather than undermines, the case for democratic institutions that emphasize provisionality, deliberation, and decentralization. Norms should be provisional so that they can be re-examined in the light of experience. Re-examination should take the form of deliberation in which diverse perspectives are brought to bear.[163] People form habits and formulate rules in order to deal effectively with their environment, but those habits and rules may congeal into blind routines. The democratic-experimentalist idea is to productively exploit encounters with dissonant experiences and 'irritations' in order to foster collective learning.

But how can norms be open to continuous re-assessment and yet provide the stability needed for effective social ordering by law? Discussion will typically begin by considering the efficacy of an existing form of co-operation in furthering its goals, but it may then reach the further stage

[160] Friedrich Hayek, Law, Legislation and Liberty, vol. 1. Rules and Order, 118 f. (1973).

[161] Charles F. Sabel and William H. Simon, 'Democratic Experimentalism', in: Justin Desautels-Stein and Christopher Tomlins (eds.), Searching for Contemporary Legal Thought (Cambridge and New York: Cambridge University Press 2017) 2; Charles F. Sabel, 'Dewey, Democracy, and Democratic Experimentalism', 9(2) Contemporary Pragmatism 35–55 (2012).

[162] Ibid, at 43.

[163] Charles F. Sabel and William H. Simon, 'Democratic Experimentalism', in: Justin Desautels-Stein and Christopher Tomlins (eds.), Searching for Contemporary Legal Thought (Cambridge and New York: Cambridge University Press 2017) 4.

where initial means-ends considerations are transformed into reconsideration of whether prior understanding of goals themselves needs revision in the light of experience. The experimentalist turn 'attenuates the distinction between enactment and implementation. Each diffuses the practice of deliberative re-assessment throughout the organization as a continuous practice'.[164] To that end—in order to avoid the myopia of localism while not falling prey to forms of dictatorial top-down regulation that are inimical to corrigibility and pluralism—experimentalism seeks to construct models of political decision which involve the interplay between a 'centre' that facilitates, supports, and co-ordinates local efforts, and 'local units' which are given autonomy to experiment with their own solutions to broadly defined problems of public policy. These relations can often be nested, for example, the centre may be a national government, but nation states can also be the lower-level actors as part of international regimes.[165] But '[t]ogether, the center and the local units set and revise goals, and the means of pursuing them in an iterative process', in an effort of progressive clarification of what, say, 'adequate education', 'access to health care services', or 'good water status' must mean. In this process of disciplined comparison, the framework goals, performance measures, and decision-making procedures themselves are periodically revised on the basis of alternatives reported and evaluated.

Radical democracy has far-reaching implications on the understanding of the concept and role of rights and of judicial intervention. Rights become *destabilization-rights*. Citizens can mobilize rights in order to seek what Unger called 'reconstructive intervention'[166] by courts to reshape an organization or a localized area of social practice frustrating the effective enjoyment of rights, for example a school or school system, prisons, or any other public institution.[167] Destabilization rights, as Sabel and Simon explain, are 'claims to unsettle and open up public institutions that have chronically failed to meet their obligations and that are substantially insulated from the normal processes of political accountability'.[168] Compared with more traditional forms of judicial intervention, courts are both more and less involved: more so, because judicial intervention aims at a 'permanent process of ramifying, participatory self-revision rather than

[164] Ibid, 7.

[165] For an example, cf. Gráinne de Búrca, 'Human Rights Experimentalism', 111 American Journal of International Law (2017).

[166] Roberto M. Unger, What Should Legal Analysis Become? (London: Verso 1999) 30 ff.

[167] Ibid.

[168] Charles F. Sabel and William H. Simon, 'Destabilization Rights: How Public Law Litigation Succeeds', 117 Harvard Law Review 1016, at 1020 (2003–2004).

a one-time readjustment to fixed criteria'; but also less so, because 'the norms that define compliance at any one moment are the work not of the judiciary, but of the actors who live by them'.[169]

By interpreting rights as *destabilization-rights*, courts can ensure the full and fair participation of stakeholders in a non-hierarchical process of debate and deliberation and thereby multiply the sites of deliberation and enhance democracy. For sure, even *reconstructive intervention* will have a constitutionalizing effect and tilt public decisionmaking in one way or another. But issues are never conclusively withdrawn from public debate and never insulated against political correction. Judicial intervention will elevate issues to the public agenda and help create a critical public sphere. The mobilization of rights by excluded or marginalized groups may generate a broader and ever more inclusive rights-discourse in society. In this sense, the concept of destabilization rights shows that constitutionalization does not mean *de-politicization*. To the contrary, courts become an interface between the various localized social spheres—such as the workplace, schools, or even nation-states—on the one hand, and a critical public, on the other. Courts can draw on the local knowledge, arguments, and expertise of stakeholders. But these arguments are subject to public scrutiny. Courts can help focus and deepen public debate, just as the public and the various stakeholders in turn can become critics of the courts, whenever the judicial preoccupation with precedent, legal coherence, and interpretation begins to distort debate.

2. Legitimation and consensus

Democratic experimentalism argues that legitimation does not require a pre-existing consensus, but *potential consensus* may be sufficient: courts can even act in anticipation of future consensus and help bringing about such a consensus by fostering transformative debate leading to consensus. But does this mean that democratic experimentalism subjects (or sacrifices) the rule of law to the vagaries of public opinion? The public may be democratically vigilant and an emancipatory public, laying siege to political and legal institutions. But judicial review simultaneously remains firmly tied to the liberalism-of-fear[170] motive, as the public is always-manipulable and may turn illiberal in just an instant.

Dialogic constitutionalism is the idea that reasonable disagreement about constitutional meaning may paradoxically produce and sustain

[169] Ibid, at 1020.

[170] Judith N. Shklar, 'Liberalism of Fear', in: Nancy L. Rosenblum (ed.), Liberalism and the Moral Life (Cambridge: Harvard University Press 1989), at 21 ff.

an ongoing antagonistic consensus about the constitutional framework itself. Each step towards a contextualization of fundamental principles provides an opportunity for the revision of the framework of those fundamental principles itself, just as the framework invites reconsideration of existing legal contextualizations which are in place and embedded in routines and institutional settlements. The dialogue never starts from nowhere: participants cannot proceed without some provisional consensus on the framework itself. This consensus is vague yet robust enough to enable participants to understand themselves, and mutually recognize one another, as bearers of legitimate interests—indeed, as participants to a shared, but unfinished constitutional project. But while the consensus does have this element of fixture, it is only *for the moment* foundational, because the application of framework principles to live political controversies provides an opportunity for the revision of the understanding of those controversies and of the constitutional framework principles themselves.

Democratic experimentalism in this way upholds the truth in fallibilism without giving away the game to scepticism. It rejects the idea that there is a set of necessary truths about 'fair balance' that it is the task of judges to discover. But this rejection does not mean that *everything* can be revised and that there is slippage. Rather, the application of law in the context of divisive social controversies is a process in time, an emancipatory process of immanent criticism, aimed at achieving *better answers* which improve, but build on, existing answers in a sense of gradual reform in the light of experience, as social conflicts are better understood. In this sense, closure and openness are intertwined; application (the contextual search for 'fair balance') is a reflection of our essence-in-the-present by being both forward- and backward-looking.

This is how one can read the discussion (and agreement) between Tim Scanlon and Frank Michelman. Scanlon quotes the following two passages from Michelman:

> The category of human rights, then, by the very notion of it—call this platonism if you will—has a strictly democracy-independent, abstract and general content. [. . .] No strictly procedural fact of democratic debate or decision can settle the question of the rightness of [. . .] relatively concrete understanding[s] of the content of human rights that may be reflected in a given country's positive law and actual practice. What settles the rightness question can only be intellectual competence—a competent accounting of the abstract and general content of human rights and of the

> apt concretization of this content for the country in question in its historical conditions.[171]

And

> It absolutely is not possible to appoint democracy to decide what democracy is ... [L]ogic bars democracy from [the] decision ... of deciding the contents of the most basic of a dedicatedly democratic country's laws, its law of lawmaking.[172]

Scanlon agrees with Michelman's 'frank Platonism' and offers an interesting comment. Michelman's statements, as Scanlon comments, remain correct, in particular, if we substitute for the term 'democracy' the expression 'the opinions of the people', meaning their opinions on such matters as the relative importance of various forms of freedom of action among other constitutionally protected liberties. The essential propositions thus are: '(1) that the legitimacy of a constitutional order depends in part on the opinions, in this sense, of those to whom it applies, and (2) that the dependence of legitimacy on opinion has limits: the support of opinion does not render any constitutional order legitimate'. Even the claim that a decision authorized by a constitution backed by democratic opinion can be rightfully enforced is a claim about right and wrong, as Platonistic a claim as any other. The 'frank Platonism' serves to highlight the fact that just any particular body of actual opinion can get it wrong:

> The democratic majority can get it wrong, conscientious judges can get it wrong, even the sense of justice unanimously shared by the members of a society can be wrong. Whether one of these has gotten it wrong or gotten it right (and whether there even is a right answer in a given case) can be determined only by the exercise of 'competent reason'. But nothing follows from this about the special standing of any particular group of persons to give authoritative answers to such questions, let alone to rule 'the masses' on the basis of their answers.

In a radically decentred, institutionally horizontalized form of constitutionalism, there is no privileged vantage-point of a hypothetical regime-designer: in part, the democratically vigilant public will provoke updating and reform of existing constitutional, and doctrinal-legal, settlements to uphold and deepen justifiability to the citizens. In part, judicial review is guardian of the—benignly inert—system of liberal safeguards (at least for

[171] Frank Michelman, 'Human Rights and the Limits of Constitutional Theory', 13(1) Ratio Juris 63–76, at 67 (2000).

[172] Frank Michelman, Brennan and Democracy (Princeton: Princeton University Press 1999) 34.

as long as that system remains in place at all). And, in part, judicial review is also associated with ideas of constitutional learning and self-revision, acting as guide and referee of discussions, instilling a sense of publicity, structure, and direction. Democratic experimentalism is, in part, a reconstructive project, but also, in part, a way of articulating unresolved practical tensions and dilemmas in the idea of constitutionalism. There is no hierarchy and no pivot of rightness, be it a Rawlsian idea of conformance with constitutional essentials or a Habermasian idea of the public sphere, but a multiplicity of review institutions interacting with each other; and that what is at stake (and endangered) is the underlying 'criterion of reciprocity' on which the possibility of self-revision and the attitude of openness to criticism depends.

The various institutional features of judicial procedure—independence, disinterestedness, impartiality, fair access, transparency, and reason-giving—facilitate dialogue and justification—gradual progression towards better answers—by forcing participants to advance considerations that not only they themselves judge to be reasons but that others can reasonably be expected to acknowledge as reasons. These institutional features emphasize the importance of substantive judicial judgment, but substantive judicial judgment serves to ignite discussion, and to extend that discussion into civil society, of contested constitutional applications, and is in this sense discursively embedded in surrounding discussion.

One may elaborate this discursive embeddedness as follows: At a relatively early stage, when a controversy is still less well-understood, the court may suggest agendas to be addressed and answered by various (groups of) stakeholders and merely indicate a discursive space for permissible outcomes by deferring to other actors with deeper knowledge of context and therefore presumptively greater legitimacy to concerned actors. Through a self-conscious choice of a broad interpretation of a fundamental right in question, the court may actively encourage complainants to invoke—in often unexpected, surprising, even unorthodox, ways—a right so as to allow for an existing consensus to be challenged. But, then, at later stages, often over repeat litigation, as judges become increasingly familiar with some generic features of situations they repeatedly confront and as progressive knowledge and a shared understanding of the conflicting stakes and interests in a particular rights-sensitive domain begin to crystallize, the court begins to exercise agenda-control. Actors charged with realizing a fair balance between competing rights may still be granted substantial autonomy in interpreting ends and re-evaluating means, but the court will require actors, as a condition for their autonomy, to reconsider their routine assumptions about what 'fair balance' means in part by restating shared commitments and in part by asking questions to be addressed and answered by one or another stakeholder group or class as the process moves along.

Finally, as answers begin to emerge, the court will intensify modalities of review and call for substantive compliance with an emergent best-practice consensus on what fair balance must mean in particular controversies and disallow the unreflective perpetuation of a practice inconsistent with the emergent understanding of what fair balance means. Democratic-experimentalist modalities of judicial review become strong-form review. The deliberation-inducing role of judicial judgments will now come to depend on the premise that judicial judgments reflect the court's considered contemporary views about constitutional meaning.

But even strong-form review is not as democracy-pre-emptive as critics allege. Courts are constantly exposed to the 'full blast'[173] of competing views and public opinions in civil society. The emphasis on substantive judicial judgment—which democratic experimentalism highlights—forces judges to construct ever franker arguments about moral principle that will, in turn, allow citizens and the wider public to join—and to continue—the constitutional-interpretive argument. Court decisions, as Post and Siegel have shown, always remain open to public disapproval, rejection, and criticism in ways that constructively rebound on judicial interpretation. Dissenting opinions by judges may contribute to that process. But those decisions will encourage and focus public political discussion of central moral issues.

The point, then is that legitimation does not rest on a stable, pre-existing consensus that antecedes judicial decision-making. Counter-majoritarian decisions may presuppose a narrow but sufficiently stable negative constitutional consensus on negative rights. But the fact remains that conscientious judges are often pressed to recognize, in hard cases, a right that hasn't been recognized before and about the merits of which there is deep, intractable—but sometimes reasonable—disagreement among democratically vigilant citizens. Judicial abstinence, paired with an attitude of deference to politics, in those situations, would cause just as much public resentment, sense of injustice, and a calling-into-question of the role of courts, as judicial overreach in 'inventing' rights. The democratic-experimentalist turn here moves beyond a stand-off and places the

[173] The condition was formulated by Frank Michelman in his Brennan and Democracy (Princeton: Princeton University Press 1999), at 59 f. For a related view, cf. Ronald Dworkin, Freedom's Law (Cambridge: Harvard University Press 1996), at 37.

emphasis on what the rule of law can be under conditions of deep moral dissensus and uncertainty: a shared framework of discussion. Substantive reasons are never isolated reasons but collaborative ones. Citizens, stakeholders, the public at large collaborate in the pursuit of the best answer as experience accumulates. Courts can facilitate this collaborative process in discursively highly differentiated societies. Abandoning courts or sharply limiting their remit offers false comfort: a loss of differentiation and complexity, in lieu of a strategy (or attitude) which harnesses these conditions of uncertainty in the service of democratic deliberation and objectivity.

In the remainder of this book, drawing on the analytic taxonomy developed in this chapter (for a summary, cf. table 1, below), I will address selected topical examples from the jurisprudence of the CJEU and of the ECtHR and, sometimes, of domestic courts, to illustrate experimentalist modalities of judicial review. In doing so, my aim is not so much to unearth a hidden judicial philosophy or 'social model' of these courts, nor is my aim an apologetic one, but my intention simply is to use the democratic-experimentalist model as a *distancing device*—in the *Brechtian* sense of a *Verfremdungseffekt*—to cast the familiar in a new light in the hope of rekindling a sense of democratic possibility.

Table 1 Summary: An Analytic Taxonomy of Non-Court Centric Conceptions of Judicial Review

	Political Liberalism (Rawls)	**Political Constitutionalism (Waldron/Bellamy/Tushnet)**	**Spherical Justice (Ackerman)**	**Democratic Constitutionalism (Post/Siegel)**	**Democratic Experimentalism**
Basis of legitimacy	Consensus on the 'central ranges' of basic negative liberties	Democratic procedure in good working order	Anti-humiliation principle	Agonistic consensus: positive conflict	Openness to self-revision
Courts	Strong-form review: courts as trustees	Weak-form review: rights-alertness mechanism	Situation sense: immanent norms (sphericality)	Judicial statesmanship and ethics of responsibility	Forum-creative and agenda-setting
Democracy and participation	Moral-theoretic: citizens as rational and reasonable	Parliamentary supremacy	Periodic citizenship; dualist democracy	Social movements: constructive uses of backlash; responsive democracy	Stakeholder democracy
Possible shortfall	Socioeconomic rights merely aspirational	Slippery slope towards antinomianism	Exceptionalism	Exceptionalism	Postponement of substantive answers

2

Adjudicating the European Social Market

Negative Constitutionalism Redux?

Les propositions Schuman ... sont révolutionnaires ou elles ne sont rien. Leur principe fondamental est la délégation de souverainité dans un domaine limité, mais décisif. [...] La coopération entre les nations ne résout rien. Ce qu'il faut chercher, c'est une fusion des intérêts des peoples européens, et non pas simplement le maintien de l'équilibre de ces intérêts.

Jean Monnet, Mémoirs (Fayard 1976), 456

One of the questions the Europeans should ask themselves, if I may hazard a suggestion, is how far-reaching they want their union to be. It seems to me that much would be lost if the European Union became a federal union like the United States. Here there is a common language of political discourse and a ready willingness to move from one state to another. Isn't there a conflict between a large, free and open market comprising all of Europe and the individual nation-states, each with its separate political and social institutions, historical memories, and forms and traditions of social policy? Surely these are great value to the citizens of these countries and give meaning to their life. The large open market including all of Europe is the aim of the large banks and the capitalist business class whose main goal is simply larger profit. The idea of economic growth, onwards and upwards, with no specific end in sight, fits this class perfectly. If they speak about distribution, it is almost always in terms of trickle down. The long-term result of this—which we already have in the United States—is a civil society awash in a meaningless consumerism of some kind. I can't believe that is what you want.

John Rawls to Philippe van Parjis, 23 June 1998[1]

[1] I would like to thank Joshua Cohen for having made this quotation available to me many years ago.

1. TRANSFORMATIONS

Are we Europeans today facing a stark choice between either embracing a large, free, and open market ('awash with consumerism'), or, in the alternative, a defensive safeguarding of individual nation-states, with their own *historical memories* and meaningful forms of social policy? This chapter argues against the sense of inevitableness and for a *tertium datur* which, as I will suggest, characterizes and defines *Euroconstitutionalism*: the initial goal of *une fusion des intérêts* of the European populations implies the possibility not only of a fusion of interests but, more ambitiously, of democratic horizons; fusion according to which an emergent shared understanding of EU-wide fundamental principles, enshrined in the Charter of Fundamental Rights of the EU (CFREU) enables critical reconsideration and transformation of institutional settlements, both at the nation-state level and in the multilevel system of the European social market, just as, crucially, a consensus on those framework-principles themselves is subject to reconsideration and transformation as experience generated from within the diverse national contexts of discovery and application accumulates.

Of the two post-war European legal orders—the Council of Europe's ECHR and the European Communities—only the ECHR was expressly founded as a human rights organization with the intention of promoting human rights and democracy in the wider Europe—and of preventing States from relapsing into totalitarianism.[2] The focus of the second of these two legal systems, now the EU, by contrast, lay in the establishment of the common market—but from the outset understood as a vehicle towards broader social and political ends. The founding treaties were silent on the matter of fundamental rights. While both legal orders were conceived as a response to World War II and the Holocaust, human rights and fundamental economic freedoms, then, were understood as belonging to, and constituting, two functionally different, mutually impermeable, and separate legal spheres.

The guiding idea—made explicit by the German tradition of a *Wirtschaftsverfassung*—was that of the EU as a liberal transnational order, held together by the principle that contracting states should not allow the political to contaminate the economic.[3] The (then) ECJ was

[2] See Andrew Moravcsik, 'The Origins of International Human Rights Regimes: Democratic Delegation in Postwar Europe', 54 International Organization 217 (2000).

[3] For theoretical foundations: Franz Böhm, 'Privatrechtsgesellschaft und Marktwirtschaft', ORDO. Jahrbuch für die Ordnung von Wirtschaft und Gesellschaft, Bd. 17 (1966), S. 75–151; Walter Hallstein, Europe in the Making (London: Allen & Unwin 1972).

correspondingly seen not as a constitutional court, but exclusively as a *Fachgericht*—a specialized court with the final judicial say on the European internal market. From this perspective an interaction, even a tangential contact between Community economic freedoms and national constitutional rights seemed impossible.[4]

But these expectations of a clean separation between the economic and the social were belied, in fits and starts, by developments. The integration project was premised on mutual restrictions on national sovereignties by the multiple national publics. This, after all, was the core message of *van Gend en Loos*[5]—the 'fountainhead of this part of the [Court's] constitutional jurisprudence'[6]—and of *Costa v. E.N.E.L.*,[7] which can both be read as an expression of the commitment made by the Member States to give reality to the promise of a 'new legal order' that is 'more than an agreement which merely creates mutual obligations' among contracting states, that 'not only imposes obligations on individuals but is also intended to confer upon them rights which become part of their legal heritage', and that '[i]s an integral part of the legal system of the Member States'. But in the 1970s the German constitutional court ('BVG'), moved less by concern for the legitimacy of an emergent European order than by preoccupations with national sovereignty and its own role as the guarantor of essential national rights (the *Wesensgehaltsgarantie* which continues to be central to the self-conception of the BVG), expressed concerns about whether EU law should also prevail in cases of conflict with fundamental rights protected by the Basic Law. There could, therefore, have been serious conflict between European and domestic law. In response to those concerns, the ECJ—in order to safeguard the principle of supremacy it sought to establish—construed the inclusion of fundamental rights in the Community law system and also the alignment of Community-interpretation with the goals of the ECHR: the Court, adopting a stance diametrically opposed to its earliest case law on the subject, proclaimed that 'fundamental rights [were] enshrined in the general principles of Community law and [therefore] protected by the Court'[8] and that the protection of fundamental rights could effectively be 'ensured within

[4] For a representative view, cf. Walter Hallstein, 'Europapolitik durch Rechtsprechung', Wirtschaftsordnung und Staatsverfassung, Festschrift für Franz Böhm, pp. 205–25, at 211f, 213.

[5] Case 26/62, *Algemene Transport-en Expeditie Onderneming van Gend en Loos NV v. Nederlandse Belastingadministratie* [1963] ECR 1.

[6] Weiler, op. cit., at 689.

[7] Case 6/64, *Costa v. E.N.E.L.* [1964] ECR 585.

[8] ECJ Case 29/69, *Stauder v. City of Ulm* [1969] ECR 419.

the framework of the structure and objectives of the Community';[9] and that the ECHR must be accorded 'special significance'[10] in this respect. In contemporary 'multilevel systems' of constitutionalism, as Kokott and Sobotta have summarized developments,

> it is possible that the level of protection of fundamental rights guaranteed by a higher level does not attain the level of protection the lower level has developed and considers indispensable. Refusing to accept the primacy of the higher level can be a proper means of responding to this deficiency.[11]

But there is an evident tension between reliance on centralized European-wide fundamental principles, on the one hand, and respect for the diversity of national traditions of constitutional law, on the other: a tension, that is, between the 'rule of law' and 'democracy', to both of which the EU is committed by Art. 2 TEU.[12] Mindful of this tension, the ECJ has been generally careful, in its recent, jurisprudentially transformative decisions, to register and defer to national interpretations of fundamental rights when the national authorities make a compelling case that they have themselves been mindful of their obligations under EU law to balance respect for fundamental rights and economic freedoms, and have done so conscientiously by the means available to them.

Because the CJEU, as a consequence of the expansion of its remit beyond the economic, must now strike a fair balance between economic freedoms and liberties, on the one hand, and fundamental and social rights, on the other, this tension between the rule of law and democracy

[9] ECJ Case 11/70, *Internationale Handelsgesellschaft mbH v. Einfuhr- und Vorratsstelle fuer Getreide und Futtermittel* [1970] ECR 1125, at 1131. Referring to this case, AG Leger in his Opinion in C-87/01—*Commission v. CEMR* [17 September 2002], at para. 64 explained: 'As we know, to establish the existence of a general principle of Community law, the Court carries out a comparative examination of national legal systems. In this connection, it is unanimously agreed that the Court does not seek to determine the arithmetical average of national laws or to fall into line with the lowest common denominator. On the contrary, the Court takes a critical approach and gives the answer which is most appropriate in relation to the structure and aims of the Community' [references omitted].

[10] ECJ, Case C-540/03 [2006], para. 35.

[11] Juliane Kokott and Christoph Sobotta, 'The Kadi Case—Constitutional Core Values and International Law—Finding the Balance?', 23(4) European Journal of International Law 1015–24 at 1018 (2012).

[12] From very different perspectives respectively: Francis G. Jacobs, The Sovereignty of Law. The European Way (Cambridge: Cambridge University Press 2007); Francis G. Jacobs, 'The State of International Economic Law: Re-Thinking Sovereignty in Europe', 11 Journal of International Economic Law 5 (2008); Takis Tridimas, General Principles of EU Law, 3rd edition (Oxford: OUP 2019); Paul Kirchhoff, 'The Legal Structure of the European Union as a Union of States', in Bogdandy/Bast (eds.), Principles of European Constitutional Law, p. 765 ff. (Oxford: Hart Publishing, 2nd edition 2009); Matthias Herdegen, 'General Principles of EU Law—the Methodological Challenge', in Ulf Bernitz, Joakim Nergelius, and Cecilia Gardner (eds.), General Principles of EC Law in a Process of Development (Alphen aan den Rijn: Kluwer 2008).

is exacerbated. Accordingly, two fundamental objections have been raised: first, a social-democratic objection, according to which the spread of proportionality analysis and experimentalist review in the CJEU's jurisprudence is a path towards a weakening of social rights against economic liberties; second, a rule-of-law based objection, according to which the Court's expansive jurisprudence—given facts of reasonable disagreement about the applied meaning of 'fair balance'—poses a threat to the integrity of domestic constitutional law. In a first step (II.), this chapter will address both these concerns in their context. In a second step (III.), with the intention to disarm these objections, this chapter proposes an analysis of representative strands of the Court's social rights jurisprudence in domains where there is a horizontal conflict between economic liberties and fundamental rights. This section will argue that, properly understood, the CJEU's jurisprudence is not as unilateral or authoritarian as the critics claim. Rather, the interaction between domestic courts and the CJEU, especially through the reference procedure, opens up a recursively dialogic space in which national administrations are compelled to explain, justify, and transform particular policy choices in the light of evolving framework principles and experience.

II. EUROCONSTITUTIONALISM BEYOND THE STATE: TWO STANDARD OBJECTIONS

A. Ordoliberalism vs. social democracy

At a first glance, to many observers the EU may appear to be an improbable illustration of the possibility of an extension of legitimacy and justice beyond the state. In contemporary European constitutional debate constitutionalism and social democracy have become antagonists, with the survival of the one seeming to require sacrifice of the other. Authors in the tradition of ordoliberalism have celebrated the Europeanization process because it seemed to ultimately disconnect constitutionalism from democratic practice and to firmly entrench a logic of market evolution that marginalizes politics. Social democrats, by contrast, have come to believe that democracy can only flourish if the solidary politics of the nation retains its sovereignty against cosmopolitan, 'constitutional' intrusions from without. Proposals to deepen constitutional integration therefore give rise to the social-democratic objection. This section offers a stylized account of both views, which more or less mirror one another.

1. Ordoliberalism: one market, many polities

One influential way to interpret the focus on markets was provided by the tradition of ordoliberalism. The ordoliberal view proceeded from the idea that the true function of constitutionalism is to protect a set of well-circumscribed economic liberties from the vicissitudes of pluralist politics, placing them beyond the reach of majorities by establishing them as legal rules and principles to be applied by independent courts. According to this framework, it was the task of the EU to implement and protect a system of open markets and undistorted competition, equipped with supremacy over the national legal systems, while the diverse Member States retain those legislative powers that prove compatible with open markets:[13] the chain binding law and democratic politics breaks.

Ordoliberalism has of course many sources and variants but it was in part inspired by a view developed by Hayek in a 1939 article of his on interstate federalism and economic individualism in which Hayek anticipated a future European 'single market'.[14] A regime of economic individualism—achieved by frontiers ceasing to be closed and by securing free economic movement across Europe—would, as Hayek argued, in fact *strengthen* democracy by unburdening it, that is, by removing perverse incentives for majority factions to form and by constricting democratic government to those fields where true agreement could be obtained. This, as Hayek believed, 'would no more than confirm the experience in the national sphere, in which it is daily becoming more obvious that democracy will work only if we do not overload it and if the majorities do not abuse their power of interfering with individual freedom'. Hayek argued that, while an 'essentially liberal economic regime'—based on the removal of 'impediments as to the movement of men, goods, and capital between the states'—was a necessary condition for the success of any 'interstate federation', also the converse was true: namely 'the abrogation of national sovereignties and the creation of an effective international order of law' was 'a necessary complement and the logical consummation of the liberal

[13] Ernst-Joachim Mestmäcker, op. cit. at 633. The German version is even more straightforward, ibid, 'Zur Wirtschaftsverfassung in der Europäischen Union', Rolf Hasse, Josef Molsberger, and Christian Watrin (eds.), Ordnung und Freiheit. Festgabe für Hans Willgerodt zum 70. Geburtstag, 263, at 274. It runs:

> Aufgabe der Gemeinschaft ist es bei dieser Betrachtung, die wirtschaftlichen Freiheitsrechte, den Binnenmarkt und das System des unverfälschten Wettbewerbs mit Vorrang vor dem Recht der Mitgliedstaaten zu gewährleisten. Den Mitgliedstaaten bliebe es überlassen, die demokratische Legitimation beanspruchenden, diskretionären Politiken in eigner Zuständigkeit, aber unter den Bedingungen offener Märkte zu betreiben.

[14] Friedrich Hayek, 'The Economic Conditions of Inter-state Federalism', V, No. 2 New Commonwealth Quarterly 131–49 (1939); reprinted in: Friedrich Hayek, Individualism and Economic Order (Chicago: University of Chicago Press 1947).

program'.[15] Because of the diversity of socioeconomic conditions among the various Member States; and because of the absence of 'common convictions and ideals, and the whole common tradition of the people of a nation state'[16] at the federal level beyond the state,

> ... the conclusion that, in a federation, certain economic powers, which are now wielded by the national states, could be exercised neither by the federation nor by the individual states, implies that there would have to be less government all around.[17]

As a result, such an economic-liberal interstate regime would help secure *peace* by eliminating causes of friction between belligerent 'communities of interest' whose territorially defined group-interests were mutually antagonistic.[18] Given the external effects of domestic measures, there would be little hope to achieve 'international order or lasting peace so long as every country is free to employ whatever measures it thinks desirable in its own immediate interest, however damaging they may be to others ...'[19]

In his 1939 piece and in subsequent writings Hayek emphasized two crucial points. First, at the international level the idea of distributive justice has no application. Even in the context of 'Western Europe', the 'moral bases [for any common ideals of distributive justice] ... are completely lacking'. The scope for moral consensus is very limited: 'as the scale increases, the amount of agreement on the order of ends decreases and the necessity to rely on force and compulsion grows'. In small communities, common views 'will exist on a great many subjects', but 'their number will become less and less the wider we throw the net'.[20] He elaborates this point in some detail: 'There exists no basis which allows us to decide whether the claims of the poor Rumanian [sic] peasant are more or less urgent than those of the still poorer Albanian ...,' and it is simply impossible 'to deliberately balance the merits of all these claims and decide between them'.[21] Given the fact of 'widely divergent ideals and values', submission to a majoritarian 'democratic procedure' to settle these conflicts would be implausible: 'English people, perhaps more than others, ... might be a minority in the [European] planning authority' and would resent the consequence that 'the main lines of the future economic development of Great Britain might be determined by a non-British majority'.[22] The clash

[15] Ibid, at 268. [16] At 263. [17] At 265. [18] At 257.

[19] Friedrich Hayek, 'The Prospects of International Order', (1944) The Road to Serfdom (London: Routledge 2007), 226.

[20] Ibid, 228. [21] Ibid, 233. [22] Ibid, 228 f.

of economic interests would ultimately translate into a 'clash of interests between whole peoples which could be decided only by force'.[23]

But, second, while the idea of distributive justice has no application, the peace-objective generates the 'need ... for an international political authority', which is able 'to restrain [states] from action which will damage others'.[24] As Hayek explained the idea, 'there must be a power which can restrain the different nations from action harmful to their neighbors, a set of rules which defines what a state may do, and an authority capable of enforcing these rules'. These quasi-constitutional rules must be 'mainly of a negative kind ... i.e. essentially the powers of the ultra-liberal "laissez-faire" state'. The rationale for this kind of negative constitutionalism beyond the state is to confine inter-state collaboration 'to the fields where true agreement can be reached ... among all those affected', while desirable forms of social and economic planning could be devolved downwards to the state or local levels where experience is abundant.[25] Such an 'ideal of international law' would express a democratic consensus. This ideal would express a form of 'federalism' in which 'certain strictly defined powers are transferred to an international authority, while in all other respects the individual countries remain responsible for their internal affairs'.[26] This kind of international-law federalism is 'nothing but the application to international affairs of democracy ... a democracy with definitely limited powers'.[27] So the Hayekian 'form of international government' expresses a form of democracy beyond the state. Although this 'ideal of international law' assumes that there are no moral bases for social and distributive justice in the sphere beyond the state, we can still 'reasonably hope to achieve'[28] in that sphere, as Hayek argued, a core negative consensus on economic liberties.

Observe that, in a similar vein, Wilhelm Röpke, another exponent of ordoliberalism, emphasized in the 1950s the '[ordo-] liberal principle [...] of the widest possible separation of the two spheres of government and economy [...] of Imperium and Dominum' as part of the ordoliberal project. By observing 'this principle of separation', indeed, by radicalizing 'the largest possible "depoliticization" of the economic sphere', it would, Röpke argued, become possible, 'to reduce to a minimum the economic significance of the coexistence of sovereign states with their different legal orders' and systems of administration and separate citizenships. As a consequence, now the 'economic process [could

[23] Ibid, 231. [24] Ibid, 238. [25] Ibid, 240. [26] Ibid, 239. [27] Ibid, 239.
[28] Ibid, 244.

be] transferred from the sphere of administration, public law, penal courts, in short, of the "State," to the sphere of the market, of private law, of property, in short of the "society" '.[29]

It may be worth noting in passing that even in its heyday, in the 1950s, ordo-liberalism never went unchallenged, not even in Germany. Thus, in 1954, in its *Investitionshilfe* judgment,[30] the *Bundesverfassungsgericht* held that the German Basic Law claimed neutrality in matters of economic policy and ordering—the Basic Law was not committed to—did not constitutionalize—a particular socioeconomic model, as the BVG insisted, but entrusted the choice of economic policy to the democratic legislature so long as fundamental rights were observed by those choices. In 1979, the BVG confirmed its position on the neutrality and the 'relative openness' of the Basic Law in matters of choice of economic policy. The only constraint on those choices was that there was no curtailment of individual freedoms guaranteed by the fundamental rights, without which 'a life in human dignity' is not possible.[31]

2. Social democracy: safeguarding the primacy of politics over economics

This section explores the social-democratic objection to deeper constitutional integration in the EU in general, and about the—allegedly detrimental, social democracy-undermining—role of the CJEU in particular. The social-democratic objection, as I hope to show, conceptually overlaps with, and is a mirror-image of, the ordoliberal 'one-market-many-states' framework of analysis. But it *normatively inverts*, the ordoliberal analysis

[29] Cf. Wilhelm Röpke, 'Economic Order and International Law', in Recueil des courses (The Hague: Martinus Nijhoff Publishers 1954), 207–70, 224.

[30] BVG 4, 7, Judgment (First Senate) of 20 July 1954, at para. 36 ff.

> Die 'wirtschaftspolitische Neutralität' des Grundgesetzes besteht lediglich darin, daß sich der Verfassungsgeber nicht ausdrücklich für ein bestimmtes Wirtschaftssystem entschieden hat. Dies ermöglicht dem Gesetzgeber die ihm jeweils sachgemäß erscheinende Wirtschaftspolitik zu verfolgen, sofern er dabei das Grundgesetz beachtet. Die gegenwärtige Wirtschafts- und Sozialordnung ist zwar eine nach dem Grundgesetz mögliche Ordnung, keineswegs aber die allein mögliche.

[31] BVG 50, 290, Judgment (First Senate) of 1 March 1979, at 141 f.:

> Das darin zutage tretende Element relativer Offenheit der Verfassungsordnung ist notwendig, um einerseits dem geschichtlichen Wandel Rechnung zu tragen, der im besonderen Maße das wirtschaftliche Leben kennzeichnet, andererseits die normierende Kraft der Verfassung nicht auf Spiel zu setzen. Allerdings darf die Berücksichtigung der Gestaltungsfreiheit des Gesetzgebers nicht zu einer Verkürzung dessen führen, was die Verfassung in allem Wandel unverändert gewährleisten will, namentlich nicht zu einer Verkürzung der in den Einzelgrundrechten garantierten individuellen Freiheiten, ohne die nach der Konzeption des Grundgesetzes ein Leben in menschlicher Würde nicht möglich ist. Die Aufgabe besteht infolgedessen darin, die grundsätzliche Freiheit wirtschaftspolitischer und sozialpolitischer Gestaltung, die dem Gesetzgeber gewahrt bleiben muß, mit dem Freiheitsschutz zu vereinen, auf den der einzelne Bürger gerade auch dem Gesetzgeber gegenüber einen verfassungsrechtlichen Anspruch hat.

by exploring the costs which the ordoliberal 'ideal of international law'—as a driver of European, market-based integration—would pose for the project of social constitutionalism which has come to define the post–World War II European nation states. The fundamental concern is that the Hayekian 'ultra-liberal' system of constitutional ordering would destructively radiate downwards into, and colonializes, the sphere of social solidarity which law and politics at the level of the nation states sought to achieve and safeguard.

There are two different (but overlapping) strands of that analysis, a more normative one, which proceeds from the fact of *legal coercion*, and a sociological one, which focuses on a solidaristic *demos*. The first asserts that the nation state—for conceptual-normative reasons—is the proper locus of egalitarian justice: political communities remain largely national, rather than transnational (a.). The second strand of analysis spells out the alleged costs for national political communities of further EU integration by asserting that the jurisprudence of the CJEU, for structural reasons, is set to bring about, and to entrench, a constitutional asymmetry between economic liberties and social rights (b.). I will address these two strands in turn.

a. The democratic-sovereigntist objection

The democratic-sovereigntist objection is that social justice implies the nation state. Consider the striking contemporary claim made by an occasional observer of the EU, the American philosopher Thomas Nagel, that the cause for any resistance against a transfer of sovereignty to supranational entities, and concomitantly against a deeper EU integration, is not merely the absence of a shared demos and a common European civil society but also, more fundamentally, the concern that a more deeply integrated EU

> would be subject to claims of legitimacy and justice that are more than the several European populations are willing to submit themselves to, [a concern, which] reflects in part their conviction that they are not morally obliged to expand their moral vulnerabilities in this way.[32]

Nagel's conception of socioeconomic justice is a distinctly—in the Rawlsian sense of the term—*political* one. Political authority—because of its coercive imposition—must meet particularly exacting normative standards: the standards associated with egalitarian justice. But Nagel argues

[32] Thomas Nagel, 'The Problem of Global Justice', reprinted in Thomas Nagel, Secular Philosophy and the Religious Temperament (New York: OUP 2010), 61–91, at 88.

that this link between coercion and egalitarian justice can only properly be established within the nation state. Nagel's democratic-sovereigntist objection essentially draws on the familiar distinction between *defensive, negative human rights, on the one hand,* and *positive* fundamental rights, on the other. Whereas negative human rights 'set universal and prepolitical limits to the legitimate use of power, [which are] independent of special forms of association', socioeconomic justice, by contrast, 'depends on positive rights that we do not have against all other persons or groups, rights that arise only because we are joined together with certain others in a political society under strong centralized control'.[33] Socioeconomic rights, for their identification and realization, depend on associative-political obligations between and among the citizens within the nation state: the citizens co-operating not only as addressees, but as *co-authors* of the legal order under which they live. Whereas the most basic *negative, defensive human rights* are 'not contingent on special institutional relations between people',[34] the 'exceptional ... positive obligations of justice'[35] and the 'heightened requirements of equal treatment',[36] however, 'are', as Nagel insists, 'contingent that way'[37] and can therefore only be saturated within the special, associative context of the sovereign nation state. The stability of any legal system of ordering presupposes the sovereign; and the unique demands which the sovereign makes on the will of its members 'bring with them exceptional obligations, the positive obligations of justice'.[38]

According to the *discontinuous political conception*,[39] which Nagel advocates, any shift from pure negative constitutionalism to positive constitutionalism must seem barred, once we move outside and beyond the state. In contrast to the moral obligations which mutually bind the citizens within the nation state, the contractual obligations created by agreements between sovereign states (such as international trade regimes), Nagel argues, are not, and cannot be, underwritten by any kind of socioeconomic justice; they are, as he says, ' "pure" contracts, and nothing guarantees the justice of their results ... like the contracts favored by libertarians [...]'.[40]

In this way, their fundamental normative differences and starting-points notwithstanding, Nagel's political liberalism and ordoliberalism both share the essential claim that social justice can have no extension beyond the state. Nagel does not spell out the institutional implications for the EU of his analysis. He suggests, however, that, as a consequence

[33] Ibid, at 73. [34] At 76. [35] At 76. [36] At 76. [37] At 76. [38] At 76.
[39] At 86. [40] Ibid, at 86.

of the discontinuity-thesis, 'constitutional sovereign authority puts a natural upper bound on the sources of law'.[41] He describes the dilemma as follows: '[i]f the EU succeeds, it will be because the attachment of Europeans to common interests and values is strong enough to contain the conflicts of interest that will inevitably remain', or the EU merely 'remains essentially a free-trade zone ... because of popular unwillingness to share sovereignty'.[42]

Prompted by Nagel's concern, then, it may be tempting to conceive of the EU as a *political project*, at least in *statu nascendi*, on a trajectory towards statehood. Given the facts of increasing interdependence and negative externalities, the EU could eventually develop political institutions and a legal system that would *transnationalize its democracies* and allow an EU-wide political space to emerge. Yet to conceive of Europe as a *political project* (with an in-built teleology towards common federal statehood), it was feared already right from the start, would raise serious concerns about an encroachment on the essential preserves of the political independence and sovereignty of the Member States themselves, embroiling them in intractable disputes about economic models and philosophies. As a close witness to the negotiations leading to the Treaty of Rome of 1957 at the time presciently observed,

> [...] although there was general agreement on the word 'Europe' there were still differences and doubts as to the nature of the Europe which was to be created, its extent and scope. There was no agreement, no common ground between the protagonists of *laissez-faire* and planning; between those who pit their faith in parliamentary action and those who preferred to appeal directly to public opinion; between those who, like the English, favored diplomatic co-operation without any surrender of sovereignty and those others who were working towards the creation, in one form or another, of a union, a United States of Europe, or a Federation. [...]
> After the frustration of the attempts to establish the primarily political community in 1953 some of the prime movers of the European movement deliberately turned their backs on the ideal of building a Europe of fifteen or seventeen nations; an ideal [...] too complex and too wide to prevent the sum of the divergent national interests from triumphing over the sum of the positive common factors. [...]
>
> Many will regard this as a defect, but possibly one of the great virtues of the [1957] Treaty [of Rome] is that it keeps as far as possible from the

[41] Thomas Nagel, 'The Limits of International Law', Thomas Nagel, Secular Philosophy and the Religious Temperament (New York: OUP 2010), 94.

[42] Ibid, 95 f.

> doctrinal disputes between supporters of a liberal and a managed economy, putting trust in the procedures which the Treaty prescribes ...[43]

So: the early focus on market integration in the Treaty of Rome was seen as a *strategy* for *avoiding* deep, unmanageable ideological conflicts that would set the Member States and populations apart, and for securing agreement *over time* on matters where agreement was possible: a form of *proceduralization*, if you will. Indeed, as Andrew Moravcsik (following Chayes and Chayes[44]) has pointed out, among the most important prerogatives which sovereignty confers on national communities under conditions of growing interdependence is the power to enter into mutual transnational arrangements which *grant reciprocal influence over each other's policies, given externalities*. In this way, 'states and their citizens gain some influence over the policies of foreign governments that impact them, in exchange for surrendering some domestic discretion over policies that impact foreign populations'.[45] The benefits, seen 'from a constitutional perspective', are not only pragmatic but, as Moravcsik argues, normative: democratic choice is expanded 'to achieve security, welfare, and other legitimate public purposes, just as a central government is necessary to achieve some purposes within a federal nation-state'.

But, as the next section will illustrate, the meaning of this *European proceduralization* has itself increasingly become subject to deep disagreements. Social democrats worry that, for structural reasons, the CJEU will read social rights adversely, putting them on the backfoot with regard to economic freedoms.

b. The social-democratic objection: the *asymmetry*-thesis

Among social democrats, concerns soon began to concentrate on what they saw as an unholy 'alliance between economic constitutionalism and the core doctrines of the ECJ'.[46] The initial hope was that the sovereignty of the nation state could be preserved and actually strengthened by membership of the Union, while European institutions could remain

[43] Jean-Francois Deniau, The Common Market. Its Structure and Purpose (1960) (Le Marché Commun, Presses Universitaires de France 1959), p. 3; and 57 f.

[44] Abraham Chayes and Antonia Handler Chayes, The New Sovereignty. Compliance with International Regulatory Agreements (Cambridge: Harvard University Press 1998).

[45] Andrew Moravcsik, The Democratic Legitimacy of the European Union: A Constitutional Perspective (ms. 2013, on file with author). See also, Andrew Moravcsik, 'Is there a "Democratic Deficit" in World Politics? A Framework for Analysis', 39(2) Government and Opposition (2004); Andrew Moravcsik, 'In Defence of the Democratic Deficit: Reassessing Legitimacy in the European Union', 40(4) Journal of Common Market Studies (40th Anniversary Edition) (November 2002).

[46] Christian Joerges, op. cit., at 74.

creatures (or agents) of national governments as their political principals. But concerned with the viability of the social-democratic national welfare state within the EU's single market, social democrats began to hold the ordoliberal analysis against the EU by normatively inverting it. They began to address what they took to be the costs which the European single market imposed on *social constitutionalism* and on the overall chances for collective democratic fate-control by the self-governing people themselves as part of the post-war national welfare state. The ECJ was seen as a main institutional driver in a Europeanization process which systematically neutralized the project of social democracy, not only by emptying it of political-economic content, but also by shifting economic governance to a supranational level where social democracy could no longer follow institutionally.[47]

According to this reading, the landmark decisions of the ECJ in the 1960s establishing direct effect and primacy of EU law[48] over national law by *judicial fiat* had the effect of entrenching exactly what the *Bundesverfassungsgericht* hitherto had refused to accept: a *constitutionalization* of the core principles of an ordo-liberal economic constitution. The judge-made doctrines of the direct effect of Community law and its supremacy over national law allowed the CJEU to interpret the commitments of Member States to create a common market *as subjective rights* of individuals and firms against these Member States, to be pleaded before national courts, and as part of a new legal order beyond the state.

Consider the *constitutional asymmetry* thesis in some more detail. The *asymmetry-argument* begins with the familiar observation that the political project of European integration was to be realized by an economic program effectuated through and by the rule of law. The pronounced emphasis on 'integration through law' in the early days had, of course, everything to do with political stagnation at various historical stages of the integration project. Integration through law could therefore be understood as an audacious but also a prudentially wise choice, insofar as transnational legality, as JHH Weiler has pointed out, helped to prevent free riding and to provide stability and continuity to any *acquis* even in periods of political instability and wavering commitment.[49] And yet, according to Fritz Scharpf's influential analysis,[50] the reliance on law also—by way of

[47] Wolfgang Streeck, 'Heller, Schmitt and the Euro', 21(3) European Law Journal 361 (2015).

[48] ECJ C-26/62, *van Gend en Loos*, 5 February 1963; Case 6/64, *Costa v. ENEL*, [1964] ECR 585, 593.

[49] Weiler, ibid.

[50] Fritz Scharpf, On the double asymmetry of European integration. Or: Why the EU cannot be a social marker economy. Max Planck Institute for the Study of Societies, MPIfG Working Paper 09/12; cf. also

an unintended consequence—fatefully led to a twofold bias: first, a bias in favour of the economic to the detriment of the social (meaning a form of socially 'embedded capitalism'[51]); second, an institutional asymmetry between law and politics. According to Fritz Scharpf's deeply sceptical analysis, 'Integration through law is now cutting deeply into the substance of the socioeconomic regimes of social market economies':[52]

> In each country, such [legitimate, but diverse socioeconomic] institutions and legacies have often been shaped by intense political conflicts and historical compromises—which is why they differ so much from one another. [...] That does not mean that they should [...] be protected against change [...], however, such changes are highly controversial in national politics and they need to be defended in public debates [...]. Instead, the supremacy of European law allows for judicial interventions that may short-circuit these political processes. [...] [These judicial interventions] need to be justified by arguments that invoke clearly important European concerns and that are highly sensitive to the specific sociocultural and politico-economic concerns that are at stake in the particular member state. This the ECJ has never attempted, and it is indeed hard to see how it could gain the necessary familiarity and empathy with the institutional traditions and the political cultures of the EU's twenty-seven member states.[53]

Yet, as Scharpf has further elaborated the dilemma, the reverse criticism must apply to the national constitutional courts and to their efforts to derive from national constitutional law criteria constraining the ECJ's interpretive monopoly with regard to the meaning of Community law. While each of these national courts can indeed be presumed to be sensitive to national concerns of identity,

> there is no reason to expect that their understandings of the 'Europe-friendliness' of their national constitutions would converge, or that they would all assign the same relative weights to the European concerns at stake. The overall result might be a chaotic form of differentiated integration through an accumulation and perhaps escalation of unilateral national opt-outs.[54]

A solution to this conundrum is, according to Scharpf, not available by judicial means—as judges would again have to define general criteria

Alain Supiot, 'Le sommeil dogmatique européen', in Revue française des affaires sociales, 2012/1 (n° 1), 185–98; ibid, La Gouvernance par les nombres. Cours au Collège de France [2012–2014] (Fayard: 2015).

[51] John Gerard Ruggie, 'International Regimes, Transactions, and Change: Embedded Liberalism in the Postwar Economic Order', 36(2) International Organization (1982).

[52] Scharpf, op. cit., at 31. [53] Scharpf, ibid, at 33. [54] Ibid.

that are unable to accommodate the legitimate diversity of national concerns—but only by *political means*: 'fair balance' ultimately is a *political question*. Instead, a solution could only be a *deconstitutionalization of European law* by way of a reduction of the scope of a European constitution.[55] An alternative 'lean constitution' should no longer include rules amounting to an economic constitution but instead ensure the protection of individual civic and civil rights. 'Instead of being bound by petrified European law, political legislation could then adopt European policies that might conflict with the "economic constitutionalism" of the present Treaties as interpreted by the Court and the Commission.'

B. The rule-of-law ('integrity-') based objection: reasonable differences of constitutional interpretation

Equally salient, among constitutional lawyers, is a second, *rule-of-law* based, objection which focuses on reasonable interpretive differences resulting from the 'phenomenon of the multidimensionality of constitutional protection'[56]—the plurality of partly overlapping, partly conflicting, non-hierarchical rights-protecting jurisdictions: domestic legal orders, EU law, the ECHR, and international law.

One influential response to the problem of reasonable interpretive differences is a negative or sceptical one: to urge leaving the constitutional path at the level 'beyond the state' and to abandon references to constitutionalism and constitutionalization altogether. The persistent worry is that the CJEU, by interpreting its mandate ever more expansively, in practical effect 'relativizes'—considerably narrows the field-of-application of—the (national) constitution to the extent that it does not stay within the 'original', contractual, state-based Treaty-framework. Thus, Dieter Grimm fears that 'international courts'—such as the CJEU and the ECtHR—may 'relativize the [national] constitution to the extent that they do not stay within the traditional framework of international law'.[57]

I will focus in this section on Dieter Grimm's influential critique. Grimm is concerned about the effects of an 'over-constitutionalization'—of there

[55] Fritz Scharpf, After the Crash: A Perspective on Multilevel European Democracy, MPIfG Discussion Paper 14/21, at http://www.mpifg.de/pu/mpifg_dp/dp14-21.pdf; ibid, 'De-constitutionalisation and majority rule: A democratic vision for Europe', 23 European Law Journal 315–34 (2017).

[56] Lech Garlicki, 'Cooperation of Courts: The Role of Supranational Jurisdictions in Europe', in 6(3&4) I•CON 509–30, at 511 (2008).

[57] Dieter Grimm, 'The Constitution in the Process of Denationalization', 12(4) Constellations 447–63, at 457 (2005). Cf. Dieter Grimm, Constitutionalism. Past, Present, and Future (Oxford: OUP 2016); and Dieter Grimm, The Constitution of European Democracy (Oxford: OUP 2017).

being 'too much constitutionalism'.[58] The constitution would no longer be a 'framework for politics', but turn into 'a blueprint for all political decisions', with the consequence that 'the administration and the judiciary marginalize the legislature'. Specifically with regard to the CJEU, Grimm fears that by 'secur[ing] the immediate validity of Community law and its precedence over national law, including national constitutions [. . .] considerably narrowed the latter's field of application, and for its part took up functions that constitutional courts possess on the national level'.[59] But that generates the risk of reasonable interpretive differences. The fact that the CJEU refuses to interpret EU law 'in the cautious manner of international law, emphasizing the will of the contracting parties and limiting adverse impacts on national sovereignty',[60] but instead 'began to interpret the European treaties in a constitutional mode ... oriented ... by an objectivised purpose' increases the EU's democratic deficit: 'the EU confirms the assertion that more constitutional law means less democracy'.[61] At the same time, these developments also pose a threat to the integrity of the (national) constitution: referring to the longstanding debate on which courts—the ECJ or the national constitutional courts—are authorized to determine whether the EU (including the ECJ) has acted *ultra vires*, Grimm raises the question 'whether the identity of national constitutions imposes an outer limit to the supremacy of European law'.[62] Agreeing with Scharpf's asymmetry analysis, he observes a 'liberalizing tendency of the ECJ's jurisprudence' meaning that, as its consequence, '[p]rivate interests expand at the expense of public interests'.[63] Grimm describes the relationship between EU-constitutionalism and domestic constitutionalism as a zero-game: the alleged loss at the national level through the expansion of EU-constitutionalism, he argues, can no longer be compensated at the EU level, because 'the European public sphere and European political discourse are weak compared with their national counterparts', largely because the 'institutions that mediate between the people and political organs of the EU are either missing or underdeveloped'[64] in the EU.

Grimm's sceptical conclusion from this is that any 'notions of constitutionalism and constitutionalization [. . .] are misleading insofar as they

[58] Dieter Grimm, 'The Democratic Costs of Constitutionalisation: The European Case', 21(4) European Law Journal 460–73 (2015) at 464.

[59] Dieter Grimm, 'The Constitution in the Process of Denationalization', 12(4) Constellations 447–63, at 457 (2005).

[60] Dieter Grimm, The Democratic Costs, at 466.

[61] Ibid, at 471.

[62] Ibid, at 467.

[63] Ibid, at 470.

[64] Ibid, at 471.

nourish the hope that the loss national constitutions suffer from internationalization and globalization could be compensated for on the supranational level'.[65] Such notions are misleading, Grimm argues, because the EU Treaties, in contrast to national constitutions, are not an expression of the self-determination of a population and thus lack proper democratic origin, contrary to what the concept of constitution requires. The EU 'does not decide upon its own legal foundation' but only 'receives this foundation from the member states which create it by an agreement concluded according to international law'.[66] Yet a further, ECJ-driven constitutionalization of the Treaties inevitably undermines that foundation.

C. Interim observation

The social-democratic and the rule-of-law based objections express deep discomfort with the Europeanization process and the role of the CJEU. The normative discontent may be summarized as follows:

- Democratic objection to proportionality or experimentalist review either as a path to an undemocratic expansion of judicial review or as path to a weakening of social rights against economic freedoms ('process over substance'; 'constitutional asymmetry');
- Rule-of-law based objection, according to which the overall integrity of domestic constitutionalism is undermined through an expansive constitutionalizing jurisprudence of the CJEU.

These are three powerful and interconnected concerns which the CJEU today faces and must come to terms with. In what follows I will contrast these concerns with contemporary developments in the CJEU's case law. I will argue that the two concerns do not carry the final word and that, instead, the European rule of law can be reconstructed and recast along democratic-experimentalist lines. The European proceduralization of law can be understood in a more dialogic sense. There is a spread of democratic-experimentalist styles of judicial intervention by the CJEU. There are affinities between the democratic-experimentalist approach and Christian Joerges' 'conflicts-law approach',[67] but also important

[65] Dieter Grimm, 'The Achievement of Constitutionalism and its Prospects in a Changed World', reprinted in: Dieter Grimm, Constitutionalism. Past, Present, Future (Oxford: OUP 2016).

[66] Ibid, at fn 20.

[67] Christian Joerges and Jurgen Neyer, 'From Intergovernmental Bargaining to Deliberative Political Processes: The Constitutionalisation of Comitology', 3 European Law Journal, 273–99 (1997); Christian Joerges, 'Social Justice in an Ever More Diverse Union', Bremen, Zentra Working Papers in Transnational

differences. Joerges' approach focuses on the democracy problem which an 'an ever stronger schism between decision-makers and those who are impacted upon by decisionmaking' under conditions of interdependence poses. Because of the proliferation of undemocratic external effects of national decisionmaking on other national communities, nation states themselves suffer from a structural democratic deficit; and the role of EU law is to 'compensate for the failings of national democracies'. Its legitimacy derives from its 'compensatory function' but is limited by the mutual respect which national communities owe each other for their economic and social concerns. The democratic experimentalist approach, in contrast, emphasizes deliberation: the CJEU enables those national communities to reconsider their policy choices in the light of shared fundamental principles. These framework-principles are themselves subject to revision and reconsideration as the experience of dealing with the diverse national contexts of discovery and application accumulates.

III. THE CJEU FROM ECONOMIC FREEDOMS TO FUNDAMENTAL RIGHTS

A. Setting the framework for proportionality analysis: the *Schmidberger* and *Omega* cases

Consider the following two, much noticed cases. In the first, *Schmidberger*,[68] the Austrian authorities had allowed a political demonstration by a grassroots-environmental group on the Brenner motorway, the main traffic-link between Northern Europe and Italy. The demonstration, though peaceful, closed the motorway completely to traffic for almost thirty hours. Schmidberger, a German transport company, argued that the effects of the Austrian authorities' conduct in allowing the closure infringed his Community right to free movement of goods under (then) Art. 28 EC [now Art. 34 TFEU] and sued Austria for damages. Thus the Court had to reconcile the conflict between Schmidberger's invocation of a fundamental economic freedom—here free movement of goods, protected under Art. 34 TFEU—and Austria's invocation of the fundamental right of its citizens, guaranteed not only under the domestic Austrian constitution but also under Art. 10

Studies, No. 62/2015; Christian Joerges, 'Unity in Diversity as Europe's Vocation and Conflicts Law as Europe's Constitutional Form', LSE 'Europe in Question' Discussion Paper Series, LEQS Paper 28/2010 (revised 2013).

[68] CJEU, C-112/00, *Eugen Schmidberger, Internationale Transporte und Planzüge v. Republik Österreich*, Judgment of the Court of 12 June 2003, [2003] ECR I-05659.

and Art. 11 of the ECHR, to freedom of expression and assembly. The Court, ignoring its earlier and adverse opinions, held that the positive obligation by a state to protect fundamental and human rights could, indeed, constitute public policy requirements sufficient to justify restrictions to basic market freedoms, provided that the restrictions were necessary and proportionate:

> [T]he interests involved must be weighed having regard to the circumstances of the case in order to determine whether a fair balance was struck between those interests. (par. 81)

In determining what constitutes a 'fair balance', the Court, furthermore, accorded the domestic authorities 'a wide margin of discretion'. Thus, after examining various factors—such as the ongoing collaboration between demonstrators, local authorities, and various motoring organizations before the event—the Court concluded that the Austrian authorities were 'reasonably entitled' (par. 93) to consider that the main aim of the demonstration could not be achieved by measures less restrictive of intra-Community trade.

In his Opinion for the case Advocate General Jacobs was careful to acknowledge, beyond the balancing of rights in any particular case, the general obligation of the Court both to give weight to the divergences between the fundamental rights catalogues of the Member States—divergences which 'often reflect the history and particular political culture of a given Member State'[69]—and to recognize that national specificities do not always trump general obligations under Community law. For that reason it cannot be

> automatically ruled out that a Member State which invokes the necessity to protect a right recognized by national law as fundamental nevertheless pursues an objective which as a matter of Community law must be regarded as illegitimate.[70]

In the second case, *Omega Spielhallen*,[71] the Court again had to balance conflicting fundamental rights and freedoms in the light of the specificities of national constitutional law. In *Omega* the German authorities had banned a laserdrome game simulating homicide. The applicant company, Omega, challenged this ban as contrary to freedom to provide services under EU law, pointing out that such games were lawfully

[69] CJEU, C-112/00 *Schmidberger*, Opinion by AG Jacobs, at 97. [70] Ibid, at 98.

[71] CJEU, C-36/02 *Omega Spielhallen—und Automatenaufstellungs—GmbH v. Oberbürgermeisterin der Bundesstadt Bonn* [2004] ECR I-9609.

marketed in the UK and that the equipment and technology were supplied by a British company and that therefore, under the principles of mutual recognition, the ban was unlawful. But for reasons of German history, human dignity is accorded special priority under the German Basic Law and the jurisprudence of the *Bundesverfassungsgericht*. A decision by the ECJ promoting the internal market despite the German concerns would risk challenges to EC supremacy; but to give primacy to the national concern for fundamental rights would be to the detriment of the internal market. The Court allowed German authorities to ban the game, but insisted that this outcome did not depend upon 'a conception shared by all Member States as regards the precise way in which the fundamental right or legitimate interest in question is to be protected'. The Court, then, considered the subject-matter to belong to a sphere properly left to the Member States.

Both cases, then, are important for the following reason: they set the stage for a balancing between negative economic liberties and fundamental positive rights at the level of EU law but in dialogue with the national legal systems. Yet in both decisions, the CJEU is eager to accommodate national diversity by emphasizing a wide margin of appreciation at the level of national legal systems. Granted, these were cases where the impact on the internal market was rather minimal. Yet, even so, the cases confirm the thesis that the spread of proportionality analysis does not automatically imply an undemocratic expansion of judicial intervention.

I will now turn to some more controversial decisions where this impact was more palpable and where fundamental social rights were involved. Critics of these decisions have argued that the European judicial constitutionalization of those rights has led to adverse effects—that is, to their dilution.

B. The sphere of work and employment

In this section I will continue to explore the penetration of substantive constitutional law into civil-society relations and also private-law relations. I will suggest that the spread of democratic-experimentalist modalities of judicial intervention does not lead to a weakening of social rights against economic liberties but is a way of *strengthening* them. In particular, I will suggest that the CJEU's rulings (analysed below) in *Viking* and *Laval* and daughter cases, and in *Kücükdeveci* and *Aziz* are continuous with one another and must be seen as part of a coherent social jurisprudence.

1. Free trade and fundamental social rights: from the *Viking* and *Laval* line of cases to *Parkwood*

In *Viking*[72] and its daughter cases, *Laval*,[73] *Rüffert*,[74] and *Luxembourg*,[75] the general question was whether overriding public interests in the protection of workers and their right to collective action could be considered equivalent to fundamental rights in their potential to restrict Community freedoms, and if so, whether the restrictions—to freedom of establishment in *Viking* and to freedom to provide services in *Laval*—were justified by the particulars of the disputes. In *Viking* and to a lesser but sufficient extent *Laval*, the CJEU affirmed the need to balance clashing fundamental rights, delegated to national entities the responsibility for determining the balance appropriate in particular cases, only intervening when the national authorities did not exercise the delegated authority. In Rüffert and Luxembourg the question is closer, but there is a reasonable case to be made for the ECJ's interpretation of the legislative authority—the Posted Workers Directive 96/71/EC—applicable to the disputes.

Viking owned a vessel that was running at a loss because of direct competition from Estonian vessels operating the same route and paying lower wages to its Estonian crew than Viking was paying under the terms of a collective bargaining agreement with the Finnish Seamen's Union ('FSU'). Viking's response was to cut its costs by reflagging the vessel to Estonia. Fearing redundancies, FSU asked ITF, an international federation of transport workers' unions to request all its affiliates to boycott negotiations with Viking. The aim was clearly to frustrate the firm's exercise of its Community right to freedom of establishment, inasmuch as the boycott would deny Viking the same treatment in the host Member State (Estonia) as that enjoyed by other economic operators established in that state. Viking applied to the Court for an injunction against the boycott.

In its decision the Grand Chamber of the ECJ extended the balancing framework established in *Schmidberger* to include the public interest in protection of worker rights, affirming that

[72] CJEU C-438/05 *International Transport Workers' Federation and Finnish Seamen's Union v. Viking Line ABP and OÜ Viking Line Eesti*, Judgment of the Court (Grand Chamber) of 11 December 2007, [2007] ECR I-10779.

[73] CJEU Case C-341/05, *Laval un Partneri Ltd v. Svenska Byggnadsarbetareförbundet, Svenska Byggnadsarbetareförbundets avdelning 1, Byggettan and Svenska Elektrikerförbundet* Judgment of the Court (Grand Chamber) of 18 December 2007, [2007] ECR I-11767.

[74] CJEU Case C-346/06, *Dirk Rüffert v. Land Niedersachsen* Judgment of the Court (Second Chamber) of 3 April 2008, [2008] ECR I-01989.

[75] CJEU Case C-319/06 *Commission of the European Communities v. Grand Duchy of Luxemburg* Judgment of the Court (First Chamber) of 19 June 2008, [2008] ECR I-04323.

> the right to take collective action, including the right to strike, must [...] be recognised as a fundamental right which forms an integral part of the general principles of Community law the observance of which the Court ensures [...]'[76]

Referring explicitly to its ruling regarding limitations on the free movement of goods in Schmidberger, the Court accordingly went on to point out that the protection of fundamental rights constitutes 'a legitimate interest which, in principle, justifies a restriction of the obligations imposed by Community law, even under a fundamental freedom guaranteed by the Treaty [...]'.[77] Indeed, the Court stresses, in *Viking* and in the subsequent *Laval* case, that economic objectives and social objectives are to be considered as co-original: that the EU has 'not only an economic but also a social purpose' and that the free trade objectives must be

> balanced against the objectives pursued by social policy, which include [...] improved living and working conditions, so as to make possible their harmonisation while improvement is being maintained, proper social protection and dialogue between management and labour.[78]

But of course balancing two rights excludes the unconditional vindication of either; so the application of the *Schmidberger* framework means that a public interest justification of collective action authorizes what is necessary to achieve the objective pursued, but no more. In *Viking* the Court states this requirement that means be proportionate to ends this way:

> ... as regards the collective action taken by FSU, even if that action could reasonably be considered to fall, at first sight, within the objective of protecting workers, such a view would no longer be tenable if it were established that the jobs or conditions of employment at issue were not jeopardised or under serious threat.[79]

The ECJ then instructs the referring domestic court to establish the relevant facts, retaining for itself the right to 'provide guidance' (par. 85) regarding the normative 'constitutional' framework under which the balancing between free market objectives and 'policy in the social sphere' must take place.

In her critique of the Court's decision in *Viking* Catherine Barnard has argued that the very fact that the Court insists on balancing between the social and the economic within the framework of proportionality means that the decision has put the 'social' on the backfoot.[80] Once collective action is viewed as a 'restriction' of the right to establishment as

[76] Par. 44. [77] Par. 45. [78] Par. 79. [79] Par. 81.

[80] Cf. Catherine Barnard, 'Employment Rights, Free Movement Under the EC Treaty and the Services Directive', Europa Institute Mitchell Working Paper Series 5/2008, at p. 14; see also Catherine Barnard,

a fundamental economic freedom, social interests have to defend themselves against the economic. The recognition of the right to strike as a fundamental social right has little more than rhetorical value, because the justifications put forward by the trade unions are subject to close scrutiny, unmitigated by references to 'margin of appreciation'.[81] But this criticism fails, because the right to strike is never absolute, but always subject to balancing and to a proportionality test—also within the domestic context. Recognition of the full spectrum of fundamental rights at the EU level entails the recognition that some rights will always 'horizontally' clash with others and that balancing is therefore inevitable. In *Schmidberger* and in *Omega* the Court considered that the protection of fundamental rights is a legitimate interest that justifies a restriction of the obligations imposed by treaty-based economic freedoms. The right to collective action to protect host country workers from social dumping is recognized as an imperative reason of general interest that can justify a restriction of economic freedoms. According to the framework established in *Schmidberger* and *Omega*, wherever possible, the Court should defer to domestic courts in striking a balance and in the application of the proportionality test. This the Court arguably did also in *Viking*. The important message in the above cases is not that social interests have to defend themselves from the economic, but that the ECJ now takes the social into account when interpreting what were once stand-alone economic rights.[82] Indeed subsequently the Court explicitly considers the dangers of 'social dumping' and considers the right to take collective action for the protection of workers against social dumping as an overriding reason of public interest.[83] Social rights, then, are not exceptions that need to be justified against a market-making rule; but fundamental freedoms and

'Social Dumping or Dumping Socialism? Case Note on Laval and Rüffert', in 67(2) Cambridge Law Journal 262–64 (2008).

[81] Cf. Catherine Barnard, op. cit.; Simon Deakin, Regulatory Competition after Laval, at: http://www.cbr.cam.ac.uk/pdf/WP364.pdf; Fritz Scharpf, The only solution is to refuse to comply with the ECJ rulings, at: http://www.boeckler.de/164_92433.html; see also Joerges/Rödl, 'Informal Politics, Formalised Law and the "Social Deficit" of European Integration: Reflections after the Judgments of the ECJ in *Viking* and *Laval*', 15(1) European Law Journal (2009), S. 1 ff.; Robert Rebhahn, Grundrechte und Grundfreiheiten im Kollektiven Arbeitsrecht vor dem Hintergrund der neuen EuGH Rechtsprechung, at: http://www.etui.org/en/Headline-issues/Viking-Laval-Rueffert-Luxembourg/2-Articles-in-academic-literature-on-the-judgements/(offset)/45.

[82] On socioeconomic rights within the domestic law context: Mark Tushnet, Weak Courts, Strong Rights (Princeton: Princeton University Press 2008) (exploring the idea of how weaker forms of judicial review may actually allow for stronger social welfare rights).

[83] Rec. 103.

fundamental rights are principles that compete at the same normative level and must be reconciled with one another.

Whereas the landmark decision in *Viking* was about a direct, 'horizontal' clash between economic freedoms and fundamental social rights, the subsequent decisions in the cases *Laval* and *Rüffert*, which concern the posting of workers, turned on the interpretation of the Posted Workers Directive 96/71/EC and the related question whether the Court in those decisions respected the legislative framework for balancing created by the Directive in the very same domain—working conditions—as in *Viking*. In *Rüffert* the Court clarified the conclusion already reached in *Laval* that a protection which is not 'required' in ways defined by the Directive cannot be justified under Art. 49 EC on the grounds of worker protection. The import of its decision is thus unintelligible without consideration of the goals and structure of the Directive.

The overall objective of the Directive is to strike a balance among three divergent policy goals: promotion of the free movement of services; protection of the workers in the host state from competition from workers from home states where labour costs and labour protection are lower; the protection of posted workers by improving their conditions of employment.[84] Its central provision is Art. 3, which requires host states to extend their protections of certain working conditions to workers temporarily posted in their territory. To do this they must use a prescribed set of instruments (statutes, administrative rule, collective bargaining agreements), applied in ways that do not result in the creation of new barriers to trade. Thus Art. 3(1) requires host states to apply to posted workers their own rules—a set of core rights—regarding matters such as maximum work periods, minimum rest periods, or minimum rates of pay, regardless of the law applicable to the employment relationship in the posted workers' home state. The crucial proviso is that those rules are set out in legislation or in some other form that is, in a relevant sense, applicable to host-state employees generally, and not aimed at 'protecting' posted workers in a way that actually protects domestic workers from exposure to foreign competitors.

What this requirement of generality exactly means was, predictably, controversial and is at the centre of the ECJ's *Rüffert* case. In *Rüffert*, the referring German court asked the ECJ whether the treaty's rules on free service delivery (the then Art. 49 EC) precluded provisions of a statute—the Public Procurement Act of Lower Saxony—requiring contractors

[84] Cf. Recital (5) of the Preamble.

to agree to pay workers deployed on the contract a minimum level of pay. Contractors had to agree to impose a similar obligation on subcontractors, and one of the enforcement mechanisms was the imposition of a 'contractual penalty' (a 'Vertragsstrafeklausel') of up to 10% of the contract's value in the case of 'culpable breach' of the provision. Minimum wages are, indeed, listed in Art. 3(1). But the Court decided that those statutory provisions were in fact precluded by Art. 3(1), because the relevant collective agreement had not been extended properly.

Davies[85] provides the necessary background: Germany did have an extension system, and its minimum-wage agreement for the construction industry—the TV Mindestlohn—had in fact been extended to all employers for the relevant region by the 'Arbeitnehmerentsendegesetz'—a federal statute which seeks to transpose Directive 96/71 into domestic law. In *Rüffert*, the contract between Lower Saxony and the building company (for the building of a prison) contained a declaration regarding compliance with the collective agreements, and, specifically with the minimum-wage provision of the 'Buildings and public works collective agreement'.[86] The difficulty was—as Lower Saxony later confirmed in response to a written question from the Court—that the 'Buildings and public works agreement', unlike the TV Mindestlohn, had not been extended and declared universally applicable within the meaning of the Arbeitnehmerent sendegesetz.[87] Nor did the case-file—as the Court observed—contain any evidence to support the conclusion that the 'Buildings and public works agreement' was nevertheless capable of being treated as universally applicable within the meaning of Art. 3(1).[88] As a result, the binding effect of the 'Buildings and public works agreement' covered only a part of the construction sector falling within its geographical area. Yet it required rates of pay well above those required by the TV Mindestlohn. Because the rate of pay had not been fixed according to the procedures laid down in Art. 3(1), it could not be considered to constitute a minimum rate of pay within the meaning of Art. 3(1).[89]

An additional issue was whether the statute of the Public Procurement Act could be rescued by Art. 3(7) of the Directive, which says that the Directive does 'not prevent application of terms and conditions of employment which are more favorable to workers'. In his Opinion in *Rüffert* AG Bot had argued that this directive does not stand in the way of an

[85] Paul Davies, 'Case C-346/06, *Rüffert v. Land Niedersachsen* [2008] IRLR 467 (ECJ)', in 37(3) Industrial Law Journal 293–95 (2008).

[86] ECJ C-346/06, Rec. 10.

[87] ECJ C-346/06, Rec. 26.

[88] ECJ C-346/06, Rec. 26.

[89] Rec. 31.

enhanced national protection of posted workers. In his view Art. 3(7) permits the eclipse of defined mandatory protective rules in force in the host State not only (as plainly intended) by the rules of the service provider's home State, if those rules are more favourable to the posted workers, but also by rules of the host state itself that do not meet the requirement of Art. 3(1).[90] The Court disagreed. Read narrowly, it argued, Art. 3(7) does indeed allow superior home state rules to trump host state rules that are inferior for posted workers. But read very broadly, as AG Bot proposed, the article would eviscerate the limits on exclusionary forms of 'protection' set out in Art. 3(1) and therefore frustrate a core purpose of the Directive: increasing cross-border provision of services—for otherwise Art. 3(7) would render Art. 3(1) meaningless.[91]

The subsequent case *Commission v. Luxembourg*[92] concerned the interpretation of Art. 3(10) of Directive 96/10. Article 3(10) allows for exceptions to the restrictions set out in Art. 3(1), provided that those exceptions are 'so crucial for the protection of the political, social, or economic order in the Member State concerned as to require compliance by all persons present on the national territory of that Member State and all legal relationships within that state'. [93] The case turned on the question whether national labour law provisions by the Grand Duchy of Luxembourg could count as 'public-order legislation' or 'public policy exceptions' within the meaning of Art. 3(10).[94] In legislation transposing the Posted Workers Directive, the Grand Duchy invoked this exemption to justify the requirement that all workers posted to its territory be linked by a written contract of employment to their home country employer, and that all rates of remuneration, not only minimum wages of any form, be indexed to the cost of living, among others. The Grand Duchy contended that the imposition of those obligations were imperative to the national public interest, inasmuch as they were deemed to be indispensable to the maintenance of good labour relations in Luxembourg. The European Commission challenged

[90] Rec. 94.

[91] ECJ, C-346/06, Rec. 33. A similar dispute, concerning, inter alia, a clause requiring an automatic adjustment of rates of remuneration to the costs of living under the law of the host state arose in Case C-319/06 *Commission v. Luxembourg*. The Grand Duchy had argued that such a clause constituted a mandatory public policy imperative under Art. 3(10) by protecting workers from the effects of inflation and thereby by ensuring good labour relations in Luxembourg. But, in response, the Court pointed out that Luxembourg had failed to provide evidence to what extent the application to workers posted in Luxembourg was capable to achieve those objectives. Rec. 53 f.

[92] Case C-319/06 *Commission of the European Communities v. Grand Duchy of Luxembourg*.

[93] Rec. 29, referring to ECJ, Joined Cases C-369/96 and C-376/96 *Arblade and Others* [1999] ECR I-8453, rec. 30.

[94] Rec. 29.

that classification, arguing that the Grand Duchy had incorrectly transposed Art. 3(1) and 3(10) into domestic law by imposing obligations on home-country undertakings beyond those permitted by Directive 96/10.

The Court agreed with the Commission. Referring to its *Omega* case, it pointed out that the notion of a public policy exemption must be interpreted strictly and cannot be determined unilaterally by each Member State, in particular when cited by a Member State as justification for a derogation from the fundamental principle of the freedom to provide services on which the Directive was based, and even if Member States were still, in principle, free to determine the requirements of public policy in the light of their national needs.[95] Thus, the concept of public policy does allow Member States a margin of discretion within the limits imposed by the Treaty and by the Directive and monitored by the Court. But Luxembourg was unable to meet its stringent burden of proof and to provide appropriate evidence to enable the necessity and proportionality of its measures which were likely to dissuade the exercise of freedom to provide services to be evaluated. So the burden of proof was on Luxembourg to show how the measures they referred to should count as public policy exemptions. Although the unions do not figure in that case, it is clear that the unions would prefer those measures and that labour relations are in some sense better, if the unions are happy. But the Grand Duchy only had cited in a general manner the objectives of protecting the purchasing power of workers and good labour relations without having established whether and to what extent the application to posted workers of a rule concerning automatic indexation is capable of achieving those objectives.[96] The case *Commission v. Luxembourg*, then, can be seen as yet another instance of a Member State—either on its own or in conjunction with trade unions—testing the limits of the margin of appreciation granted by the Posted Workers Directive. The outcome in each of the above cases depends not on a general—quasi-legislative—statement by the Court as to how the multipolar conflict between freedom of services; protection of posted workers against social dumping; protection of host state workers against competition from home state workers; should be resolved. Rather, the Court offers a proceduralizing and contextualizing approach to the underlying fundamental conflict within the enlarged EU between the commitment to a liberal market economy and social policy commitments: the Court obligates the parties to the conflict, via the referring court, to do the balancing that is necessary here, thereby shifting

[95] Rec. 30 ff.; 49 f. Cf. also the Opinion by AG Trstenjak, at para. 42.

[96] Rec. 52 f.

the burdens of providing mutually acceptable justifications to the parties themselves.

Critics of the decisions particularly in *Laval* and *Rüffert* have objected to the alleged 'lack of loyalty by the Court with regard to the democratic process at European level'.[97] The legislative intention in adopting Directive 96/71/EC, they argue, was to co-ordinate the statutory protection of posted workers, but not to interfere with national regulation of collective actions. The preamble of the Directive explicitly states in recital 22—which is not discussed by the Court—that the Directive 'is without prejudice to the law of the Member States concerning collective action to defend the interests of trades and professions'.[98]

But read in the light of the foregoing observations, the outcome in *Laval* and *Rüffert* and *Commission v. Luxembourg* does not appear to be an attack on the right to bargain collectively or on workers' rights more generally. In her nuanced assessment of the case law, AG Kokott comments:[99]

> In this respect, I would like to emphasise one particular aspect to which many critics, who, for example, consider the *Laval* judgment an indicator of the demise of the right to strike, do not pay sufficient attention in my view. One should be aware of the fact that the Court of Justice, in the

[97] Jonas Malmberg and Tore Sigeman, 'Industrial Actions and EU Economic Freedoms: The Autonomous Collective Bargaining Model Curtailed by the European Court of Justice', 45 Common Market Law Review 1115–46, at 1145 (2008).

[98] Ibid; Joerges / Roedl, op. cit.; for further background, cf. B. Bercusson, 13(3) European Law Journal 279–308 (2007) . Moreover, critics accuse the Court of establishing a state of affairs proposed by the Commission in the Bolkestein directive on services (Proposal COM (2004) 2 final); a proposal which was subsequently withdrawn in the democratic process leading to the final Services Directive 2006/123/EC. But the complex history of the Directive weights against this reading and supports rather the argument that in deciding not to follow the AG Bot the Court acted within the legislative framework and so remained faithful to the compromise achieved by the democratic process at the European level. In Davies' definitive account, the legislative history is the story of attempts to reconcile the desire to increase crossborder service with continued autonomy of domestic labour law. The labour importing Member States had in this situation a strong hand because of the ECJ's *Rush*-jurisprudence, according to which Community law does not preclude Member States from extending their legislation, or collective labour agreements, to any person who is employed, even temporarily, within their territory, no matter in which country the employer is established. Nonetheless, providers and users of crossborder services in the construction industry and the European Commission allied to press for some restrictions on host-state discretion in area, given the recognition of the need for at least a minimal harmonization on the provision of services. The initial proposal by the Commission was to impose a time condition: The ECJ's *Rush* ruling would only apply to postings of more than three months; however, the Member States did not accept this policy. The eventual compromise was a directive which recognizes the primacy of the law and collective agreements in the host country as the regulatory framework for the employment conditions of posted workers, but limits the measures having such primacy to a narrowly defined core of mandatory rules defined in Art. 3(1). The exacting research undertaken by Menz on national response strategies to Europeanization suggests that complex arrangements at the national level are widespread and that judicial vigilance with regard to those arrangements is legitimate.

[99] http://www.bmas.de/coremedia/generator/26986/2008__07__16__symposium__eugh__kokott.html.

> relevant judgments, ruled only on the particular question referred for a preliminary ruling. [. . .] For example, in the *Laval* judgment it underlined the national context in which the collective measures were embedded. [. . .] The Court of Justice has not made a *general* statement on the relation between fundamental freedoms and fundamental rights. In particular, it has not found in its recent rulings in question that the right to strike or, worse, human dignity must in principle take second place to fundamental freedoms. Rather, fundamental freedoms and fundamental Community rights are at the same level and must be harmonised. By placing particular emphasis on the specific characteristics of the cases, the Court of Justice, in my view, clearly shows its intention to diversify its rulings on the basis of the particularities of future proceedings referred for preliminary rulings.

The recent ruling in *Sähköalojen ammattillitto*[100] illustrates this intention to diversify. ESA, a company established in Poland and carrying on business in the electricity sector, posted workers to its Finnish branch on a long-term basis. Maintaining that ESA did not pay them the minimum remuneration that was due to them under the Finnish collective agreements for the electricity sector, the workers concerned individually assigned their outstanding pay claims to the *Sähköalojen ammattiliitto*—a Finnish trade union in the electricity sector—so that it could recover those claims—an amount of over 6 Mil. Euro—from ESA. In its ruling, the CJEU dismissed ESA's argument that because Polish law prohibited the ceding of claims arising from an employment relationship to a trade union the *Sähköalojen ammattiliitto* did not have standing to act and bring proceedings on behalf the posted workers. Rather, what mattered was that under Finnish law the *Sähköalojen ammattiliitto* had standing to bring proceedings on behalf of the Polish workers and that the assignment of claims with a view of their recovery for the posted workers was in conformity with Finnish law. An important implication of that finding was that posted workers have the right to join a trade union in the host state—meaning that in this way their status is becoming more similar to that of workers exercising their economic freedoms.

Moreover, referring to its *Laval* judgment, the CJEU reiterated that Directive 96/71 aims to ensure 'a nucleus of mandatory rules for minimum protection' for posted workers.[101] Member States must therefore ensure that, whatever the law applicable to the employment relationship, in the framework of the transnational provision of services, undertakings

[100] CJEU, *Sähköalojen ammattiliitto ry v. Elektrobudowa Spółka Akcyjna*, C-396/13, Judgment of 12 February 2015, ECLI:EU:C:2015:86.

[101] At rec. 29.

guarantee workers posted to their territory the terms and conditions of employment covering the matters listed in Art. 3(1) of Directive 96/71. The Court emphasized that the aim of Art. 3(1) is to strike a fair balance: on the one hand, it seeks to 'ensure a climate of fair competition between national undertakings and undertakings which provide services transnationally'; but, on the other hand, Art. 3(1) at the same time also seeks to ensure that 'posted workers will have the rules of the host Member State for minimum protection as regards the terms and conditions of employment relating to those matters applied to them while they work on a temporary basis in the territory of that Member State'.[102] Yet Directive 96/71 has not harmonized at EU level the material content of those mandatory rules for minimum protection of posted workers. It refers to the national law or practice of the Member State to whose territory the worker is posted for the definition of the minimum rates of pay. Hence, the task of defining what are the constituent elements of the minimum wage, for the application of that directive, remains a matter for the law of the Member State of the posting, but only in so far as that definition does not have the effect of impeding the freedom to provide services between Member States. For example, allowances and supplements which are not defined as being constituent elements of the minimum wage by the law or practice of the (host-) Member State to whose territory the worker is posted cannot, under the Directive, be considered to be elements of the nucleus of mandatory rules for minimum protection.[103] The Court thus seeks to reconcile the need for a nucleus of minimum protection for posted workers with the employers' freedom to provide services transnationally. The ruling thus provides a strong incentive *for trade unions to collaborate transnationally* and establish *transnational regimes* among themselves at EU level, specifying the parameters for equal treatment of posted workers in the host states. One goal of such agreements, for example, would lie in ensuring that the Polish employer cannot claim back the wages which were won by *Sähköalojen ammattiliitto* before Finnish courts back the posted workers once they return to Poland. In this way, the line of cases originating from *Viking* and *Laval* and its daughter cases to *Sähköalojen ammattiliitto*, most recently, can be seen as providing the incentives for experimentalist regime-building in the social sphere beyond the State and, in this way, as deliberation-enhancing.

Consider, finally, a constellation concerning the protection of employees in the event of a transfer of undertakings from public to private.

[102] At rec. 30. [103] At rec. 36.

In those constellations, collective agreements applied to the individual employment relationships between the employer and his employees by virtue of a reference made to those agreements in the contracts of employment. But the general issue raised was whether, once a business has been transferred, a transferee employer may still be compelled to apply the terms and conditions arising from collective agreements adopted after that transfer. In other words, the question arose whether the transferee employer was obliged to apply the terms and conditions arising from (employee-friendly) future amendments made to the collective agreement even after the transfer. Clauses in employment contracts can operate either statically or dynamically: this depends on whether they refer only to a particular collective agreement in force ('statistic') or also to any future changes that will be made to that agreement ('dynamic'). So-called *static clauses* thus refer to a specific collective agreement, and only to the version of that agreement which is in force at the time of the transfer. By contrast, *dynamic referral clauses* may also refer to future modifications to the agreements, which involve changes to those rights and obligations. In practice, dynamic reference clauses therefore are more favourable to employees than merely static ones: the parties to the employment contract agree that certain material provisions of the employment relationship that exists between them must be dynamically determined and updated by an external legal framework and continue to evolve. The terms and conditions applicable are therefore those provided for in the collective agreements periodically negotiated by the competent peek organizations.

The facts in *Mark Alemo-Herron and Others v. Parkwood Leisure Ltd*[104] were as follows: the Lewisham London Borough Council in 2002 contracted out its 'leisure-services' to a private sector undertaking, which then in May 2004 sold the business to *Parkwood*, another private sector undertaking. The employees became part of that company. The initial public-sector employment contract between the Lewisham Borough and the employees in question referred to terms and conditions negotiated by the local government collective bargaining body ('NJC'). These terms and conditions contained a so-called *dynamic clause* automatically adopting the terms agreed in future agreements. But *Parkwood*, as a private sector undertaking, did not participate in the NJC. When a new agreement with NJC was reached in June 2004—with retrospective effectiveness from 1 April 2004—*Parkwood* took the view that this agreement was not binding on it, and thus refused to grant its employees a pay increase negotiated

[104] CJEU, *Mark Alemo-Herron and Others v. Parkwood Leisure Ltd*, Judgment of 18 July 2013: Case C-426/11.

under the new agreement. Yet under the so-called 'dynamic approach' which existed in the UK, dynamic clauses referring to collective agreements negotiated and agreed after the date of transfer were enforceable even against a transferee who was not party to the collective agreement. In contrast to the dynamic approach, a 'static approach'—which, for example, is used in Germany—holds that collectively agreed rules become part of the employment contract with the content only that they possess at the time when the business is transferred, and that they are not automatically updated after the transfer. The referring UK Supreme Court wanted to know whether the existing UK 'dynamic approach' was consistent with EU law.

The question turned on the interpretation of Art. 3(3) of the Transfer of Undertakings Directive 2001/23 which stipulates that '[t]he transferor's rights and obligations arising from a contract of employment or from an employment relationship existing on the date of a transfer shall, by reason of such transfer, be transferred to the transferee'. AG Villalón argued that the Directive *allowed* UK-style dynamic clauses such as the one at issue: the legitimate aim of such clauses was to promote the safeguarding of terms and conditions more favourable to employees by means of a reference to a collective agreement that will apply them.[105] But the CJEU disagreed, pointing out that the Directive 'does not aim solely to safeguard the interests of employees in the event of transfer of an undertaking' but

> seeks to ensure a fair balance between the interests of those employees, on the one hand, and those of the transferee, on the other. More particularly, it makes clear that the transferee must be in a position to make the adjustments and changes necessary to carry on its operations.[106]

The CJEU held that Art. 16 of the CFREU—which guarantees the 'freedom to conduct a business'—also covered freedom of contract as a fundamental right. But the dynamic clause seriously reduced *Parkwood's* contractual freedom in a way that was liable 'to adversely affect *the very essence* of its freedom to conduct a business', because *Parkwood* did not have any possibility of participating in the negotiation process of collective agreements concluded after the date of the transfer. Because *Parkwood* was not represented in the collective bargaining body at issue, it was unable to negotiate the aspects determining changes in working conditions for its employees with a view to its future economic activity. The dynamic clause thus limited the room for manoeuvre necessary for *Parkwood* to make the necessary adjustments and changes and therefore failed to

[105] Opinion, at rec. 39. [106] Rec. 25.

guarantee a fair balance between *Parkwood's* interests and those of its employees. As a consequence, *Parkwood's* 'contractual freedom [was] seriously reduced to the point that such a limitation [was] liable to adversely affect the very essence of its freedom to conduct a business'. Hence, the UK-style dynamic approach was inconsistent with the Directive. So, from *Alemon-Heron* follows that, while Member States can in principle, on the basis of Art. 8 of Directive 2001/23, opt to make contractual clauses referring to collective agreements dynamic, the exercise of that option is nonetheless subject to the condition of respect for fundamental rights, in particular the transferee's CFREU-freedom to conduct a business. However, the transferee's freedom to conduct a business is violated where the transferee is unable to participate in the process of negotiating collective agreements concluded after the date of the transfer.

Commentators sharply criticized the Court's deployment of the Charter to the effect of what they thought was 'an aggressive protection of the constitutional value of freedom of contract'[107] and listed *Parkwood* as being among the progeny of *Viking* and *Laval* in posing a threat to Europe's social fabric. Hugh Collins, for example, argued that 'it would . . . be wrong to follow *Alemo-Herron* down the dark alley, which was first mapped by the US Supreme Court in *Lochner v. New York*, of permitting Charter rights to block social measures that inevitably involve interference with market freedoms'.[108] In a similar vein, Stephen Weatherill objects that an '[a]ppreciation of the dual function of harmonization—market-making *and* social protection—has gone missing in *Alemon-Herron* . . . and been replaced by a vision which is blind to the particular concerns of a group—workers—who lack the economic power to bargain effectively on an individual basis'.[109] Martijn Hesselink concurs and argues that the ruling 'has a distinctly libertarian flavour to it and seems partisan . . .'[110] So the worry is that the CFREU *blocks*—rather than enables—a socially desirable transformation of private-law relations.

[107] Stephen Weatherill, 'Case Note. Use and Abuse of the EU's Charter of Fundamental Rights: On the Improper Veneration of "Freedom of Contract" ', 10(1) European Review of Contract Law 167–82 (2014), at 172 ff. Jeremias Prassl, 'Freedom of Contract as a General Principle of EU Law? Transfers of Undertakings and the Protection of Employer Rights in EU Labour Law', 42 Industrial Law Journal 434 (2013).

[108] Hugh Collins, 'Building European Contract Law on Charter Rights', ibid (ed.), European Contract Law and the Charter of Fundamental Rights (Cambridge, Intersentia 2017), 1–32, at 29.

[109] Stephen Weatherill, The Internal Market as a Legal Concept (Oxford: OUP 2017), at 206 f.

[110] Martijn Hesselink, 'The Justice Dimensions of the Relationship between Fundamental Rights and Private Law', Hugh Collins, European Contract Law and the Charter of Fundamental Rights, op. cit., at 189.

But it is important to place that criticism further in context. The case giving rise to the earlier judgment in *Werhof* concerned a statically worded reference clause and a claim by the employees that that clause should be interpreted as being dynamic.[111] The situation at issue in the case in *Asklepios*, decided after *Alemon-Herron*, was the reverse.[112] Here, the reference clause was worded dynamically. Faced with the employees' claim that the amendments to the collective agreement referred to by that clause, made after the transfer of the business, were enforceable against the transferee, the referring German court wanted to know whether Directive 2001/23 precluded that clause from being dynamic.

Again, in *Asklepios*, there were successive transfers. Workers were employed at a hospital owned by the local authority. The local authority transferred the hospital to a limited liability company (GmbH), then, two years later, the part of the hospital business where the workers were employed was transferred to KLS FM, also a limited liability company not belonging to any employers' association which had negotiated and participated in the adoption of a collective labour agreement. But the employment contracts between the workers and KLS FM contained a dynamic referral clause providing that their employment relationship would be governed, as was the case before the transfer, by the Federal framework collective agreement for employees of municipal authorities and businesses, 'BMT-G II', and also, in the future, by the collective agreements supplementing, amending, and replacing it. Subsequently, the part of the business where the workers were employed was transferred from KLS FM to *Asklepios*, another company in the group of undertakings in the hospital sector. *Asklepios* was neither bound to the BMT-G II nor to any other collective agreement for the public service.

The Court, again, pointed out that Directive 2001/23 'does not aim solely to safeguard the interests of employees in the event of transfer of an undertaking, but seeks to ensure a fair balance between the interests of those employees, on the one hand, and those of the transferee, on the other', and that 'the transferee must be able to assert its interests effectively in a contractual process to which it is party and to negotiate the aspects determining changes in the working conditions of its employees with a view to its future economic activity'. But because the German legal provisions did provide for the possibility, even after the transfer, for

[111] CJEU, C-499/04, *Hans Werhof v. Freeway Traffic Systems GmbH & Co. KG*, Judgment of the Court (Third Chamber) of 9 March 2006, [2006] ECR I-02397.

[112] CJEU, C-680/15 and C-681/15, *Asklepios Kliniken Langen-Seligenstadt GmbH v. Felja*, Judgment of 27 April 2017 [2017] IRLR 653.

the transferee to adjust the working conditions existing at the date of the transfer, either consensually or unilaterally, those domestic provisions were consistent with the Directive and Art. 16 CFREU. Hence dynamic clauses can be legitimate under EU law, provided that national law allows the possibility for the transferee to make adjustments both consensually and unilaterally. The CFREU does not block *ipso facto* social measures but requires national legislation to provide the transferee with the possibility for adjustments.

In each of these cases the Court has insisted on the necessity of striking a fair balance between economic liberties and socioeconomic rights. Given the institutional complexity of the issues involved, the Court has refused to resort to traditional 'command-and-control' strong-form interventions in the pursuit of fair balance. *Laval* and *Viking* and daughter cases involved the clash of economic interests between workers from old Europe and those from the new Member States after Eastern enlargement, and *Parkwood* a choice between the *British* and the *German* model of social protection. In each of these decisions, the Court responded through *proceduralization* by inviting social actors, including the trade unions, to form a contextualization regime in which stakeholders themselves could develop substantive standards and remedies that meet the requirement of fair balance.

Contrary to the prevailing sentiment in the literature, these developments do not lend support to the constitutional asymmetry thesis. To the contrary, the Court's intervention has triggered legislative innovation. In 2014 the so-called Enforcement Directive 2014/67/EU concerning the posting of workers in the framework of the provision of services was approved. The Directive's objective is to establish a common framework that provides Member States with effective tools to distinguish genuine posting from abuses and circumvention, for example, by enabling the authorities of a receiving host Member State to request the authorities in the sending home Member State to verify that the posting company genuinely performs substantial activities, other than pure administrative activities. To combat abuse and circumvention, the Directive seeks to increase the awareness of posted workers and companies about their rights and obligations and to improve co-operation between national authorities in charge of posting; and the Directive also empowers trade unions and other parties to lodge complaints and take legal and administrative action against the employers of posted workers, if their rights are not respected, and establishes a system of administrative penalties and fines across the Member States if the requirements of EU law on posting are not respected. In 2016 plans were underway to revise the 1996 Posted Workers Directive so as to ensure that social dumping has no place in the EU by eliminating unwanted incentives to use posting as a means to exploit ever growing wage differences between the Member States and by making universally applicable collective agreements mandatory for posted workers in all economic sectors. The judicial interventions have triggered a process of transnational regime-building. The emergent regime enables a process of meaningful engagement between various stakeholders themselves and aims at ensuring an appropriate level of protection of the rights of posted workers for the cross-border provision of services.

2. Transformative modernization of national law by the CJEU: the example of age discrimination in employment (*Mangold* and *Kücükdeveci*)

The CJEU's decisions in *Mangold* and *Kücükdeveci* concern the interpretation of Directive 2000/78/EC establishing a general framework for equal treatment in employment and occupation. The overall objectives of the Directive is 'to lay down a general framework for combating discrimination on the grounds of religion or belief, disability, age or sexual orientation as regards employment and occupation, with a view to putting into effect in the Member States the principle of equal treatment'. Both decisions, in particular in *Kücükdeveci*, illustrate the Court's transformative role in updating and modernizing national labour law by increasing the standard of social protection afforded to employees *beyond the level hitherto envisaged by domestic law*.

The *Mangold* case concerned the question whether old age discrimination is a general principle of Community law.[113] Mr Mangold, then fifty-six years old, concluded with Mr Helm, a practicing lawyer, a fixed-term employment contract. The duration of the contract was based on the statutory provision of the German Art. 14(3) TzBfG which is intended to make it easier to conclude fixed-term contracts with older workers, defined as those aged fifty-two or more years, by permitting conclusion of a fixed-term employment contract without having to provide a justification for this limitation.[114] The parties had agreed that there was no reason for

[113] CJEU Case C-144/04, *Werner Mangold v. Rüdiger Helm*, Judgment of the Court (Grand Chamber) of 22 November 2005, ECLI:EU:C:2005:709.

[114] Article 14(1) TzBfG permits the conclusion of fixed term contracts if there are objective grounds for doing so, as enumerated in a list. Article 14(2) TzBfG permits the conclusion of up to three fixed term employment contracts without objective justification for the first two years of employment with a specific employer ('new employment exception'). Article 14(3) TzBfG permits conclusion of a fixed-term employment contract without justification, if the worker has reached the age of fifty-eight by the time the fixed-term contract begins; a threshold which was later lowered to the age of fifty-two for the period

the fixed term of this contract other than that set out in Art. 14(3) above; all other grounds for limiting the term of employment accepted in principle by the legislature were expressly excluded from this agreement. Indeed, the parties to the conflict—both lawyers—had deliberately sought for a way for having Art. 14(3) TzBfG declared incompatible with EC law; so the legal dispute was, in this sense, artificial. According to Mr Mangold, the limitation of his contract was, although in keeping with Art. 14(3) of the TzBfG, incompatible with the Framework Agreement, which aims at improving the quality of fixed-term work by ensuring the application of the principle of non-discrimination and at preventing the abuse arising from the use of successive fixed term contracts, and with Directive 2000/78. Mr Helm, by contrast, took the view the that Clause 5(1)(a) of the Framework Agreement, which allows member states to introduce anti-discrimination measures 'in a manner which takes account of the needs of specific sectors and/or categories of workers', permitted the use of fixed-term contracts, in this case older workers. The period prescribed for the implementation of Directive 2000/78/EC into domestic law had neither expired when the fixed-term employment contract was concluded nor when the decision was handed down.

The ECJ's central—and controversial—finding was that 'the principle of non-discrimination on grounds of age must be ... regarded as a general principle of Community law' (par. 75). Consequently, the 'observance of the general principle of equal treatment, in particular in respect of age, cannot as such be conditional upon the expiry of the period allowed the Member States for the transposition of a directive intended to lay down a general framework for combating discrimination on the grounds of age' (par. 76). The Court stated that Directive 2000/78 does not itself lay down the principle of equal treatment in the field of employment and occupation; rather, 'the source of the actual principle underlying the prohibition of those forms of discrimination' is to be found 'as is clear from the [first] and fourth recitals in the preamble to the Directive, in various international instruments and in the constitutional traditions common to the Member States' (74). According to the Court, it is therefore 'the responsibility of the national court, hearing a dispute involving the principle of non-discrimination in respect of age, to provide [...] the legal protection which individuals derive from the rules of Community law and to ensure that those rules are fully effective, setting aside any provision of national

between 2003 and 2006. Article 14(3) also prohibits the transformation of an employment contract of unlimited duration into a fixed-term contract.

law which may conflict with that law [and] to guarantee the full effectiveness of the general principle of non-discrimination in respect of age' (77 f.).

Mangold's critics have accused the Court of a judicial usurpation of prerogatives that—given the policy conflict at stake between the policy of opening-up labour markets to older workers and the policy of implementing the principle of non-discrimination on grounds of age—should belong to the national legislators. They take issue with the impact of judicial lawmaking on domestic democratic choices and call for a greater degree of sensitivity to concerns of subsidiarity, democratic legitimacy, and institutional balance.

Thus, former German president Roman Herzog argued that the ' "general principle of Community law" was a fabrication', which 'the ECJ more or less pulled out of the hat, […] acting not as part of the judicial power but as the legislature', crossing the line to 'invent[ing]' EU law and thereby 'undermin[ing] the competences of the Member States even in the core fields of national powers'.[115] Similarly, AG Geelhoed, in his Opinion in *Chacón Navas*, pointed to 'potentially far-reaching consequences, economic and financial, which such prohibitions of discrimination may have in horizontal relationships among citizens and in vertical relationships between public authorities and interested citizens' and which are best addressed by national legislators. The ECJ's contention that non-discrimination on grounds of age must be regarded as a general principle of EC law amounts to the 'creation of an Archimedean position, from which the prohibitions of discrimination defined in Article 13 EC can be used as a lever to correct, without the intervention of the authors of the Treaty or the Community legislature, the decisions made by the Member States in the exercise of the powers which they—still—retain'. But the implementation of non-discrimination prohibitions entails 'painful, if not tragic, choices when weighing up the interests in question, such as the rights of disabled or older workers versus the flexible operation of the labour market or an increase in the level of participation of older workers'; choices which are the domain of the legislator. In a similar vein, AG Mazak considers it a (89) 'bold proposition and a significant move',[116] and (94) 'far from compelling', to judicially infer, (89) 'solely

[115] Roman Herzog and Lüder Gerken, 'An Article on the EU Constitution', in 'Welt am Sonntag' dated 14 January 2007, English version at http://swpat.ffii.org/07/01/herzog_eu/herzog_eu_orig0701.en.pdf.

[116] Opinion AG Mazak in Case C-411/05, *Félix Palacios de la Villa v. Cortefiel Servicios SA*, delivered on 15 February 2007, ECLI:EU:C:2007:106.

from the general principle of equal treatment, the existence of a specific prohibition of discrimination on the ground of age'.

By contrast, AG Sharpston agreed with the ECJ in *Mangold* that 'the origins of the principle [...] lie neither in Directive 2000/78 as an implementing directive, nor indeed in Art. 13 EC as such. They must be found in a prior time and place'.[117] But she also pointed out that this does not render Art. 13 EC or Directive 2000/78 redundant and that 'any argument to the effect that if a principle prohibiting discrimination on grounds of age had already existed, Art. 13 EC or Directive 2000/78 would have been unnecessary is fundamentally misconceived'. It is, according to her, 'precisely *because* the general principle of equality has now been recognized also to include equality of treatment irrespective of age that an enabling legislative provisions such as Art. 13 EC becomes necessary and is duly used as the basis of legislative intervention'.[118] Indeed, '[d]etailed legislation will be needed [in order to] to classify the application of particular criteria in particular circumstances as acceptable or unacceptable and to give binding legal effect to that classification'.[119]

Martijn Hesselink believes the *Mangold* ruling remains 'problematic from the point of view of justice because it sets aside a more democratically legitimate reading of a general principle of EU law'[120] and because reasonable pluralism prompts judicial deference to interpretations with a strong deliberative-democratic basis, especially where the fundamental rights issue was explicitly addressed in the legislative process. But AG Sharpston's interpretation was confirmed in the CJEU's subsequent decision in *Kücükdeveci*.[121] The underlying facts were as follows: Seda Kücükdeveci was born in February 1978. She had been employed by Swedex, a private company, from June 1996 (that is, from the age of eighteen) onwards. Swedex dismissed her by letter of 19 December 2006 with the effect from 31 January 2007, taking account of the statutory notice period under the German civil code. Seda Kücükdeveci contested her dismissal before the local German labour court, arguing that the period of notice should have been four months, not one month, corresponding to ten years' service and pursuant to a provision in the German civil code

[117] Opinion AG Sharpston, in Case C-427/06, *Birgit Bartsch v. Bosch und Siemens Hausgeräte (BSH) Altersfürsorge GmbH*, delivered on 22 May 2008, at 44.

[118] At para. 50. [119] At para. 56.

[120] Martijn Hesselink, 'The Justice Dimensions of the Relationship between Fundamental Rights and Private Law', Hugh Collins (ed.), European Contract Law and the Charta of Fundamental Rights (Cambridge: Intersentia 2017), 167–96, at 190.

[121] CJEU Case C-555/07, *Seda Kücükdeveci v. Swedex GmbH & Co. KG*, Judgment of the Court (Grand Chamber) of 19 January 2010, [2010] ECR I-00365.

(BGB) originating in a law from 1926. Insofar as that provision provided that periods of employment completed before the age of twenty-five were not to be taken into account in calculating the notice period, those norms of the civil code, she argued, discriminate on grounds of age in ways disallowed by Art. 13 EC [now: Art. 10 TEU] (which authorizes the Community legislature to 'take appropriate action to combat discrimination based on sex, racial or ethnic origin, religion or belief, disability, age, or sexual orientation') and, in particular, by EU Directive 2000/78—the period of transposition of which into national law had already expired by the date of the dismissal—and which must therefore be disapplied. The dispute was one between private parties. An important difference to *Mangold* was that the CFREU was now binding law. The CJEU held that Directive 2000/78 'merely gives expression to, but does not lay down, the principle of equal treatment in employment and occupation', including the principle of non-discrimination on grounds of age as its specific application enshrined in Art. 21 CFREU: '[i]n those circumstances it for the national court . . . to provide . . . the legal protection which individuals derive from European Union law and to ensure the full effectiveness of that law, disapplying if need be any provision of national legislation contrary to that principle . . .'[122]

Three important conclusions follow from the CJEU's ruling. First, the designation of rights guaranteed by directives as fundamental rights strengthens the right to rely on them even in proceedings between private parties. The Court thus confirmed a principal tenet of its highly controversial previous *Mangold* judgment: national courts must give full effect to the general principle of Community law prohibiting age discrimination by setting aside any provision of national law which may conflict with Community law, even when the time-limit for the transposition by the domestic legislature had not yet been reached.[123]

Secondly, equally importantly, while firm on the principle, the CJEU stopped short of proposing detailed (quasi-) legislative solutions itself: the CJEU did not enter the terrain of 'legislation with political latitude'. The general principle of non-discrimination on the basis of age serves as a platform from which an aggrieved individual—Seda Kücükdeveci—was able to challenge as unfair, and to force reconsideration of, a domestic legislative compromise of 1926—a compromise defended by the German government as still adequate—against the backdrop of changed contemporary circumstances. There are constitutionally resonant interests on

[122] C-144/04, of 22 November 2005, at 50 f., 56. [123] Ibid.

all sides in this multipolar conflict; and 'painful, if not tragic, choices'[124] have to be made between: the rights of disabled and older workers versus the flexible operation of the labour market; the interests of older workers versus those of younger workers in a fair level of participation in the labour market. Making such choices means stopping treating both older and younger workers as objects of stereotypes (as the German Government did in the *Seda Kücükdeveci* case) and reinstating them as participants in a discursive employment-process. But a familiar standard concern is: whom to trust more when resolving such conflicts and when making such choices—elected governments (and legislatures) working alone, or governments (legislatures) working under the limits monitored by (European) judges applying constitutional norms to the best of their understandings? The *Seda Kücükdeveci* case suggests a nuanced answer: an answer which, on the one hand, unequivocally keeps the judiciary in the game, but which, on the other hand, does not assign the judiciary the task to issue a set of definite and final top-down prescriptions displacing legislative judgments. Even if—indeed, because—the case is decided, *the dialogue*, both in the domestic system and at the EU level about a new and fairer compromise, *remains open*: a compromise which moves beyond stereotypical assumptions about age and which is no longer merely guided by a purely economic analysis of market flexibility but considers the individual employee;[125] and which reflects awareness of the implications of age discrimination on individual self-perception and membership in a political community.

Third, the power of a national court to disapply a domestic provision which it considers incompatible with EU law cannot be restricted by a national rule making the setting aside of national legislation subject to a prior declaration of unconstitutionality by the *Bundesverfassungsgericht*. And such a national rule cannot *oblige* the national court to make a reference to the CJEU: the national court's discretion as to whether to refer cannot be transformed into an obligation: '[b]y reason of the principle of the primacy of European Union law [...] contrary national legislation

[124] Thus the characterization by AG Geelhoed in C-13/95 (*Chacon Navas*), rec. 50.

[125] For an early, perceptive criticism of the domestic German approach to old-age discrimination, cf. Sp. Simitis: 'A society which wilfully blocks access to employment on the basis of disqualifying assertions is, to say the least, well on its way to totalitarian structures. Hence, the quest for a "rational," market-oriented view operates, strange as it may sound, on the same lines as the interventionist policies it condemns. In both cases, individuals are instrumentalized, the historical and societal factors determining the perception of the ability to work are disregarded and the psychological implications of a deliberate marginalization are ignored.' 'Denationalizing Labor Law: The Case of Age Discrimination', 15 Comparative Labor Law Journal 321, at 337 (1993–1994).

which falls within the scope of European Union law must be disapplied',[126] without the national court being *compelled* to invoke the assistance of the preliminary reference procedure. Thus, in *Seda Kücükdeveci* the Court dramatically strengthened the position of a vulnerable, weaker party to employment contracts by finding that the protection of individuals against age discrimination contrary to Community law cannot be reduced by national law after (and as a consequence of) the expiry of the transposition period afforded to the domestic legislature, since the meaning and purpose of the Community law principle in question was *to increase their protection*.

Indeed, the German Bundesverfassungsgericht (BVG) in *Honeywell*[127] refused to consider the ECJ's decisions in *Mangold* and *Kücükdeveci* as a judicial development of the law *ultra vires*. The BVG acknowledged that freedom of contract was, on the one hand, an essential expression of private autonomy—but also emphasized, on the other hand, the importance of safeguarding the social concerns of weaker market-participants. The BVG recognized that fixed-term contracts, while enhancing flexibility, come with a lot of uncertainty for workers—hence the need for legislative intervention into private autonomy in order to reconcile competing legitimate interests.[128] In striking a fair balance between private autonomy and the social, Union law—as autonomous law—and national constitutional law have to co-operate and to take each other's legitimate perspectives into account[129] and must avoid unilateral answers: the BVG will monitor and police the principle of conferral only 'on the basis of manifest transgressions of competence or on the basis of the exercise of competence in the area of constitutional identity which is not assignable'.

> Ultra vires review may only be exercised in a manner which is open towards European law ... The Court of Justice is ... not precluded from refining the law by means of methodically bound case-law. [But] [f]urther development of the law ... is above all not permissible where case-law makes fundamental policy decisions over and above individual cases or as a result of the further development of the law causes structural shifts to occur in the system of the sharing of constitutional power and influence. [But] the Court of Justice has a right to tolerance of error ...[130]

[126] At rec. 54. This aspect was later confirmed and strengthened in CJEU Joined Cases C-188 and C189/10 *Melki and Abdeli* [2010] ECR I-5667.

[127] Bundesverfassungsgericht, Order of the Second Senate of 6 July 2010 - 2 BvR 2661/06, at para. 58; 66.

[128] At para. 50. [129] At para. 57. [130] At para. 66 and 77.

The procedural point in *Kücükdeveci* was subsequently confirmed in *Melki*,[131] which addressed a situation, arising under French law, where a domestic court considers that a provision of national law is not only contrary to EU law, but also unconstitutional under the national constitution. According to an important 2008 amendment of the French Constitution, any citizen was allowed to bring proceedings before the ordinary courts to challenge the consistency of a domestic legislative provision with the rights and freedoms guaranteed by the French Constitution. The French implementing law provided that, where the compatibility of a French law with both the Constitution and EU law were at issue, the domestic court had to stay proceedings (except in cases of urgency of where the liberty of the individual was at stake) and to give 'priority' to initiating a domestic interlocutory procedure for constitutionality review under the French Constitution. The referring *Cour de Cassation* in *Melki* was accordingly concerned about a resulting clash between its EU obligations and its obligations under domestic constitutional law, because the requirement to refer 'as a matter of priority [. . .] to the national court responsible for reviewing the constitutionality of laws'[132] might adversely affect its ability to make a preliminary reference under Art. 267 TFEU.

In its response, the CJEU insisted that a Member State may not reserve to a constitutional court the power to examine the compatibility of national law with EU law and preclude domestic courts from making a reference. The priority mechanism was therefore compatible with EU law only under the condition that national courts remained free to refer to the CJEU for a preliminary ruling at any stage in the proceedings and to disapply, at the end of the procedure, any legislation in question if they hold it to be contrary to EU law.[133] *Melki* thus accords with *Kücükdeveci*.

In its remarkable *Conley King* ruling,[134] the CJEU ruled that the right for every worker to paid annual leave, which is set out in Art. 31(2) CFREU, must be regarded as a 'particularly important principle of EU social law' and Member States 'must not make the very existence of that right . . . subject to any preconditions whatsoever'.[135] Again, and as before in

[131] CJEU Joined Cases C-188 and C-189/10 *Melki and Abdeli* [2010] ECR I-5667.

[132] At para. 31.

[133] Subsequently, in its ruling following the CJEU, the *Court de Cassation* was able to avoid altogether the prior examination by the *Conseil constitutionnel*, which the priority mechanism had the objective of rendering compulsory, by examining the substance of the case and by declaring the impugned domestic provision inconsistent with EU law. Cf. at http://ec.europa.eu/dgs/legal_service/arrets/10c188_en.pdf.

[134] CJEU, Case C-214/16, *Conley King v. The Sash Window Workshop Ltd et al.*, Judgment of 29 November 2017 [2018] IRLR 142.

[135] CJEU, Case C-214/16, at 32 and 34.

Kücükdeveci, the ruling illustrates the transformative role of an EU fundamental social right in shaping private-law relations. The ruling concerned the interpretation of Working-Time Directive 2003/88, which—referring to principles of the International Labour Organisation (ILO)—lays down minimum safety and health requirements for the organization of working time, also with regard to minimum periods of annual leave (Art. 1(2)(a)) and requires Member States to ensure that every worker is entitled to annual paid leave of at least four weeks (Art. 7(1)). But Mr King had worked for his employer on the basis of a self-employed commission-only contract for more than twelve years until his retirement and was paid on a commission-only basis. When he took annual leave, it was unpaid, and now, upon his retirement, Mr King sought to recover payment for his annual leave, taken and not paid and untaken, for the entire period of his engagement. In its response to the referring Court of Appeal of England and Wales, the CJEU ruled, first, that EU law precluded a situation in which the worker had to take his leave before establishing whether he has the right to be paid in respect of that leave. Otherwise—if the worker was forced to take leave without pay and only then bring an action to claim payment for it, as required by UK law—the worker might be dissuaded from taking that leave which would frustrate '[t]he very purpose' of the right to paid annual leave which 'is to enable the worker to rest and to enjoy a period of relaxation and leisure'.[136] But the Directive 'treats the right to annual leave and to a payment on that account as being two aspects of a single right'.[137] UK law therefore also deprived the worker of the right to an effective remedy, enshrined in Art. 47 CREU.

Second, and equally importantly, the Court ruled that EU law also precluded UK national provisions and practices which prevented a worker from carrying over and accumulating paid annual leave rights which the worker had not been able or willing to exercise because of the employer's refusal to remunerate that leave. The Court here emphasized that the Directive serves not only the protection of workers but also the protection of employers who are 'faced with the risk that a worker will accumulate periods of absence of too great a length and the difficulties in the organisation of work which such periods might entail'.[138] But the protection of the employer's interest in *Conley King* could not be classified as 'strictly necessary' because an employer who does not allow a worker to

[136] CJEU, Case C-214/16, at 37.

[137] CJEU, Case C-214/16, at 35.

[138] CJEU, Case C-214/16, at 55.

exercise his or her right to paid annual leave for mere reasons of convenience 'must bear the consequences'.[139] For if the right to paid annual leave could be extinguished in this way, that 'would amount to validating conduct by which an employer was unjustly enriched to the detriment of the very purpose of that directive, which is that there should be due regard for workers' health'.[140]

One need not explicitly refer to Paul Lafargue's treatise on *Le droit à la paresse*[141] to see that the emphasis on the right to paid annual leave as a *principle* shaping private-law relations serves an important *pro-democratic rationale*: this right allows individuals to understand themselves not only as entirely subsumed under the role as workers or employees, living in a position of total and immediate dependence (or, as in the case of Mr Conley King, of fictitious self-employment), but also as free and equal citizens in a self-governing polity. The right to paid leave as a 'particularly important principle of EU social law' thus becomes a *democratic right*, and the CJEU's ruling in this way, however surreptitiously, contributes to an attenuation of the EU's democratic deficit.

C. Unfair terms in consumer contracts: Directive 93/13/EEC as a regime

At the beginning of the twentieth century, Max Weber wrote

> New demands for a 'social law' to be based upon such emotionally colored ethical postulates as 'justice' or 'human dignity,' and directed against the very dominance of a mere business morality, have arisen with the emergence of the modern class problem ... By these demands, legal formalism itself has been challenged. Such a concept as economic duress, or the attempt to treat as immoral, and thus as invalid, a contract because of a gross disproportion between promise and consideration, are derived from norms which, from the legal standpoint, are entirely amorphous and which are neither juristic nor conventional nor traditional in character but ethical and which claim as their legitimation substantive justice rather than formal legality.[142]

The threat to legality, as Weber added, is compounded not only by the 'status ideologies of the lawyers themselves', but also by the 'demand for

[139] CJEU, Case C-214/16, at 63. [140] CJEU, Case C-214/16, at 64.

[141] Paul Lafargue, *Le Droit à la paresse* (1880/1883), English translation at: https://www.marxists.org/archive/lafargue/1883/lazy/index.htm.

[142] Max Weber, 'Economy and Society: An Outline of Interpretive Sociology', Guenther Roth and Claus Wittich (eds.) (Berkeley: University of California Press 1978) 886.

"judicial creativeness" at least where the statute is silent'.[143] Today, many will reject Weber's value scepticism, but also agree that the hope for an overlapping consensus on a conception of justice undergirding constitutional law comes to something too strong. Yet, as I will argue in this section, Europeanization and proceduralization suggest a constructive way beyond this impasse.

The theme of *modernization* of wayward national law is prominent in the sphere of consumer protection when it comes to consumer concluded contracts between banks (acting as creditors) and vulnerable individuals acting as consumers. A fundamental problem any modern system of private law must address is how to combine two types of provisions: those that are intended to facilitate private ordering through voluntary transactions; and those setting out certain mandatory terms that are intended to protect vulnerable consumers against risks inherent to free market transactions. Directive 93/13/EEC[144] responds to this problem as follows: with regard to *contractual terms* which have 'not been individually negotiated', the Directive assumes the consumer typically to be 'in a weak position vis-à-vis seller or supplier, as regards both his bargaining power and his level of knowledge' and therefore 'aims to replace the formal balance which the contract establishes between the rights and obligations of the parties with an effective balance which re-establishes equality between them'[145] by providing that unfair terms are non-binding on the consumer (Art. 6). In order to assist national courts in their task of determining whether a specific term is actually unfair, an Annex of the Directive contains, as an interpretive aid,[146] 'an indicative and non-exhaustive list' of seventeen terms 'which may be regarded as unfair'.[147] To catch what this list

[143] As Weber famously added: '[b]eing confined to the interpretation of statutes and contracts, like a slot machine into one which just drops the facts (and the fees) in order to have it spew out the decision (plus opinion), appears to the modern lawyer as beneath his dignity'.

[144] For authoritative accounts, cf. Norbert Reich, General Principles of EU Civil Law (Cambridge: Intersentia 2014); Hans Micklitz and Norbert Reich, 'The Court and the Sleeping Beauty: The Revival of the Unfair Contract Terms Directive (UCTD)', 51 Common Market Law Review 771–808 (2014); Hans-Wolfgang Micklitz and Betül Kas, 'Overview of Cases before the CJEU on European Consumer Contract Law (2008–2013)—Part I', 10(1) European Review of Contract Law 1–63 (2014); Oliver Gerstenberg, 'Constitutional Reasoning in Private Law: The Role of the CJEU as an Interpreter of Directive 93/13', European Law Journal (2015).

[145] E.g. CJEU, Joined Cases C-240/98 to C-244/98 *Océano Grupo Editorial and Salvat Editores* [2000] ECR I-4941.

[146] Stephen Weatherill, EU Consumer Law and Policy (Cheltenham: Edward Elgar Publishing 2013), at 149 ff.

[147] Art. 3(3) of the Directive.

does not a general clause in Art. 3(1) defines as unfair any contractual term, not individually negotiated, that

> contrary to the requirement of good faith, [...] causes a significant imbalance in the parties' rights and obligations arising under the contract, to the detriment of the consumer.

With regard to ancillary *national procedural law*, Art. 7 (1) requires Member States to 'ensure that, in the interests of consumers and of competitors, adequate and effective means exist to prevent the continued use of unfair terms in contracts concluded with consumers by sellers or suppliers'. Indeed, Art. 7 (1) of the Directive can be seen as a specific expression of Art. 19(1) TEU which delegates the responsibility for 'providing remedies *sufficient* to ensure effective legal protection in the fields covered by Union law'[148] to the Member States and their domestic courts acting as Union courts.

In response to references from national courts, the CJEU has begun to transform the long-dormant Directive into a regime, first, by developing an evolving EU-wide black or grey list of understandings of *unfairness* through which it regulates market behaviour. For example, the CJEU has begun to clear the market of exclusive jurisdiction clauses;[149] of excessive penalty clauses for late payment and an arbitration clause which did not allow the consumer to choose a legal representative unless the consumer payed a contractual penalty;[150] of intransparent and unilateral price increase clauses;[151] of commercial practices involving incomplete or false information;[152] and of clauses leading to a serious impairment of the legal situation in which the consumer is placed by reason of relevant national legal provisions.[153]

Second, the Court has acted as an *updating mechanism with regard to national procedural law* and the remedies it provides. For example, the CJEU

148 My emphasis.

149 Joined Cases C-240/98 to C-244/98 *Océano Grupo Editorial and Salvat Editores* [2000] ECR I-4941; Case C-243/08 *Pannon* [2009] ECR I-4713; *VB Pénzügyi Lízing* C-137/08.

150 C-76/10—*Pohotovosť s. r. o. v. Iveta Korčkovska* Judgment of 16 November 2010. The case involved a disabled consumer living on an invalidity pension amounting to EUR 370 per month who had borrowed a sum of approximately EUR 633, having entered into a credit agreement with Pohotovosť, a credit company. On the basis of a final and enforceable arbitral award, the credit company sought an enforcement order to recover from the consumer the sum of EUR 3.467.

151 C-472/10 of 26 April 2012; CJEU Case C-92/11—*RWE Vertrieb AG v. Verbraucherzentrale Nordrhein-Westfalen e.V.* Judgment of 21 March 2013.

152 C-453/10—*Jana Pereničová, Vladislav Perenic v. SOS financ spol. s. r. o.*, judgment of 15 March 2012.

153 C-226/12—*Constructora Principado SA v. Álvarez* of 16 January 2014; C-280/13—*Barclays Bank SA v Sara Sánchez García*.

has introduced a new procedural remedy into national procedural law by obliging national courts to examine *of their own motion* all the contractual terms falling under the Directive's remit so as to ascertain their unfairness, even in the absence of an express application by the consumer (but not against the will of the consumer). The Court has extended this *obligation* not only to situations where the contested term was *in fact unfair* but where the unfairness of the term *was merely suspected* but could be established with full certainty;[154] extended the ex-officio control to arbitration clauses [155] and to actions for an injunction, thereby linking individual and collective redress;[156] has required Member States to prevent the trader from circumventing the level of consumer protection envisaged by the Directive;[157] has strengthened the deterrent effect of Art. 6 (1) of the Directive *by extending the invalidity of unfair terms to all contracts concluded by the same defendant under the same standard contract terms*;[158] and has required domestic courts to structure the domestic adversarial legal process around and the constitutional guarantee, in Art. 47 EUCFR, of an effective remedy and a fair trial: once a term has been found a term to be unfair, the domestic judge must inform the parties to the adversarial procedure of that fact and must 'invite each of them to set out their views on that matter' and provide them 'with the opportunity to challenge the views of the other party'.[159]

The landmark case C-415/11 *Mohammed Aziz*[160] dramatically confirms these transformations. This much-noted case is important for two reasons. First, *Aziz* offers a vivid illustration of the devastating impact of the economic and financial crisis in Europe on vulnerable individuals, in particular in strongly exposed countries like Spain: many consumers had mortgaged their family homes to secure unaffordable loans

[154] Cf. C-618/10—*Banco Español de Crédito SA [Banesto] v. Joaquín Calderón Camino* of 14 June 2012; C-76/10—*Pohotovosť s. r. o. v. Iveta Korčkovska* of 16 November 2010; CJEU C-472/11—*Banif Plus Bank Zrt v. Csaba Csipai, Viktória Csipai*, of 21 February 2013; CJEU C-488/11—*Brusse v. Jahani*, Judgment of 30 May 2013; C-472/10—Invitel—of 26 April 2012.

[155] C-76/10—*Pohotovosť s. r. o. v. Iveta Korčkovska* of 16 November 2010.

[156] C-472/10 of 26 April 2012 (Invitel).

[157] C-618/10—*Banco Español de Crédito SA [Banesto] v. Joaquín Calderón Camino* of 14 June 2012.

[158] C-472/10 of 26 April 2012. For a case-report and analysis, cf. Stephanie Law, Fabrizio Cafaggi, 'Unfair Contract Terms—Effect of Collective Proceedings—C-472/10, *Invitel*' (5 August 2013); Evelyne Terryn, Gert Straetmans, and Veerle Colaert (eds.), Landmark Cases of EU Consumer Law—In Honour of Jules Stuyck (Cambridge: Intersentia 2013).

[159] CJEU C-472/11—*Banif Plus Bank Zrt v. Csaba Csipai, Viktória Csipai*, of 21 February 2013—para. 29; CJEU C-488/11—*Brusse v. Jahani*, Judgment of 30 May 2013, at 52.

[160] CJEU (First Chamber), C-415/11—*Mohamed Aziz v. Caixa d'Estalvis de Catalunya, Tarragona i Manresa (Catalunyacaixa)*—Judgment of 14 March 2013.

and subsequently lost their homes due to a malign combination of over-indebtedness, lopsided contract-terms, and ancillary national procedural law regimes that prioritized the interests of traders in fast, 'simplified' enforcement over the interests of vulnerable consumers. Second, *Aziz* is illustrative of a growing judicial emphasis on the role and efficacy of fundamental social rights in private-law relationships. As AG Wahl emphasized in a subsequent (post-*Aziz*) case,

> I should stress [...] that where the property concerned by the [national enforcement] procedure at issue is the consumer's home, there must be specific guarantees. Failure to provide such guarantees may prove problematic from a fundamental rights perspective. Indeed, the loss of a family home is one of the most extreme forms of interference with the rights of the consumer. As respect for the home is a right guaranteed under Article 7 of the Charter of Fundamental Rights of the European Union, in the light of which Directive 93/13 must be interpreted, any person at risk of an interference of this magnitude should be able to have the proportionality of such a measure reviewed by an independent judicial body.[161]

Aziz concerned the availability of remedies to a consumer objecting to the unfairness of a term of a mortgage loan agreement.[162] Mr Aziz, a Moroccan worker in Spain had used his family home as a security for a mortgage loan. But the mortgage loan contract concluded between him and the Spanish bank contained several arguably unfair terms—for example an acceleration clause, allowing the bank, in the event of consumer default with just one of monthly instalments, to *automatically* recall the totality of the loan and to make a unilateral quantification of the amount owed. In addition, in case of arrears, the bank under Spanish law was entitled to initiate simplified enforcement procedures, which precluded any consideration of the fairness of the contract provisions. When Mr Aziz fell behind with his monthly payments, the bank invoked this process, and, as a result, Mr Aziz was evicted from his home. The home

[161] Opinion in Case C-482/12, *Peter Macinský, Eva Macinská v. Getfin s. r. o., Financreal s. r. o.* (delivered on 21 November 2013), at 82, referring to the ECtHR's ruling in *Rousk v. Sweden*, Application no. 27183/04, of 25 July 2013 (Fifth Section), at 137:

> the loss of one's home is a most extreme form of interference with the right to respect for the home. Any person at risk of an interference of this magnitude should in principle be able to have the proportionality of the measure determined by an independent tribunal in the light of the relevant principles under Article 8 of the Convention. [...] The decision-making process leading to the measures of interference must also have been fair. The Court will therefore attach particular weight to the existence of procedural safeguards.

[162] CJEU (First Chamber), C-415/11—*Mohamed Aziz v. Caixa d'Estalvis de Catalunya, Tarragona i Manresa (Catalunyacaixa)*—Judgment of 14 March 2013.

was sold, by auction, at only half its value. Under Spanish procedural law, the owner could only protest the fairness of terms in the mortgage in separate declaratory proceedings concerning the validity of the title, and even then the court could not prevent an auction of property by ordering provisional suspension of enforcement. As a consequence, as AG Kokott explained in her Opinion in *Aziz*, even if the enforcement of the mortgage was based on an unfair loan term, the consumer would be unable, under Spanish law, to prevent the definite and always irreversible loss of ownership: 'it would thus be sufficient for sellers or suppliers [. . .] to initiate [simplified] mortgage proceedings so as to deprive consumers [. . .] of the protection of the Directive, that being [. . .] contrary to the Court's case-law [. . .]'.[163] The ordinary domestic court must be in a position to determine whether an impugned contract term 'is appropriate for securing the attainment of the objectives pursued by it in the Member State concerned and does not go beyond what is necessary to achieve them'[164]—an analysis which may entail, as AG Kokott explained, 'an overall assessment of the advantages and disadvantages associated with the term for both parties'.[165]

The CFEU in its ruling essentially followed AG Kokott's Opinion. The Directive 'must be interpreted as precluding legislation of a Member State ... which ... does not allow the court ..., which does have jurisdiction to assess whether ... a term is unfair, to grant interim relief, including, in particular, the staying of those enforcement proceedings ...' Moreover, the CJEU held that in order to assess whether indeed a 'significant imbalance' between the parties arises 'contrary to the requirement of good faith', 'it must be determined whether the seller or supplier, dealing fairly and equitably with the consumer, could reasonably assume that the consumer would have agreed to the term concerned in individual contract negotiations'. In other words, the Court extended proportionality analysis into private law. The ordinary domestic court must *of its own motion* determine whether an impugned contract term is 'appropriate for securing the attainment of the objectives pursued by it in the Member State concerned and does not go beyond what is necessary to achieve them'.[166]

Aziz led to further litigation. In the aftermath of *Aziz*, the Spanish legislature amended the provisions relating to enforcement proceedings against mortgaged assets by introducing the possibility for the party

[163] Ibid, at 62. [164] CJEU *Aziz*, at 74. [165] AG Kokott, in *Aziz*, at 93.

[166] CJEU *Aziz*, at 74.

opposing the mortgage enforcement proceedings to object to those proceedings on the ground that the contractual clause upon which the enforcement was based was unfair. But the legislative amendment gave rise to a new problem which came to the fore in *Sánchez Morcillo*.[167] While the newly amended Spanish civil procedure allowed an appeal to be brought by the consumer (debtor) which, if successful, would terminate enforcement proceedings, the amended civil procedure did not allow the consumer (debtor) whose objection was unsuccessful to appeal against the judgment at first instance which ordered the enforcement procedure to be carried out. The CJEU's First Chamber held that the amended Spanish procedural system still did not resolve the problems which *Aziz* had brought to the limelight: the system still had the effect of exposing consumers and their family in an unacceptable way to the risk of losing their home in an enforced sale. The purely compensatory nature of the remedy that might be awarded to the consumer, if the underlying clause was found to be unfair, would confer on the consumer only an incomplete and insufficient level of protection. Moreover, the imbalance between the procedural rights available to the consumer, on the one hand, and to the seller or supplier on the other hand, simply mirrored the imbalance existing between the parties to the agreement, contrary to Art. 47 of the EU Charter of Fundamental Rights, which guarantees the right to a fair trial.

Aziz thus illustrates the Court's role in *raising* the level of consumer protection by elaborating an EU-wide conception of *unfairness*.

D. Freedom of contract and media pluralism

The *Sky* case, decided by the CJEU's Grand Chamber in 2013,[168] further illustrates the CJEU willingness to embed freedom of contract in a constitutional framework. The case concerned the right of TV broadcasters to produce short news reports of events of public interest using material of other broadcasters, who had acquired the right to use these materials on an exclusive basis. At issue was the compatibility with the EU Charter of Fundamental Rights of Art. 15 of the Audiovisual Media Services Directive 2010/13, which provides that 'for the purpose of short news reports, any broadcaster established in the [European] Union has access on a fair, reasonable and non-discriminatory basis to events of high interest to the public which are transmitted on an exclusive basis by a broadcaster under

[167] CJEU (First Chamber), Case C-169/14, *Juan Carlos Sánchez Morcillo, María del Carmen Abril García v. Banco Bilbao Vizcaya Argentaria*, SA, Judgment of 17 July 2014.

[168] CJEU [GC], Case C-283/11, *Sky Österreich GmbH v. Österreichischer Rundfunk*, Judgment of 22 January 2013.

their jurisdiction'. The overall aim of the Directive is to strike a complex balance: on the one hand, 'to promote pluralism through the diversity of news production and programming across the [European] Union', in accordance with Art. 11 of the EU Charter of Fundamental Rights, but also 'to safeguard the fundamental freedom to receive information and to ensure that the interests of viewers in the [European] Union are fully and properly protected ...',[169] on the other. The Directive thus limits the contractual freedom of the holders of exclusive rights in two ways: they are neither allowed to freely decide with which broadcasters they may wish to enter into an agreement regarding access, nor are they allowed to freely decide on the price to be charged for access to the signal for the purpose of making short news reports. Art. 15(6) provides that the exclusive-rights holder is required to authorize *any other broadcaster* in the EU to make short news reports 'without being able to seek compensation exceeding the additional costs directly incurred in providing access to the signal'. Among the questions referred by the Austrian *Bundeskommunikationssenat* was whether Art. 15(6) of the Directive was compatible with Art. 16 of the Charter—'[t]he freedom to conduct a business in accordance with European Union law and national laws and practices'.

In its response, the CJEU's Grand Chamber confirmed that in principle Art. 16 also covered freedom of contract, including the freedom to choose with whom to do business and to determine the price of a service, and that there was an interference with that right. But, importantly, the Grand Chamber went on to say that contractual freedom 'is not absolute, but must be viewed in relation to its social function' and 'may be subject to a broad range of interventions on the part of public authorities' in the public interest.[170] The public interest lay in the aims mentioned in rec. 48 and 55 of the Directive—the promotion of media pluralism and the guarantee to receive information under Art. 11 of the Charter. In particular, the Grand Chamber was concerned that a provision for compensation might 'deter or even prevent certain broadcasters from requesting access for the purpose of making short news reports and thus considerably restrict the access of the general public to the information. Hence, the interference with freedom of contract was justified:

> In the light, first, of the importance of safeguarding the fundamental freedom to receive information and the freedom and pluralism of the media guaranteed by Article 11 of the Charter and, second, of the protection of the freedom to conduct a business as guaranteed by Article

[169] Directive 2010/13, rec. 48; 55. [170] At para. 45 f.

> 16 of the Charter, the European Union legislature was entitled to adopt rules such as those laid down in Article 15 of Directive 2010/13, which limit the freedom to conduct a business, and to give priority, in the necessary balancing of the rights and interests at issue, to public access to information over contractual freedom.[171]

The ruling illustrates the search for a context-sensitive and social-sector specific fair balance when it comes to determining the scope of private contractual autonomy under EU law. Private autonomy is not absolute but must accommodate countervailing constitutionally sensitive legitimate interests in media pluralism and in the public's access to multiple sources of information.

IV. CONCLUSION

I have argued that the decisions in *Viking* and *Laval* and daughter cases, and in *Kücükdeveci* and in *Conley King* and *Aziz* are continuous with one another and must be seen as part of a coherent jurisprudence. They exemplify the expansion of substantive constitutional law into private law and civil-society relations. The decisions serve to illustrate, in response to that expansion, the proliferation of a democratic-experimentalist modality of judicial review that moves away from a command-and-control form of judicial intervention towards a more indirect form of intervention which is focused on the forum-creative role courts can play in instigating and managing a process of meaningful engagement in which multiple stakeholders, in various spheres of economic life, can come together and collaborate to identify solutions that fulfil the requirement of fair balance.

An influential contemporary critique of the democratic-experimentalist model that echoes the Scharpfian objection is that proceduralization dilutes fundamental social rights by emphasizing process over substance: social rights, according to this view, are weakened as against economic liberties.

For example, against the specific backdrop of the South-African constitutional experience, Sandra Liebenberg and Katharine Young object to protecting socioeconomic rights by allowing claimants to participate in decisions affecting them, instead of giving them substantive rights to demand certain outcomes: the 'engagement with the normative content of

[171] At para. 66.

rights is too procedural at the cost of substance ...'[172] First, Liebenberg and Young argue that experimentalism is normatively insufficiently ambitious by weakening the '"equalizing" power of courts', a power which they associate with necessarily strong substantive standards of review: 'reliance is primarily placed on the outcome of ongoing deliberative engagements to develop the normative content of rights. These processes do not contemplate that courts themselves apply normative standards and values, independently from the parties' own expression'. Second, Liebenberg and Young argue that experimentalist remedies further marginalize the vulnerable because participation requires resources that the poor or the vulnerable lack and because experimentalist adjudication fails to adequately address the power imbalances between the parties. If the potential pay-off for expensive litigation is only a 'weak' right—which offers enhanced procedural obligations as opposed to concrete benefits—then litigation may simply not be worth the expense and effort. Third, Liebenberg and Young object that experimentalism detracts from the society-wide redistributive aspirations of socioeconomic rights which require 'a national-scale redistribution of resources, services and opportunities may be needed before experimentalist methods can meaningfully be contemplated'. Thus, as Liebenberg and Young conclude, 'many central tenets of democratic experimentalism contain built-in structural biases that systematically advantage the strong and disadvantage the weak';[173] and '[e]xperimentalism steers participants to seek collaborative solutions that accommodate market efficiency concerns (typically to be the credo of the more economically powerful) ...'[174] This critique restates the social-democratic objection discussed above.[175]

But as *Aziz* illustrates, there can be no doubt that the judicially developed protection against disproportionate consequences of unfair terms

[172] Sandra Liebenberg and Katharine G. Young, 'Adjudicating Social and Economic Rights: Can Democratic Experimentalism Help?', in Helena Alviar García et al. (eds.), Social and Economic Rights in Theory and Practice: Critical Inquiries (2015), 237, 251–53, at 219.

[173] At 221. [174] At 222.

[175] But notice that in her recent writings, Sandra Liebenberg (drawing on the work of Susan Sturm) has developed an approach that closely resembles the democratic-experimentalist approach by emphasizing the idea of meaningful engagement, cf. Liebenberg, S., 'Remedial Principles and Meaningful Engagement in Education Rights Disputes' PER / PELJ 2016(19). Using the same South-African context as his foil, Brian Ray has forcefully challenged the assumption underlying Liebenberg's and Young's objection that a stronger substantive standard of review is necessary to fulfil their potential. A close analysis of the South African Constitutional Court's jurisprudence, Ray argues, throws into doubt the view that the proceduralization of the social rights necessarily leads to deference and ineffectiveness and, quite to the contrary, confirms the view that the Court operating in a procedural mode 'might be more effective than a jurisprudence that develops a stronger set of abstract constitutional principles'. Brian Ray, Engaging With Social Rights (Cambridge: Cambridge University Press 2016), at 367 f.

(such as the loss of a home) is also a vindication of a *democratic value* which resonates with restoring equal citizenship. Judicially developed EU law opened up a *forum* for principled consideration of personhood and citizenship in the sphere of economic life, which was particularly important at a time of grave financial turmoil and also in the face of a striking national recalcitrance to address the problem adequately of its own motion. European (private) law may in fact mitigate, rather than exacerbate, the much-bemoaned European democratic deficit. The judicial process at least implicitly highlighted the human-rights dimension of seemingly mundane consumer contracts disputes.

While the Court in this way strengthened democracy, it also—in response to standard separation of powers concerns—softened judicial finality but without compromising principle. The Court exerted its role not so much by pushing Member States in directions they may not wish to go, but rather by setting the stage for, and instigating, a process of gradual interpretive clarification of what, say, *unfairness* in consumer contracts consists of in substance and what remedial steps, by what sort of actors, are in order 'to replace the formal balance which the contract establishes [. . .] with an effective balance [. . .]'. The judicial acquis may be seen as illustrative of an emergent 'non-hierarchical'[176] or citizen-based[177] understanding of the EU multilevel-system of law. Proportionality-analysis becomes a process of discursive benchmarking and collaborative governance. As the experimentalist process moves along over successive references, the decentralized application of the framework concept of unfairness in the Directive opens the opportunity for an (upward-) revision. At subsequent stages, as a fuller understanding of a regulatory problem emerges, the Court intensifies its powers of review and demands compliance with an emergent best-practice consensus without, however, ever claiming a door-closing last word. The EU multilevel system thus enables vulnerable consumers to put national law and politics under pressure to reform and overcome insularity.

[176] Hugh Collins, op. cit., at 205 ('not a hierarchical process'). [177] Cf. Reich, op. cit.

3

Democratic Experimentalism and the Public Sphere

Freedom of Conscience, Free Speech, and Non-Discrimination

Feelings of injury and insult have mattered most, especially when they come together to impel a leap of consciousness, in which a quickened expectation of decent treatment is combined with a more definite feeling of what human dignity in some simple sense is owed; and once emergent, these attitudes and passions disseminate themselves by ordinary if belated insight, by imitation, and by the attractiveness of gradually established example.

George Kateb, Human Dignity
(Cambridge: Harvard University Press 2011) 3

I. INTRODUCTION

This chapter argues that democratic-experimentalist forms of judicial review should not be confined to socioeconomic rights but can also be invoked with negative liberties and dignitarian personal rights. An apparent dilemma is this: on the one hand, modern, pluralist democracies are increasingly, and often irreconcilably, divided when it comes to fundamental choices which affect and express the self-understanding of a polity as a whole in matters such as, say, the right to religious freedom, free speech, the rights of transsexuals, and so forth. And yet, on the other hand, there is an ever-accelerating reliance on courts and the judiciary for addressing those fundamental choices. As, for example, the former AG Sir Francis Jacobs has observed, 'many fundamental choices for society are now made, and probably have to be made, not by legislature, not by the executive, but by courts'[1]—including, in Europe, *courts beyond the state*,

[1] Sir Francis Jacobs, The Sovereignty of Law. The European Way. Hamlyn Lectures (Cambridge: Cambridge University Press 2007), 1.

such as the ECtHR and the CJEU. If this observation is correct; and if the judiciary's influence extends beyond settling disputes and seeps into all aspects of society, codifying the values of our times, doesn't this overstretch the resources of consensus-based legality?

The claim that democratic experimentalism here can play a role and even may 'come to the rescue', as it were, of liberal legalism may appear counterintuitive and simply a bridge too far. Critics will see democratic experimentalism more as part or symptom of a contemporary malaise than as part of the solution to the problem. They invariably raise a rule-of-law based objection against a seemingly undisciplined expansion of rights discourse and point to the spectre of a politicization of the judiciary under the guises of proportionality analysis. In the context of modern, contemporary societies' culture wars, the use of the language of rights, as critics see it, inevitably raises the stakes: rights are rescued from, and insulated against, the political process and become non-negotiable possessions of those who can claim them, thus diminishing the chances for moderation, civility, and compromise. Justiciable individual rights give courts—and, *a fortiori* in the European system, also courts beyond the state—precedence over the political process. But if ever more individual and social interests can be turned into rights claims, say, to circumstances in which dignity would be protected, as a consequence of morally generous (or licentious, as the critics see it) judicial interpretations, then a key role of the rule of law—to ensure that the political process is founded on consent—would be thrown into jeopardy. Such a development would not only imply a severe democratic deficit, but, and equally importantly, it would also endanger the rule of law itself: the end of that process may be the dilution of the idea of individual rights themselves. Contentious issues that divide modern societies would no longer be allowed to percolate in politics, but would be transformed into irreconcilable, non-negotiable, and seemingly undecidable clashes between human rights. As a consequence, judges would be drawn into the crucible of pluralistic politics. They would eventually no longer be applying consensually shared legal norms and standards, known in advance, but would be led to substitute their own transient moral preferences or opinions for the rule of law, thereby exposing themselves to the influence of changing and volatile public opinion and moods which may or may not be consistent with the rule of law after all.

In response to this rule-of-law based objection, I will argue in this chapter that the critique is too broad and lacks nuance: *ab abusu ad usum non valet consequentia*. Courts can play a benign proceduralizing role. The critics' conception of consensus is too narrow. It assumes a pre-existing consensus and ignores the discursive mutual interplay between courts, stakeholders, and the general public, and the ongoing interplay between law and social values in societies that are constantly changing. As I will show, judges are constantly and inevitably seized with disputes which involve novel, morally sensitive, and socially divisive questions where there just is no pre-existing consensus, and to simply assume that such a consensus exists itself often amounts to a partisan view. Instead of relying on a pre-existing consensus, I will argue that courts can exert a proceduralizing role by instigating debate and deliberation that may eventually lead to a consensus. In other words, courts can rely on *potential consensus* and act in anticipation of an emergence of such a consensus in time. In this way, proceduralizing judicial intervention may over time help 'impel a leap of consciousness' and a change of 'attitudes and passions' that may 'disseminate themselves ... by the attractiveness of gradually established example', in the sense of George Kateb's formulation.

While reflecting changing social values, law can even move ahead of social values, and where necessary, trigger social change. An advantage of courts is that they operate on a case-by-case basis, following a problem-solving approach. What makes deliberation possible is some preliminary agreement on certain specific instances or examples of injustice—for example on the plight of religious minorities or of transsexuals (cf. below). Deliberation then aims at generating principles of some general scope and then to connect those general principles with concrete, contextualized judgments—similar to a Rawlsian reflective equilibrium, but in the more proceduralist sense of an ongoing and interminable mutual revision between frameworks and their applications in the light of experience. The procedure constantly invites and requires stakeholder-participation, even of hitherto marginalized voices, and meaningful engagement with them. Deliberation, which in this way reaches out into society, constantly rebounds on judicial judgments.

But the deliberation-inducing role of judicial intervention also depends on procedures which allow for discursive differentiation and which invite self-revision. In this chapter, I will suggest that the European multilevel system of constitutionalism favours, indeed facilitates, this kind of ongoing self-revision or immanent criticism and that Convention rights, in their institutional dimension, can be mobilized as destabilization rights to trigger that process. Courts beyond the state—such as the European Court of Human Rights but also the CJEU—provide a forum where petrified domestic routines can be reconsidered in the light of shared European-wide experience, and sometimes an emergent shared understanding of principle. Judicialization beyond the state strengthens the rule of law, rather than weakening it, and enhances the objectivity of judicial judgments.

This chapter will accordingly explore both these aspects of the deliberation-enhancing role of judicial intervention in the core domain of personal rights by considering in particular the jurisprudence of the ECtHR. In a first step (Section II), I focus on multilevel governance by analysing the parameters of European supervision of national authorities by the European Court of Human Rights. Crucial is the concept of a *decentralized review* of human rights by the national courts themselves; the ECtHR *devolves* or *delegates* to the domestic level a measure of co-responsibility for the joint development of Convention Rights. The margin-of-appreciation doctrine is the crucial device of devolution. The Convention thus ceases to be an exclusively international law regime and becomes *also-national law* in all the Contracting States. The ECtHR's supervisionary role accordingly is that of a backstop European review of the review carried out by the national courts. But the Convention also ceases to be an exclusively international law regime in a different sense: it serves as a transnational constitution of discussion aimed at extending beyond the state an overlapping consensus on the applied meaning of key fundamental legal principles.

Accordingly, in a second step (Section III), I address selected topical issues. First, I will consider the example of freedom of conscience, which in Europe emerged after many centuries of religious persecution. I will show that, many unresolved controversies notwithstanding, *religious diversity* in Europe has now come to be seen as an objective principle and political value, which is associated with democracy, and which has begun to radiate into many spheres of social life, such as schools and even private-sector employment. Second, I turn to the proceduralization of the clash between free speech and personality rights. Third, I will consider personality rights in the context of gender and same-sex marriage. I will suggest that this is a domain which illustrates how the European parameters of review can themselves be exposed to the 'full blast'[2] of further ongoing discussion in the light of experience and, hence, to ongoing transformation.

The topics chosen are inevitably selective but perhaps representative of the moral conflicts contemporary democracies face. They illustrate the forum-creative role courts—and even courts beyond the state—can

[2] On this concept, cf. Frank Michelman, Brennan and Democracy (Princeton University Press 1999).

play in allowing 'feelings of injury and insult' to 'come together to impel a leap of consciousness' in an emergent European public sphere and in channelling a process of society-wide deliberation.

II. MULTILEVEL CONSTITUTIONALISM

This section explores how the Strasbourg Court has, in a dialogue with the German *Bundesverfassungsgericht*, begun to discover and establish a *regime* combining the *decentralized* enforcement of Convention Rights with *centralized* European supervision.

A. The ECtHR and the German *Bundesverfassungsgericht*: the *emergence* of a regime

The ECtHR's landmark *von Hannover (No. 2)*[3] ruling in 2012 concerned a clash between the right to freedom of expression and the right to respect for private life in the context of the publication of photos showing the private life of celebrities in the rainbow press.

In the past, in order to resolve those clashes, German courts relied on the hard and fast concept of 'figure of contemporary society par excellence' (*'absolute Person der Zeitgeschichte'*), which afforded complainants with only minimal protection against press intrusions. The German Copyright (Arts Domain) Act (*'Kunsturhebergesetz'*) of 1907 provides, in Section 22(1), that a person's images could only be disseminated with the express consent of the person concerned. But under Section 23(1) no. 1, images portraying an aspect of contemporary society were exempted from the obligation to obtain consent, but again only on condition that their publication did not interfere with a 'legitimate interest' of the person concerned. In interpreting these statutory provisions and their key open-textured concepts (such as 'legitimate interest'), the ordinary civil courts were required to observe and balance fundamental rights guaranteed under the German Basic Law such as the freedom of the press (and the interest of the public in being informed), on the one hand, and general personality rights, on the other. According to the balance struck by the ordinary courts in Germany, and confirmed by the *Bundesverfassungsgericht* in a landmark decision of 1999, 'figures of contemporary society par excellence' were protected *only* if a 'standard of physical seclusion' applied: that is, if the complainant was in a secluded

[3] ECtHR, *von Hannover v. Germany (No. 2)*, Application nos. 40660/08 and 60641/08, Judgment of 7 February 2012.

place with the objectively recognizable aim of being alone.[4] The BVG's physical-seclusion standard required '(1) a local seclusion to which someone has withdrawn to be alone; (2) that this wish to be alone is recognisable by an objective person; and (3) that the person, confiding in the seclusion, behaves in a manner in which he or she would not behave in the broad public'.[5]

The Strasbourg Court, by contrast, in its 2004 *von Hannover (No. 1)*[6] judgment rejected the physical seclusion standard as 'too vague' and as too 'difficult for the person concerned to determine in advance'.[7] Instead, the ECtHR developed a different, more contextualizing approach, which it restated in its 2012 *von Hannover (No. 2)* Grand Chamber ruling.[8] According to this new approach, the national courts are required to apply the following contextual criteria in striking a balance: namely, whether the photos do contribute to a debate of general interest; the role or function of the person concerned; the 'fundamental distinction ... between reporting facts capable of contributing to a debate in a democratic society, [...], and reporting details of the private life of an individual who does not exercise such functions' where the sole aim is that of 'satisfying public curiosity';[9] the 'conduct of the person concerned prior to publication';[10] the way in which the photo or report are published and the manner in which the person concerned is represented in the photo and the circumstances in which the photos were taken.[11]

The *Bundesverfassungsgericht*, in an Order of 2008,[12] adopted the contextualizing approach. The *Bundesverfassungsgericht* now emphasized

[4] Cf. the (then) landmark judgment of the Bundesverfassungsgericht of 15 December 1999, BVerfGE 101, 361.

[5] *Bundesverfassungsgericht*, BVerfGE (1999) 101, 361, at para. 72.

[6] ECtHR, *von Hannover v. Germany (No. 1)* Application no. 59320/00, Judgment of 24 June 2004.

[7] ECtHR, *von Hannover (No. 1)*, at 72, 74, and 75:

> The Court finds it hard to agree with the domestic courts' interpretation of section 23(1) of the Copyright (Arts Domain) Act, which consists in describing a person as such as a figure of contemporary society *'par excellence'*. Since that definition affords the person very limited protection of their private life or the right to control the use of their image ..., the Court considers that, [...], the Act has to be interpreted narrowly to ensure that the State complies with its positive obligation under the Convention to protect private life and the right to control the use of one's image. [...] As a figure of contemporary society *'par excellence'* [the applicant] cannot—in the name of freedom of the press and the public interest—rely on protection of her private life unless she is in a secluded place out of the public eye and, moreover, succeeds in proving it (which can be difficult). [...] In the Court's view, the criterion of spatial isolation, although apposite in theory, is in reality too vague and difficult for the person concerned to determine in advance.

[8] ECtHR, *von Hannover v. Germany (no. 2)*, Applications nos. 40660/08 and 60641/08, Judgment of 7 February 2012.

[9] Ibid, at para. 110. [10] Ibid, at para. 111. [11] Ibid, at para. 112–13.

[12] *Bundesverfassungsgericht*, Order of 26 February 2008—1 BvR 1602/07.

that in striking a fair balance, ordinary civil courts, when interpreting ordinary civil law, 'must have regard to the relevant guarantees contained in the European Convention on Human Rights'[13] and are thus obliged to incorporate the ECtHR's case law into the respective 'partial legal area of the national legal system' (such as the private law system). Only 'if the protective scope of a relevant fundamental right [of the Basic Law] was wrongly or incompletely determined, its weight not measured accurately and thus erroneously included in the weighing, or when the weighing contradicts other standards of constitutional law, in particular also constitutionally relevant standards in the European Convention on Human Rights', would there be a breach of the German constitution, justifying correction by the BVG.[14]

In the light of these transformations, the ECtHR's Grand Chamber in *von Hannover (No. 2)* was now willing to grant the domestic German courts—the *Bundesverfassungsgericht*, but also the German *Federal Court of Justice*—a wide margin of appreciation:

> [w]here the balancing exercise has been undertaken by the national authorities *in conformity with the criteria laid down in the Court's case-law*, the Court would require strong reasons to substitute its view for that of the domestic courts.[15]

In particular, the ECtHR's Grand Chamber agreed that the German courts had 'attached fundamental importance to the question whether the photos, considered in the light of the accompanying articles, had contributed to a debate of general interest. They also examined the circumstances in which the photos had been taken'.[16] Hence, in striking a fair balance,

> the national courts explicitly took account of the Court's relevant case-law. Whilst the Federal Court of Justice had changed its approach following the *von Hannover (1)* judgment, the Federal Constitutional Court, for its part, had not only confirmed that approach, but also undertaken a detailed analysis of the Court's case-law in response to the applicants' complaints that the Federal Court of Justice had disregarded the Convention and the Court's case-law.[17]

The Grand Chamber confirmed its approach in *Aksu v. Turkey*,[18] which concerned a complainant of Roma origins who objected to comments

[13] Ibid, at 49. [14] Ibid, at 76.

[15] ECtHR, *von Hannover v. Germany (No. 2)*, at para. 107 [my emphasis, OG]. [16] Ibid, at para. 124.

[17] Ibid, at para. 125.

[18] ECtHR [GC], *Aksu v. Turkey*, Application nos. 4149/04 and 41029/04, of 15 March 2012.

about the Roma that were included in academic and educational publications published or part-financed by the Turkish Ministry of Culture:

> If the balance struck by the national judicial authorities is unsatisfactory, in particular because the importance or the scope of one of the fundamental rights at stake was not duly considered, the margin of appreciation accorded to the decisions of the national courts will be a narrow one. *However, if the assessment was made in the light of the principles resulting from [the ECtHR's] well-established case-law, the Court would require strong reasons to substitute its own view for that of the domestic courts, which consequently will enjoy a wider margin of appreciation.* [my emphasis, OG]

So the Strasbourg Court has established a contextualizing regime: the national courts will benefit from a wide margin of appreciation as long as they take the broad framework criteria developed by the Strasbourg Court as their guidance. In developing these framework criteria, the ECtHR exerts a transformative and modernizing role with regard to domestic private law and constitutional law. A rather formalistic concept—the physical seclusion standard—is replaced by a more context-sensitive regime which, arguably, is more responsive to the legitimate interests of stakeholders. But once an overlapping consensus between the ECtHR and the national constitutional courts on this contextualizing regime has crystallized, the ECtHR then 'accepts pluralism over uniformity, as long as the fundamental guarantees are effectively observed', as Dean Spielmann, its President, has described the regime.[19] The ECtHR under those circumstances does not substitute its own view for that of the domestic courts but is willing to *devolve to the national level* co-responsibility for ensuring the observance of Convention rights. The concept of margin of appreciation becomes co-extensive with the concept of a *decentralized domestic-courts based review* of Convention rights. And, *mutatis mutandis*, decentralized review may feed into—and may legitimize—the evolutive interpretation of the Convention as a living instrument by the ECtHR. In this way, frameworks and their applications mutually transform one another, confirming the structure of democratic-experimentalist modalities of judicial intervention.

B. A brief excursion on the generalization of the emergent regime

The emergent democratic-experimentalist regime has broader application. In its *'Brighton Declaration'* of 19 and 20 April 2012, the *High Level*

[19] Dean Spielmann, 'Whither the Margin of Appreciation?', UCL, Current Legal Problems Lecture of 20 March 2014, at http://www.echr.coe.int/Documents/Speech_20140320_London_ENG.pdf.

Conference on the Future of the European Court of Human Rights has expressed 'the determination of the States Parties to ensure effective implementation of the Convention at national level by taking the following specific measures, so far as relevant':

> (iv) Enabling and encouraging national courts and tribunals to take into account the relevant principles of the Convention, having regard to the case law of the Court, in conducting proceedings and formulating judgments; and in particular enabling litigants, within the appropriate parameters of national judicial procedure but without unnecessary impediments, to draw to the attention of national courts and tribunals any relevant provisions of the Convention and jurisprudence of the Court...

This commitment by the State Parties 'to take into account' the principles of the Convention and to strengthen the role of litigants accordingly mirrors and summarizes judicial developments.

In its 2004 order in *Görgülü v. Germany*,[20] a rather mundane child custody case, the *Bundesverfassungsgericht* took an important step towards enhancing the position of the Convention in the German legal order, but on the other hand it also clearly showed the limits in implementing the ECtHR's judgments into national law by insisting that the enforcement must never be a 'schematic' one.

In a previous judgment of 26 February 2004, a chamber of the ECtHR unanimously found that the impugned decisions by German courts on custody and the exclusion of the right of access violated Art. 8 of the Convention because those courts had failed to sufficiently take into account the best interests of the child. However, the civil court seized with the matter, the *Naumburg Higher Regional Court*, refused to implement the Strasbourg Court's judgment based on the assumption that it was not directly bound by it. According to the *Naumburg Higher Regional Court*,

> ... the [earlier 2004 ECtHR Chamber-] judgment bound only the Federal Republic of Germany as a subject of public international law, but not its bodies, authorities and the bodies responsible for the administration of justice, which are independent under Article 97.1 of the Basic Law.... As a result of the status of the European Convention on Human Rights as ordinary statutory law below the level of the constitution, the ECHR was not functionally a higher-ranking court in relation to the courts of the States parties. For this reason, neither in interpreting the European Convention on Human Rights nor in interpreting national fundamental rights could domestic courts be bound by the decisions of the ECHR.

[20] *Bundesverfassungsgericht*, Order of the Second Senate of 14 October 2004—2 BvR 1481/04.

But the *Bundesverfassungsgericht* disagreed, ruling that the *Naumburg* court had failed to 'take sufficient account' of the earlier ECtHR judgment and that its decision therefore 'violate[d] Article 6 [right to marriage and family life] of the Basic Law in conjunction with the principle of the rule of law'.[21] The *Bundesverfassungsgericht* began to elaborate a new, and more theoretically grounded, approach to the implementation of the Court's judgments in German law, in part, motivated by the conflict in the *von Hannover* case[22] which had started shortly before. According to this new approach, '[t]he authorities and courts of the Federal Republic of Germany are obliged, under certain conditions, to take account of the European Convention on Human Rights as interpreted by the ECtHR in making their decisions'.[23] The *Bundesverfassungsgericht* clarified that the binding effect of a decision of the ECtHR 'extends to all state bodies and in principle imposes on these an obligation ... to end a continuing violation of the Convention and to create a situation that complies with the Convention'.[24] But the *Bundesverfassungsgericht* also spelled out where the limits of the implementation of the ECtHR's judgments lay. The implementation must never be a merely 'schematic enforcement', but has to take the effects on the national legal system into account.[25]

Within the German hierarchy of norms, the Convention figures as a 'federal statute', and this ranking means that its guarantees 'are not a direct constitutional standard of review in the German legal system'. In practice, this means that '[a] complainant can therefore not *directly* challenge the violation of a human right contained in the European Convention on Human Rights by a constitutional complaint before the Federal Constitutional Court'.[26]

But while the Convention only ranks as a federal statute, its role is enhanced by the fact that it still has a 'constitutional significance'.[27] *Constitutional significance* means that the Convention can 'influence the interpretation of the fundamental rights and constitutional principles of the Basic Law'. The Convention and the case-law of the ECtHR thus 'serve ... as guides to interpretation in determining the content and scope of fundamental rights and constitutional principles of the Basic Law', but only 'provided that this does not lead to a restriction or reduction of protection of the individual's fundamental rights under the Basic Law—and this the Convention itself does not desire'.[28] This constitutional significance

[21] Ibid, at 64.

[22] Cf. ECtHR, *von Hannover v. Germany (No. 1)* Application no. 59320/00, Judgment of 24 June 2004.

[23] Ibid, at 29. [24] Ibid, at 30. [25] Ibid, at 47. [26] Ibid, at 30 and 32. [27] Ibid, at 33.

[28] Ibid, at 32.

must be seen as 'the expression of the Basic Law's commitment to international law (*Völkerrechtsfreundlichkeit*)'.[29] The German Constitution 'aims to incorporate the Federal Republic of Germany into the community of states as a peaceful member having equal rights in a system of public international law serving peace'.[30] The *Bundesverfassungsgericht* understands itself as 'indirectly in the service of enforcing international law'[31] and as contributor to 'a joint European development of fundamental rights (*gemeineuropäische Grundrechtsentwicklung*)'.[32]

But while, on the one hand, the Convention has constitutional significance, there also exists, on the other hand, an important reservation of sovereignty vis-à-vis the Convention:

> The Basic Law is clearly based on the classic idea that the relationship of public international law and domestic law is a relationship between two different legal spheres and that the nature of this relationship can be determined from the viewpoint of domestic law only by domestic law itself [. . .]. The commitment to international law takes effect only within the democratic and constitutional system of the Basic Law.[33]

'The Basic Law'—the *Bundesverfassungsgericht* continued—'does not waive the sovereignty contained in the last instance in the German constitution'[34] and it 'does not seek a submission to non-German acts of sovereignty that is removed from every constitutional limit and control'.[35] This statement may appear surprising, as it seems to conflict with the avowed *Völkerrechtsfreundlichkeit* of the Basic Law. Yet the practical consequence of the reservation of sovereignty is that the domestic implementation of ECtHR judgments must never be a 'schematic enforcement',[36] but has to take the effects on the national legal system and on its partial legal orders—such as private law—into account.[37] Domestic courts 'must discernibly consider the decision and, if necessary, justify understandably why they nevertheless do not follow the international-law interpretation of the law'.[38]

The Bundesverfassungsgericht went on to say that this idea of a *non-schematic enforcement* is specifically important in the context of *private law* where Convention rights may be invoked by both sides of the civil law dispute. But in proceedings before the ECtHR there is an asymmetry: the only party to these proceedings is, apart from the complainant, the State party affected, but not the original defendant; and this asymmetry may pose a threat to the integrity of private law:

[29] Ibid, at 33. [30] Ibid, at 33. [31] Ibid, at 61. [32] Ibid, at 62. [33] Ibid, at 34.
[34] Ibid, at 35. [35] Ibid, at 36. [36] Ibid, at 47, 50. [37] Ibid, at 49. [38] Ibid, at 50.

> Precisely in cases in which national courts, as in private law, have to structure multipolar fundamental rights situations, it is always important that various subjective legal positions are sensitively weighed against each other, and if there is a change in the persons involved in the dispute or a change in the actual or legal circumstances, this weighing up may lead to a different result. There may therefore be constitutional problems if one of the subjects of fundamental rights in conflict with another obtains an ECHR judgment in his or her favour against the Federal Republic of Germany and German courts schematically apply this decision to the private-law relationship, with the result that the holder of fundamental rights who has 'lost' in this case and was possibly not involved in the proceedings at the ECtHR would no longer be able to take an effective part in the proceedings as a party.[39]

In order to protect the integrity of national law, the domestic courts, in taking into account decisions of the ECHR, accordingly 'must include the effects on the national legal system in their application of the law. This applies in particular with regard to a partial system of domestic law whose legal consequences are balanced and that is intended to achieve an equilibrium between differing fundamental rights':[40]

> The decisions of the ECtHR may encounter national partial systems of law shaped by a complex system of case-law. [. . .] [T]his may happen in particular in family law and the law concerning aliens, and also in the law on the protection of personality [. . .], in which conflicting fundamental rights are balanced by the creation of groups of cases and graduated legal consequences. [. . .] it cannot be the desired result of the international-law basis nor express will of the ECHR for the ECHR through its decisions itself to undertake directly any necessary adjustments within a domestic partial legal system.[41]

So the 'friendliness to international law' takes effect *within the—albeit very broad—framework of the constitutional system of the German Basic Law*. The effect of the Convention is mediated or filtered by the national legal system and in this sense an *indirect* one. The main constraint is that domestic courts must 'justify understandably' any deviations from 'international-law interpretation of the law'.

But the indirect effect of the Convention is robust enough to leave the door open to transformation of domestic law in the light of transformative values contained in the ECHR:

[39] Ibid, at 50. [40] Ibid, at 57. [41] Ibid, at 58.

> it must at all events be possible, on the basis of the relevant fundamental right, [for a complainant] to raise the objection in proceedings before the Federal Constitutional Court that state bodies disregarded or failed to take into account a decision of the ECHR.

This *procedural* or *dynamic element* enables a complainant to *indirectly* challenge the violation of a Convention right before the German Federal Constitutional Court by arguing that in the interpretation of a fundamental right under the Basic Law the jurisprudence of the ECtHR relevant to the coinciding Convention right was disregarded; *mutatis mutandis*, the procedural component consolidates the role of the *Bundesverfassungsgericht* in co-monitoring the violation of Convention rights. Because the door thus remains open to a transformation of domestic law in the light of (sometimes) emancipatory values enshrined in the ECHR at the behest of aggrieved individuals, this procedural or dynamic dimension resonates with the democratic-experimentalist concept of destabilization rights. Convention rights can be mobilized in innovative ways within domestic rights discourse by aggrieved individuals as an *argument* to induce deliberation about the adequacy—as measured against the normative promise of the ECHR—of domestic doctrinal-legal understandings of a domestic constitutional right in question.

The *Bundesverfassungsgericht* has subsequently clarified its position in the context a different dispute. In 2009, the ECtHR had to consider a German law, which had been upheld by the *Bundesverfassungsgericht*, on the imposition and unlimited duration of *preventive detention*—allowing further detention of convicted criminals beyond their initial prison sentence in the interest of public security—to be a violation of the Convention.[42] In that ruling, the ECtHR criticized the insufficient distinction, in German *criminal law*, between *preventive detention* and *punishment*. As a consequence of the Strasbourg ruling, the *Bundesverfassungsgericht* reversed its previous decision on detention orders, notwithstanding the final and binding effect of its previous jurisprudence, because the decisions of the ECtHR contained 'new aspects for the interpretation of the Basic Law', and reasoned:

> The openness of the Basic Law to international law [*Völkerrechtsfreund lichkeit*] expresses an understanding of sovereignty that not only does not oppose international and supranational integration, it presupposes and expects it. Against this background, the 'final word' of the German

[42] *M. v. Germany* Application no. 9359/04, 17 December 2009.

> Constitution is not an obstacle to an international and European dialogue of courts but rather its normative foundation.[43]

Subsequently, in 2011, in its ruling *Mork v. Germany*, the ECtHR in turn acknowledged the *Bundesverfassungsgericht's* position was as follows:

> In its judgment, the Federal Constitutional Court stressed that the fact that the [German] Constitution stood above the Convention in the domestic hierarchy of norms was not an obstacle to an international and European dialogue between the courts, but was, on the contrary, its normative basis in view of the fact that the Constitution was to be interpreted in a manner that was open to public international law (*völkerrechtsfreundliche Auslegung*). In its reasoning, the Federal Constitutional Court relied on the interpretation of Article 5 and Article 7 of the Convention made by this Court in its judgment in the case of *M. v. Germany*. [. . .]
>
> The Court takes note [. . .] of the reversal of the [BVG's] case-law concerning preventive detention [. . .]. It welcomes the Federal Constitutional Court's approach of interpreting the provisions of the Basic Law also in the light of the Convention and this Court's case-law, which demonstrates that the court's continuing commitment to the protection of fundamental rights not only on national, but also European level.[44]

This confirms the concept of decentralized review. The applied meaning of Convention rights is not dictatorially imposed 'from above' by the ECtHR but an ongoing interim result of a collaborative process between the ECtHR and national constitutional courts. This collaborative process may ultimately enhance the rule of law. The regime is less premised on existing consensus only, but on hybridization and potential consensus: on procedure and deliberation aimed at bringing about—at widening and deepening—an overlapping consensus in the light of shared experience.

III. SUBSTANCE

A. Freedom of conscience

> *[Under the influence of political liberalism] guaranties for certain intellectual freedoms, especially freedom of conscience, have been included in the concept of democracy, so that a social order which does not contain such a guaranty would not be considered democratic, even if the procedure for its creation and application guarantees the participation of the governed in the government.*

[43] BVerfG, 2 BvR 2365/09 vom 4.5.2011, at 89:

> Die Völkerrechtsfreundlichkeit des Grundgesetzes ist damit Ausdruck eines Souveränitätsverständnisses, das einer Einbindung in inter- und supranationale Zusammenhänge sowie deren Weiterentwicklung nicht nur nicht entgegensteht, sondern diese voraussetzt und erwartet. Vor diesem Hintergrund steht auch das 'letzte Wort' der deutschen Verfassung einem internationalen und europäischen Dialog der Gerichte nicht entgegen, sondern ist dessen normative Grundlage.

[44] Case *Mork v. Germany*, Application nos. 31047/04 and 43386/08 of 9 June 2011, at 31 and 54.

Hans Kelsen, Foundations of Democracy, in: Ethics, Vol. 66, No. 1, Part 2: Foundations of Democracy, (Oct., 1955), pp. 1–101, at 3.

[T]he ideal of democratic citizens ... also expresses a willingness to listen to what others have to say and being ready to accept reasonable accommodations or alterations on one's own view.... This preserves the ties of civic friendship . . .

John Rawls, Political Liberalism (New York: Columbia University Press 1993), 253

In its two paragraphs Art. 9 of the European Convention on Human Rights sets out both the essence of religious freedom and its limitations:

1. Everyone has the right to freedom of thought, conscience and religion; this right includes freedom to change his religion or belief and freedom, either alone or in community with others and in public or private, to manifest his religion or belief, in worship, teaching, practice and observance.
2. Freedom to manifest one's religion or beliefs shall be subject only to such limitations as are prescribed by law and are necessary in a democratic society in the interests of public safety, for the protection of public order, health or morals, or for the protection of the rights and freedoms of others.

Hence, it is only the freedom to manifest one's religion that may be subjected to limitations on the grounds specified, not freedom of thought, conscience, and religion in itself. But what is the proper scope, what are the limits of that freedom to manifest one's religion? And what is the role of courts in determining the proper scope?

Comparing the 'dominant European tradition' with the 'subtly different American conception', Martha Nussbaum has claimed that '[m]ost Europeans [...] have been content to send signals to minorities that the community's form of life is structured by the majority religion, and that they don't think that this creates a problem for the equality of citizens—or, if they do see a problem, they are willing to live with it'.[45] But this claim may be contrasted with the ECtHR's insistence that the guarantee of freedom of thought, conscience, and religion, including the freedom not to belong to a religion, imposes on States a 'duty of neutrality and impartiality'.[46] In explaining what neutrality and impartiality mean and

[45] Martha Nussbaum, Liberty of Conscience. In Defense of America's Tradition of Religious Equality (New York: Basic Books 2008), at 25.

[46] ECtHR [GC], *Lautsi and Others v. Italy*, Application no. 30814/06, Judgment of 18 March 2011, at 60.

what the justification for this duty is, the Strasbourg Court has insisted that religious pluralism is an *important good* in a democratic society, and indeed, one of its very foundations. In the first case under Art. 9 to come before the ECtHR, it held that

> freedom of thought, conscience and religion is one of the foundations of a 'democratic society' within the meaning of the Convention. It is, in its religious dimension, one of the most vital elements that go to make up the identity of believers and their conception of life, but it is also a precious asset for atheists, agnostics, sceptics and the unconcerned. The pluralism indissociable from a democratic society, which has been dearly won over the centuries, depends on it.[47]

Just as the affirmative right to practice a religion implies the negative right to practice no religion and to remain 'unconcerned', so the negative guarantees of 'freedom of thought, conscience and religion', in their institutional or affirmative dimension, lay the *foundations* for a 'democratic society'—a pluralistic sphere of public debate and deliberation for resolving public moral disputes about issues that affect the lives of all citizens. In its institutional dimension, then, the recognition of a *non-public sphere of freedom of conscience and religion*, while it shelters that sphere from unwanted incursions, also *unburdens* the sphere of public debate and deliberation of irresolvable problems, religious disagreements being the clearest example. By taking these matters off the political agenda, a constitution can, as political theorist Stephen Holmes has influentially argued, *enable discussion* about those matters that cannot be removed from the agenda. As Holmes argues, '[b]y helping secularize politics, religious freedoms also help democratize collective life. Legal protections of individual conscience ... do not merely shield the private; they also disencumber the public'.[48] As a consequence, remaining moral controversies are made more amenable to deliberation and compromise in the crucible of politics in a liberal political culture.

But the idea of 'disencumbering the public' by applying *rules of omission* may still be insufficient to adequately capture the institutional and proceduralizing dimension of the right to freedom of conscience. A deliberative conception of that right, on which democratic experimentalism draws, adds the further dimension of freedom of conscience as an *also-political right*: a *destabilization right*. For the idea of taking

[47] ECtHR [Chamber], *Kokkinakis v. Greece*, Application no. 14307/88, Judgment of 25 May 1993.

[48] Stephen Holmes, 'Gag Rules or the Politics of Omission', in Stephen Holmes (ed.), Passions and Constraint (Chicago: University of Chicago Press 1995), 207.

certain matters off the public agenda, of course, always implies the need for an ongoing process of public deliberation among the citizens themselves about the grounds and reasons why this should be done in order to be able to distinguish between those questions that can reasonably be omitted from the public agenda and those that cannot.[49] The content of a liberal political culture must itself be subject to dialogue and ongoing self-revision in the crucible of deliberative politics. It is here where *diversity* and the 'pluralism indissociable from a democratic society' come to matter—not only as a cultural given or a fact of life to be accommodated, but as an objective democratic value to be actively endorsed.

For in order for a shared liberal political culture to remain open to constant self-revision, democratic citizens have an interest in hearing from the other—from outsiders and hitherto marginalized groups. Religious freedom is not only a private negative right but also by the same token can in this sense be mobilized as a political right. In its inward-looking dimension, of course, it protects and assigns value to the *forum internum*, in contradistinction to the political forum. But in its outward-looking dimension, the guarantee of freedom of religion is a political right by giving voice to the hitherto marginalized and despised. The rationale for a morally generous reading of the right to religious freedom is thus not merely to impose a negative barrier against excessive state intervention (by providing private spaces of withdrawal and escape) but to construe it as a destabilization right that creates and sustains the possibility for new views to undermine false forms of social cohesion and closure and to empower individuals and groups to challenge existing institutional settlements—in anticipation of a more encompassing, more tolerant, and inclusive consensus.

Accordingly, this section will explore, against the backdrop of the European experience, the role of freedom of conscience both as a defensive negative right and as an *inclusive political* or *deliberative right*—indeed, as a *destabilization right*—that not only expresses the value of religious pluralism in contemporary European society in the abstract but has also begun to transform multiple spheres of civil society, ranging from schools to private and public employment and to the wider public sphere itself.

[49] See John Rawls, Political Liberalism (New York: Columbia University Press 1993), at 151 (in fn. 16), drawing on Stephen Holmes.

1. Germany: freedom of conscience in public schools (Bundesverfassungsgericht: *Headscarf I* and *II*)

When Fereshta Ludin, a German citizen born in Afghanistan, declared she would wear the Muslim headscarf not only in private but also in the class room, the School board rejected her application to become a teacher in a State school in the *Land Baden-Württemberg*.[50] Ms. Ludin explained that without covering her hair in public she would feel naked; and that to wear the headscarf is for her a way of both expressing her religious conviction as a Muslim woman and of 'being a person' given her specific biography. Ms. Ludin also explained that while she was aware of public anxieties about the headscarf, she did not wear it as a political symbol or provocation or with the purpose of influencing pupils in religious matters. There had never been any conflicts or complaints during her employment as a teacher on probation.

In response, the school-board pointed to anxieties about the headscarf in German society, and argued that Ms. Ludin's headscarf must be considered as a 'danger' to the cohesion of and pedagogic climate in state schools. From 'an objective standpoint', the board argued, the headscarf is not merely a private religious symbol, but must be understood as a symbol of cultural (self-) segregation, and thus as an explicitly political symbol prone to elicit strong reactions of rejection and polarization. In state elementary schools, pupils would be exposed to this symbol at a very early age. And while there had been no conflicts with either pupils or parents when Ms. Ludin was a teacher on probation, her wearing the headscarf in class would have the 'objective effect of cultural disintegration', as the school board put it—'without possibility of escape'.

In Germany, religious freedom is guaranteed by Art. 4 I and II of the German Basic Law. The guarantees, in response to the Nazi past, are very broad and emphatic; Section I reads: 'Freedom of faith and conscience, and freedom of creed religious or ideological, are inviolable.' And section II adds: 'The undisturbed practice of religion is guaranteed.' Thus, the right to religious freedom and to freedom of conscience is guaranteed, under the German Basic Law, without reservation and as an 'absolute right'. Only restrictions which are immanent to the Basic Law itself (*verfassungsimmanente Schranken*) are legitimate.

In its 5–3 *Headscarf I* judgment, the *Bundesverfassungsgericht* held that the school-board's decision to reject Ms. Ludin's application was unconstitutional. The Court's Opinion emphasized the importance of freedom

[50] 2 BvG 1436/02, Judgment of 24 September 2003 ('*Headscarf I*'), and 1 BvR 471/10 and 1 BvR 1181/10, Order of 27 January 2015 ('*Headscarf II*').

of conscience as a principle—a principle not to be understood in terms of a 'strict separation between State and religion', but permitting State-involvement with religion for the purpose of encouraging, protecting, or sustaining religious diversity, in the wider society and in State schools. But the Bundesverfassungsericht refused to say that the headscarf is not a 'danger'. And this refusal carried large legal and political consequences. In particular, it made the headscarf subject to State regulation. The Court majority rejected the school-board's decision solely on the ground that Baden-Württemberg lacked, at the time, any statutory law *explicitly authorizing* the school-board to ban the teacher-headscarf as a matter of danger-prevention. But the Court explicitly left the legislatures of the *Länder* free to produce statutes banning the teacher-headscarf and to decide to keep pupils away from the religious references evoked by the outer appearance of teachers, in order to avoid conflicts with pupils, parents, or other teachers right from the start. According to the BVG, such a headscarf-statute *could* encourage the exploration of religious differences. But, as the BVG went on to argue, the state legislators could also reasonably come to quite different conclusions. They could, for example, reasonably conclude that increased religious diversity generates an increased potential for conflicts, conflicts which schools are increasingly less able to cope with. And within weeks of the decision, a majority of German *Länder* announced plans to pass such laws.

The BVG's Order of 27 January 2015 (*Headscarf II*) essentially concerned the compatibility with the German Basic Law of the *Schulgesetz (SchulG)* of the *Land Nordrhein-Westphalen* of 15 February 2005. The *SchulG* imposed a strict prohibition on teachers to publicly express any 'views of a political, religious, ideological or similar nature which are likely to endanger, or interfere with, the neutrality of the Land with regard to pupils and parents, or to endanger or disturb the political, religious and ideological peace at school'. Without mentioning the Muslim headscarf explicitly, the *SchulG* prohibited any 'conduct that might create the impression among pupils or parents that a teacher advocates against human dignity, the principle of equal treatment, fundamental freedoms or the free democratic order'. But the *SchulG* created an exception for 'Christian and occidental educational and cultural values' by declaring that the public presentation ('Darstellung') of those values did not contradict the prohibition the statute imposed.

In its ruling, the BVG departed from the framework of its earlier *Headscarf I* ruling and declared the *SchulG* void due to its incompatibility with Art. 3 III sentence 1 and Art. 33 III of the Basic Law which prohibit discrimination on religious grounds generally and also with regard to eligibility for public office. To justify a strict ban of the teacher headscarf, the BVG now argued, it is never sufficient for there to be *a mere abstract danger to the peace at school or to the neutrality of the state*. Rather, there always has to be a *sufficiently specific danger* for the ban to be lawful. The BVG was unequivocal in saying that merely wearing an Islamic headscarf does not already in itself constitute a sufficiently specific danger and does not have the effect of promoting Islam or even proselytizing. Only in conflict situations, where the threshold of a sufficiently specific danger to school peace or to state neutrality has been crossed, would it be reasonable to expect the educational staff to refrain from following a religious rule, perceived as imperative, to cover their heads. Because the *Schulgesetz (SchulG)* of the Land Nordrhein-Westfalen had failed to establish a differentiating regime, the BVG considered it to be a 'disproportionate' interference with the applicants' right to freedom of faith.

The BVG provided a framework for a legislative regime by indicating where the balance between various constitutionally protected interests lay.

- First, and importantly, the interference with freedom of conscience had to be considered a serious one: the general ban of the teacher headscarf effectively meant that mainly Muslim women were denied access to the teaching profession and were kept away from qualified positions in ways that undermine the requirement to achieve real equality of women in practice.
- Second, there is no general constitutional right of pupils to be spared of exposure: neither the pupils' negative religious freedom nor the parents' corresponding educational rights are impaired by a teacher wearing clothes with a religious connotation, at least as long as the teachers do not verbally promote their faith or try to influence the pupils.
- Third, a general assumption—unsupported by additional facts—that wearing the headscarf per se signals opposition to human dignity and hostility to ideas of gender equality and a free democratic basic order is impermissible. In particular, such a presumption cannot be based on the fact that there are some Islamic schools of thought which reject these ideas.
- Fourth, interdenominational schools—which are open to all faiths—mirror the religious-pluralist society; and it is precisely their task to convey to pupils the idea of tolerance with regard to other religions and ideologies. 'It has to be possible,' the BVG explained, 'to lead a life according to this ideal, even if this entails wearing clothes with a

religious connotation, as—apart from the headscarf—the Jewish kipah, the nun's habit, or symbols such as a cross worn visibly.'

- Fifth, the idea of state neutrality must be understood as embracing diversity. Neutrality is not a 'distancing attitude in the sense of a strict separation of state and church', but an 'open and comprehensive' one, which is aimed at 'encouraging freedom of faith equally for all beliefs'. In particular, the BVG insisted that there were no tenable reasons for discriminating against manifestations of religious beliefs that were not traceable back to Christian-occidental cultural values and traditions; nor were there any tenable justifications for favouring expressions relating to Christian or Jewish faith. Existing constitutional references to Christianity, in various constitutions of the *Länder*, were meant to refer to secularized values of Christianity only.

Critics of *Headscarf II* argued that the ruling overtaxed the ability of schools for dialogue. But, of course, schools constitute a 'special environment', in John Dewey's words, in which new bases of active tolerance can be learnt and constructed through processes of defining and addressing common concerns.[51] Schools put a headscarf-wearing teacher in a position to explain to pupils, parents, and colleagues both the meaning of the headscarf and the great good of mutual respect and tolerance. Schools, at the same time, put pupils, parents, and colleagues in a position to explain to the teacher (and to themselves) their concerns with immanent restrictions on or limits of religious freedom and tolerance, with gender equality and secularization more generally. Exposure in school to religious commitment can foster an understanding of the reality of modern societies and help pupils, from an early age on, to learn the importance and techniques of mutual tolerance. The protective function of the state is to promote dialogue within schools—not by prohibitions, but by helping schools to construct themselves as self-organizing and autonomous spheres of deliberative encounter and critical contention, as schools of discourse.

A reverse criticism was that the ruling still did not go far enough. For it still used the language of danger prevention and failed to draw the conclusion that the headscarf is not a threat. Even when the teacher wears the headscarf merely as a way of 'being a person' as a Muslim woman and, hence, *not as a political symbol*, a ban is still possible in situations of conflict where the threshold of a sufficiently specific danger to school

[51] Quoted in Michael Walzer, Spheres of Justice. A Defense of Pluralism and Equality (New York: Basic Books 1983), 199. Compare with Michael Walzer, On Toleration (New Haven: Yale University Press 1999), 71 ff.

peace has been crossed. But situations of conflict may not be attributable to the teachers, who, as in both cases before the BVG, were perfectly loyal to the constitution, but to the veto of the most excitable in society who believe that Islam has no place in Germany and who accordingly may generate incidents of conflict to trigger a sense of 'specific danger' and a ban. That—possible—outcome, which is consequence of the language of danger prevention, appears at odds and inconsistent with the very idea of freedom of conscience as a subjective individual right, and there appears to be a remaining inconsistency in the BVG's approach.

2. The ECtHR: crucifixes in Italian state schools

The idea of schools as mirrors of social pluralism and sites of dialogue has also been a prominent element in the *Lautsi* ECtHR judgment concerning the permissibility of *crucifixes* in Italian state schools. The ECtHR here adopted a position different from that of the German *Bundesverfassungsgericht*, which in its 1995 Crucifix-ruling had struck down as unconstitutional a Bavarian law requiring the public display of crucifixes in state schools. The BVG at the time argued that the impugned Bavarian law had created a situation where 'the individual is exposed without possibility of escape to the influence of a particular faith, to the acts through which it is manifested and to the symbols in which it is presented'.[52]

By contrast, in *Lautsi* the ECtHR's Grand Chamber ruled that no violation of the Convention could be found:

> Firstly, the presence of crucifixes is not associated with compulsory teaching about Christianity [. . .]. Secondly, [. . .] Italy opens up the school environment in parallel to other religions. The Government indicated in this connection that it was not forbidden for pupils to wear Islamic headscarves or other symbols or apparel having a religious connotation; alternative arrangements were possible to help schooling fit in with non-majority religious practices; the beginning and end of Ramadan were 'often celebrated' in schools; and optional religious education could be organised in schools for 'all recognised religious creeds.' Moreover, there was nothing to suggest that the authorities were intolerant of pupils who believed in other religions, were non-believers or who held non-religious philosophical convictions.[53]

[52] Bundesverfassungsgericht, BVerfGE 93, I I BvR 1097/91, Judgment of 16 May 1995, para. C(II)(1).

[53] ECtHR [GC], *Lautsi and Others v. Italy*, Application no. 30814/06, Judgment of 18 March 2011.

So, the guiding idea was that schools are sites of dialogic encounter and that state neutrality means that the State must *promote* pluralism and discourse in education as a fundamental feature of a democratic society.[54]

3. The ECtHR: reasonable accommodation of freedom of conscience in the sphere of private-sector and public-sector employment (*Eweida and Others*)

One of the questions before the ECtHR in *Eweida and Others*[55] concerned the open (but discreet) wearing by the first applicant, Ms. Eweida, who was employed by British Airways, of a cross, in breach (at the time) of her conditions of employment, which sought to project a certain corporate image. The ECtHR found that there was an interference with Ms. Eweida's right to manifest her religion under Art. 9 and that the UK domestic authorities had been in breach of their positive obligation under Art. 9 to sufficiently protect that right. Importantly, the Strasbourg Court held that, because of the importance of religious freedom and pluralism in a democratic society,

> where an individual complains of a restriction on freedom of religion in the workplace, rather than holding that the possibility of changing job would negate any interference with the right, the better approach would be to weigh that possibility in the overall balance when considering whether or not the restriction was proportionate.[56]

Taking the view that 'a healthy democratic society needs to tolerate and sustain pluralism and diversity',[57] the Strasbourg Court insisted that the protection must also fully take effect in *private* employment relations and not only in the public sector, in particular as there was 'no evidence of any real encroachment on the interests of others'.[58]

The debate about the legal situation of the third applicant in *Eweida and Others*, a public sector employee, is of particular interest. The applicant had refused to agree to be designated as a registrar of civil partnerships because of her orthodox Christian view that marriage is the union of one man and one woman for life. She believed that same-sex unions are contrary to God's will and that it would therefore be wrong for her to participate in the creation of an institution equivalent to marriage between a same-sex couple. When she joined

[54] For an insightful discussion, cf. Myriam Hunter-Henin, 'Believing in Negotiation: Reflection on Law's Regulation of Religious Symbols in State Schools', in: François Guesnet, Cécile Laborde, and Louis Lee (eds.), Negotiating With Religion: Cross-Disciplinary Perspectives (London: Routledge 2016).

[55] ECtHR, *Eweida and Others v. the United Kingdom*, Application nos. 48420/10, 59842/10, 51671/10, and 36516/10, Judgment of 15 January 2013.

[56] Ibid, at 83. [57] Ibid, at 94. [58] Ibid, at 95.

the public service in 1992 and in 2002 became a registrar in the Borough of Islington (London), her job did not include officiating at same-sex partnership ceremonies. Initially she was permitted to make informal arrangements with colleagues to exchange work so that she did not have to conduct civil partnership ceremonies. But in March 2006 two of the applicant's colleagues complained that her refusal to carry out such duties was discriminatory. In April 2006, the Borough of Islington formally informed her that, in its view, refusing to conduct civil partnerships could put her in breach of its Code of Conduct and might be contrary to the Borough's policy of being 'an employer and a public authority wholly committed to the promotion of equal opportunities and to requiring all its employees to act in a way which does not discriminate against others'. Yet the applicant had never publicly expressed her beliefs to service users or tried to impose her beliefs on others. But her refusal to carry out civil partnerships began causing rota difficulties and putting a burden on others and there had been complaints from homosexual colleagues (but never from users of the service) that they felt victimized. Because of her religiously motivated refusal to perform civil partnerships, the applicant faced formal grievance procedures and eventually lost her job. The UK Court of Appeal concluded that the applicant's wish to have her religious views respected should not be allowed '... to override Islington's concern to ensure that all its registrars manifest equal respect for the homosexual community as for the heterosexual community'.

The ECtHR remained divided over the issue. The Court's majority found there was no violation of Art. 9 ECHR. It observed that same-sex couples are in a relevantly similar situation to different-sex couples as regards their need for legal recognition and protection of their relationship—hence the Islington policy pursued a legitimate aim. The majority then argued that a balance had to be struck between the applicant's rights and the 'rights of others'—that is the rights which the Borough's anti-discrimination policy aimed to secure and which were also protected under the ECHR. With regard to that balance, according to the majority, the Borough enjoyed a broad margin of appreciation which it had not exceeded. Yet the majority's finding that no violation of Art. 9 could be found provoked sharp criticisms by a Dissenting Opinion by Judges Vučinić and Gaetano, who pointed out that common-sense practical compromises could easily have been found which would not force registrars to act against their consciences and allow them to quietly step aside.

4. The CJEU: headscarves in private-sector employment

Is there a contradiction in the Charter of Fundamental Rights of the European Union? The CJEU's decisions in *Achbita*[59] and *Bougnaoui*[60] raised the question of the efficacy of the right to religious freedom—which is reaffirmed in Art. 10(1) of the Charter—in the sphere of private employment.[61] Is a private employer, exercising his right to conduct a business which is recognized in Art. 16 of the Charter, permitted to dismiss a female employee of Muslim faith, employed in a customer-facing role, if she refuses to remove the headscarf at work? Both cases raise the question of how to construe, in the light of these horizontally clashing principles, the concept of a 'genuine and determining occupational requirement' in Art. 4(1) of the Employment Equality Framework Directive 2000/78.

The only—but legally significant—difference between both cases was that in *Achbita* the employing company had enacted a so-called neutrality code banning the display of religious symbols at work, whereas in *Bougnaoui* there was no such code. Thus, in *Achbita*, a case originating in Belgium, the applicant had worked for some time as a receptionist for her employer—a company offering security and guarding services, but also reception services, to private and public customers—wearing the headscarf exclusively outside working hours. When she announced that, in future, she firmly intended to wear a headscarf during working hours as well, for religious reasons, she was dismissed on the basis of a codified strict company 'neutrality' policy which had already been in place as an occupational requirement when the applicant had joined the company and to which she had never objected in the past.

In *Bougnaoui*, a case originating in France, the applicant, who was employed as a design engineer for a company specializing in advice, engineering, and specialized training for the development of decision-making solutions, was told that her headscarf had 'embarrassed a number of ... employees' of a company client the applicant had visited. As a consequence, the employing company required her, 'in the interest of the business and for its development', not to wear the veil on future visits to that client. When the applicant refused to agree, the company dismissed her, stating also that due to her 'professional competence

[59] CJEU [Grand Chamber] Case C-157/15, *Samira Achbita and Centrum voor gelijkheid van kansen en voor racismebestrijding v. G4S Secure Solutions NV*, Opinion by AG Kokott delivered on 31 May 2016.

[60] CJEU [Grand Chamber] Case C-188/15, *Asma Bougnaoui, Association de défense des droits de l'homme (ADDH) v. Micropole SA*, 14 March 2017, with Opinion by AG Sharpston delivered on 13 July 2016.

[61] For a thoughtful discussion of these cases, cf. Myriam Hunter-Henin (2017), Lessons from the European Court's Hijab rulings, at https://www.ucl.ac.uk/european-institute/analysis/2016-17/religious-discrimination.

and ... potential' it had hoped for a long-term collaboration. In its written and oral submissions, the company also placed great emphasis on the fact that the proportion of Ms. Bouganoui's working time during which she was in contact with customers and thus prohibited from wearing an Islamic headscarf was not greater than 5 per cent.

In *Bagnaoui* the CJEU's Grand Chamber ruled that 'a "genuine and determining occupational requirement" ... refers to a requirement that is objectively dictated by the nature of the occupational activities concerned or of the context in which they are carried out. It cannot, however, cover subjective considerations, such as the willingness of the employer to take account of the particular wishes of the customer.'[62] So, the dismissal, as it was based on those particular—potentially bigoted—customer wishes not to be exposed to the applicant's headscarf, was unlawful.

The decision in *Achbita*—where a neutrality code was in place—proved to be more controversial. Employees may generally display religious symbols in the workplace. But private employers may prohibit the wearing of the Muslim headscarf if they have enacted an internal corporate neutrality code and if there are good reasons. A corporate neutrality code does not in itself constitute a form of direct discrimination. But a national court may still come to the conclusion that there was indirect discrimination, if the internal code has been applied selectively, for example, only to Islamic headscarves but not to other religious symbols. But, importantly, the employer's 'desire to display, in relations with both public and private sector customers, a policy of political, philosophical or religious neutrality must be considered legitimate'. Hence, '[a]n employer's wish to project an image of neutrality towards customers relates to the freedom to conduct a business that is recognised in Article 16 of the Charter and is, in principle, legitimate',[63] notably when employees come into contact with the employer's customers.

The CJEU's Grand Chamber by and large followed AG Kokott's Opinion. In her Opinion in *Achbita*, AG Kokott emphasized the 'social sensitivity inherent in this issue',[64] which raised the question of how much difference and diversity an open and pluralistic European society must tolerate and, conversely, how much assimilation it is permitted to require from certain minorities.[65] The fundamental right to religious freedom, as she

[62] Case C-188/15, *Asma Bougnaoui, Association de défense des droits de l'homme (ADDH) v. Micropole SA*, at rec. 40.

[63] CJEU [Grand Chamber] Case C-157/15, *Samira Achbita and Centrum voor gelijkheid van kansen en voor racismebestrijding v. G4S Secure Solutions NV*, at rec. 37, 38.

[64] Opinion AG Kokott, at rec. 2.

[65] Opinion AG Kokott, at rec. 3.

was adamant, is 'one of the foundations of a democratic society ... and an expression of the system of values on which the European Union is founded'. Accordingly, these values 'also have repercussions, at least indirectly, on private employment relations'. And this means that, within the framework of Directive 2000/78, 'it is important to take due account of those values, from the point of view of the principle of equal treatment, when seeking to strike a fair balance between the interests of employers and employees'.[66]

Yet, at the same time, she took the view that 'the application of that directive must not adversely affect the national identities of the Member States' and that national identity must be 'taken into account in the interpretation of the principle of equal treatment'.[67] As she wrote,

> the Luxembourg Court does not necessarily have to prescribe a solution that is uniform throughout the European Union. Rather, it would be sufficient, in my opinion, for the Court to indicate to the national court all of the material factors that it must take into account in carrying out the proportionality test but otherwise to leave to that court the actual task of striking a balance between the substantive interests involved.[68]

And, in addition to urging caution and judicial deference, she also suggested, as regards to those 'material factors' to be considered by the referring national court, that in a constellation where the code required from employees only neutrality in relation to their own religious beliefs, but did not impose on them an active obligation to adopt a particular religious etc. position, '[a] duty simply to exercise restraint in such a way can be expected of employees'.[69] This is so, because 'unlike sex, skin colour, ethnic origin, sexual orientation, age or a person's disability, the practice of religion is not so much an unalterable fact [but] one ... over which the employees concerned can choose to exert an influence. While an employee cannot "leave" his sex, skin colour, ethnicity, sexual orientation, age or disability "at the door" upon entering his employer's premises, he may be expected to moderate the exercise of his religion in the workplace, be this in relation to religious practices, religiously motivated behaviour or (as in the present case) his clothing.'[70]

The Grand Chamber's ruling, in its deference to national law and politics, seems reminiscent of the CJEU's decision in *Omega*. Yet one may wonder, when comparing the *Achbita* and *Bougnaoui* rulings, whether the

[66] Opinion AG Kokott, at rec. 113.
[67] Opinion AG Kokott, at rec. 32.
[68] Opinion AG Kokott, at 99.
[69] Opinion AG Kokott, at 120.
[70] Opinion AG Kokott, at 114.

Court has drawn a distinction without a difference. One may wonder why the existence *vel non* of a neutrality code should matter and dictate different outcomes. As a consequence of *Achbita*, companies are likely to introduce neutrality codes, if they feel under (even only potential) pressure from 'particular wishes of the customer' to do so, and religiously observant Muslim women may be driven out of (parts of) the labour market. A fair and obvious question, then, is why the rationale in *Bougnaoui*—not to bow to the most excitable in society when an important principle is at stake—should not equally have applied in *Achbita*.

My remarks can only be somewhat speculative. Perhaps the Grand Chamber felt that the CJEU, and EU law generally, lack the legitimacy to exert a stronger, culturally transformative role, given the perceived 'democratic deficit' of both. In the absence of an existing EU-wide consensus, the Grand Chamber was not prepared to make a bet on a future or emergent consensus in civil society by simply declaring corporate neutrality codes legally irrelevant even in constellations just as the present one, where the headscarf was merely a personal, not a political, statement—and simply a common occurrence in contemporary society. Perhaps, in a horizontal conflict as the present one, to the Grand Chamber the economic freedom to conduct a business in Art. 16 of the Charter appeared as more fundamental and tangible—expressing a quasi-natural private-law baseline expectation—and as less open-textured, less vague, and hard-to-define, and more easily judicially manageable at the point of application. Perhaps that is what the situation looked like to the CJEU as an essentially economic court. The right to religious freedom then is qualified by the right to conduct a business: In the sphere of private employment, the former can be exercised only within the framework provided by the latter as the master-right.

A democratic experimentalist reading would have come to the opposite outcome in *Achbita*. The inspiration here is a distinctly political-liberal one: personal rights—because of their connection to the democratic principle—are accorded a primacy over economic liberties. Economic liberties are valued, as Thomas Nagel has written, 'not as an essential part of individual liberty but as indispensable features of the economic system … [They are] the consequence, and not the foundation, of the justice of economic institutions'.[71] So, from a democratic-experimentalist perspective, the right to conduct a business is qualified by the right to religious freedom. It is, of course, true that the sphere of private

[71] Thomas Nagel, Rawls and Liberalism, op. cit., at 67.

employment—the corporate world—is different from, say, the sphere of public schools which was at issue in the German BVG's teacher-headscarf decisions and where the BVG insisted that '[i]t has to be possible … to lead a life according to this ideal [of tolerance with regard to other religions and ideologies], even if this entails wearing clothes with a religious connotation …' But *Achbita* invites the question of why similar considerations should not equally apply also in corporate workplaces, which in a similar way today mirror a morally diverse society and are sites of encounter and engagement and of democracy.

5. The ECtHR: full-face veils in the public space

Related dilemmas arise when it comes to laws banning the full-face veil from public places. A still ongoing debate in several European countries focuses on whether wearing the burqa in public was consistent with the rules of civility and of 'living together' in modern western-European societies, in particular, in France.[72]

In the ECtHR's case in *S.A.S. v. France*,[73] the applicant—a 24-year-old French citizen living in France but born in Pakistan and belonging to the Sunni-tradition—submitted that as a devout Muslim and as a matter of free personal choice she wore the burqa and niqab in accordance with her religious faith, culture, and personal convictions in public and in private, but not systematically. But she wished to be able to wear it in public when she chose to do so, depending in particular on her spiritual feelings. She did not claim that she should be able to keep the niqab on when undergoing a security check, at the bank or in airports, and she agreed to show her face when requested to do so for necessary identity checks.

Debate in France had started when the then French President Nicolas Sarkozy stated in June 2009 that religious face veils were 'not welcome' within France. In July 2010, the *Assemblée nationale* passed the *Loi interdisant la dissimulation du visage dans l'espace public*[74] by a vote of 335–1,[75] which provided that, except under specified circumstances, 'no one can, in the public space, wear clothing intended to hide the face'.[76] The ban applied

[72] For a comprehensive engagement with the contemporary French debate, cf. Myriam Hunter-Henin, 'Why the French Don't Like the Burqa: Laïcité, National Identity and Religious Freedom', 61 International Comparative and Law Quarterly 613–39 (2012). For some further background, cf. also Dominique Schnapper, L'ésprit démocratique des lois (Gallimard: 2014), in particular at pp. 145 ff.

[73] ECtHR [GC], *S.A.S. v. France*, Application no. 43835/11, Judgment of 1 July 2014.

[74] Cf. at http://www.assemblee-nationale.fr/13/projets/pl2520.asp.

[75] http://www.assemblee-nationale.fr/13/scrutins/jo0595.asp.

[76] 'Nul ne peut, dans l'espace public, porter une tenue destinée à dissimuler son visage.'

to the burqa, a full-body covering, if it covers the face.[77] The bill defined 'public space' very broadly, including streets, markets, and private businesses, as well as government buildings and public transportation. It imposed a fine of up to €150, and/or participation in citizenship education, for those who violate the law. French voters overwhelmingly, by a margin of 80 per cent, supported the ban on facial veils.[78] In September 2010, the French Senate, by a vote of 246–1, with 100 abstentions, voted the bill into law. The bill was accompanied by an 'explanatory memorandum'. The memorandum considered the full face veil to be incompatible with the fundamental requirements of living together ('vivre ensemble'[79]) in French society.[80]

The Grand Chamber of the ECtHR, by a 15–2 majority, held that the French ban did not violate Art. 8 and Art. 9 of the ECHR because France had to be accorded a margin of appreciation in this matter.

[77] As the explanatory memorandum says, re Art. 4,

> Même si une partie des femmes qui portent des tenues dissimulant leur visage semble le faire volontairement, cette pratique résulte aussi, pour certaines d'entre elles, d'une contrainte. C'est la raison pour laquelle le projet vise expressément ce cas et apporte résolument son soutien à la défense des droits des femmes. On ne saurait admettre en effet qu'une femme soit contrainte, pour quelque raison que ce soit, de dissimuler son visage et de se couper ainsi de toute relation normale avec l'extérieur.

[78] On some of the background, cf. Steven Erlanger, The New York Times, 13 July 2010, at http://www.nytimes.com/2010/07/14/world/europe/14burqa.html?_r=0. The sole opposing vote was cast by a centre-right member of the Assembly, Daniel Garrigue, who was quoted as saying 'to fight an extremist behavior, we risk slipping toward a totalitarian society'.

[79] 'Si la dissimulation volontaire et systématique du visage pose problème, c'est parce qu'elle est tout simplement contraire aux exigences fondamentales du « vivre ensemble » dans la société française.'

[80] The memorandum stated:

> France is never as much itself, faithful to its history, its destiny, its image, than when it is united around the values of the Republic: liberty, equality, fraternity. Those values form the foundation-stone of our social covenant; they guarantee the cohesion of the Nation; they underpin the principle of respect for the dignity of individuals and for equality between men and women.
>
> [. . .] Even though the phenomenon at present remains marginal, the wearing of the full veil is the sectarian manifestation of a rejection of the values of the Republic. Negating the fact of belonging to society for the persons concerned, the concealment of the face in public places brings with it a symbolic and dehumanising violence, at odds with the social fabric. [. . .]
>
> The voluntary and systematic concealment of the face is problematic because it is quite simply incompatible with the fundamental requirements of 'living together' in French society . . . [and] directly runs counter to rules that are essential to the Republican social covenant, on which our society is founded . . . [and], even in cases where it is voluntary or accepted, clearly contravenes the principle of respect for the dignity of the person . . . not only [. . .] the dignity of the individual who is confined in this manner, but also the dignity of others who share the same public space and who are thus treated as individuals from whom one must be protected by the refusal of any exchange, even if only visual . . . [and] goes hand in hand with the public manifestation of a conspicuous denial of equality between men and women . . .

The Grand Chamber's majority explained that neither respect for equality between men and women, nor respect for human dignity, could justify a ban:

> a State cannot invoke gender equality in order to ban a practice that is defended by women—such as the applicant—in the context of the exercise [of her rights], unless it were to be understood that individuals could be protected on that basis from the exercise of their own fundamental rights and freedoms.[81]

While wearing the full face veil is 'the expression of a cultural identity which contributes to the pluralism that is inherent in democracy'; and there was no evidence for considering that 'women who wear the full-face veil seek to express a form of contempt against those they encounter or otherwise to offend against the dignity of others'.[82] The French Government had failed to show that there was a general threat to public safety which could justify a blanket ban as 'necessary in a democratic society'.[83]

But the majority accepted that ensuring the ground rules of social communication and more broadly the requirements of 'living together'—as stated in the explanatory memorandum—did constitute a legitimate legislative aim and an aspect of the 'rights and freedoms of others' within the meaning of the explicit reservations under which the rights to freedom of conscience and freedom of expression in Art. 8 and Art. 9 ECHR are placed.

In its search for a fair balance, the majority, on the one hand, accepted that 'the face plays an important role in social interaction' and that individuals who are present in places open to all 'may not wish to see practices or attitudes developing [. . .] which would fundamentally call into question the possibility of open interpersonal relationships, which, by virtue of an established consensus, forms an indispensable element of community life within the society in question'. Yet the majority, on the other, also agreed with the applicant that the ban 'restricted the reach of pluralism',[84] since it prevented certain women from expressing their personality and beliefs. The majority explicitly addressed the 'complex dilemma' which the blanket ban necessarily caused for women in the applicant's position, since the ban 'may have the effect of isolating them and restricting their autonomy'. It was therefore 'understandable that the women concerned

[81] At rec. 119. [82] At rec. 120. [83] At rec. 139. [84] At rec. 153.

may perceive the ban as a threat to their identity'.[85] Indeed, the majority expressed a strong concern with Islamophobia and warned that 'a State which enters into a legislative process of this kind takes the risk of contributing to the consolidation of the stereotypes which affect certain categories of the population and of encouraging the expression of intolerance, when it has a duty, on the contrary, to promote tolerance'.[86]

But the majority ultimately took the view that the question whether wearing the full-face veil in public places was compatible with the requirements of 'living together' in France in essence constituted 'a choice of [French] society'.[87] The majority accepted the French Government's argument that the French legislature had been seeking to protect 'a principle of interaction between individuals', which it considered essential for upholding pluralism, tolerance, and broadmindedness in French society.[88]

The dissenting opinion, by contrast, rejected the very idea that the general concept of 'living together' fell under any of the rights and freedoms guaranteed within the ECHR. They argued that feelings of fear and uneasiness were not so much caused by the veil itself, but by the 'philosophy' that was attributed to it, such as the 'dehumanizing violence' and 'self-containment' of women 'effaced' from the public space. Yet not only had these interpretations been called into question by the applicant, but there also is no right not to be shocked or provoked by different models of cultural or religious identity, even those that are very different from French and European life-styles. In other words, the right to private life should also be seen as comprising the right not to communicate and not to enter into contact with others in public places—the right to be an outsider.[89] The blanket ban, according to the minority, was therefore a sign of selective pluralism and restricted tolerance[90] and also could not be expected to have the desired effect of liberating women presumed to be oppressed, but is likely to further exclude them from society and aggravate their situation.[91]

6. Concluding observation

The rulings on freedom of conscience by the *Bundesverfassungsgericht*, the CJEU, and by the ECtHR illustrate the role and limits of constitutional adjudication under circumstances of uncertainty and deep moral dissensus. The judiciary's service to democracy, in each of these cases, lies in clarifying the overarching, yet open-textured, constitutional commitments

[85] At rec. 146. [86] At rec. 149. [87] At rec. 153. [88] At rec. 153.

[89] Dissenting Opinion by Judges Nußberger and Jäderblom, at rec. 8. [90] At rec. 14.

[91] At para. 21.

that provide structure to an ongoing and unresolved public debate and in providing a structure of discussion.

In doing so, courts can rely on a kind of social-sphere-by-sphere 'comparative' constitutionalism which compares, and differentiates, not only between national legal orders, but also, and perhaps more fundamentally, between the normative requirements which different social spheres pose against the backdrop of an evolving shared understanding of principle. Schools—as in the two German cases—are themselves sites of dialogue which mirror dialogue in society. The BVG's progression from *Headscarf I—II* can be seen as a constitutional learning process that in part moves along in sympathetic critical consultation with changing public opinion and in part reflects its unresolved divisions and tensions. The cases *Achbita* and *Bougnaoui*, by contrast, raised for the CJEU the question whether the corporate sphere of private employment is so fundamentally different—that is the question why one shouldn't equally say that the workplace mirrors a morally diverse society and is a site of dialogue, too, where the civic virtues of tolerance can be tested and learned.

In response to AG Kokott's worry about the CJEU prescribing a solution that is uniform throughout the European Union, one may point out that the fundamental principles which make up an EU-wide liberal political culture are not an imperial third force overriding embedded diverse community norms but can be seen as a statement of an emergent overlapping consensus among the various—not only national, but 'spherical' professional and civil-society—communities. The Court could have chosen to contribute to the formation of such an overlapping consensus without defaulting on legitimacy. And in response to AG Kokott's argument that a duty to exercise restraint can be expected of female employees wishing to wear the headscarf even at work, because, contrary to disability, skin colour, age, etc. the practice of religion is an aspect of an individual's private life over which the employees concerned can *choose* to exert an influence, one may wonder whether this view is plausible and even realistic. As political philosopher Joshua Cohen has observed,

> Religious views set demands of an especially high order—perhaps transcendent obligations—on their adherents. Moreover, if we see these requirements from the believer's standpoint, we cannot see them as self-imposed—chosen by the agent. [...] [I]f we believe about these requirements ... then we do not believe that the adherent chooses to place herself under these demands. The content and stringency of these demands are

fixed instead by the content of the convictions, which the adherent believes true, not by the adherent's endorsement of these convictions.[92]

But if the stringency or religious views in this way depend on their content, not on the believer's choice or facts of his or her endorsement, then we must also accept that preventing a person from fulfilling religious demands for reasons the person is compelled to regard as insufficient is to deny this person standing as an equal citizen and full and equal membership—a failure of democracy. The fact that this happened in private-employment relations seems immaterial from a democratic perspective and therefore should not have dictated the outcome.

In the ECtHR cases, the self-understanding of the ECHR as a merely subsidiary instrument was influential. In *S.A.S. v. France*, the Court deferred to what it took to be a majoritarian-democratic ethical choice of French society about its collective identity. Even if one disagrees with the judgment on grounds of the view that the modern state should refrain from imposing on its citizens what in the German debate was called a *Leitkultur* ('core culture') to regulate their everyday interactions, the judgment can still be seen as forum-creative: it opened up a transnational arena of public discourse where competing lines of argument can be displayed, weighed, and fought over, and also where, at the behest of aggrieved individuals, the importance of freedom of conscience as a universal principle that radiates into all spheres of life is acknowledged.

All this may not amount to very much, court-sceptics might say, but it is certainly more than nothing: adjudication provides an important service to both democracy and the rule of law by injecting an element of moral complexity and sometimes clarity into public debate which is often short-circuited by resurgent majoritarian impulses and passions. Adjudication succeeds by showing what the stakes, concerns, and agreed-upon principles are—and sometimes where the balance lies. This *forum-creative* role can have a positive effect on public opinion and in this way help the process in which common values develop in society.

B. Freedom of speech and the protection of personality rights

Article 10(1) ECHR provides that the right to freedom of expression 'shall include freedom to hold opinions and to receive and impart information and ideas without interference by public authority and regardless of frontiers'. Article 10(2) provides that freedom of expression 'may be subject to

[92] Joshua Cohen, 'Democracy and Liberty', in Philosophy, Politics, Democracy (Harvard 2009), 243 .

such formalities, conditions, restrictions or penalties as are prescribed by law and are necessary in a democratic society' and lists a number of public interest exceptions, among them 'the protection of the reputation or rights of others'. This section explores the ways in which the problem of fair balance has been proceduralized by the Strasbourg Court—and whether the proceduralization is normatively adequate, and by what standards. To that end, I will more clearly than before distinguish between proportionality analysis and democratic-experimentalist techniques of judicial review. I will begin with a somewhat controversial use by the ECtHR of the margin of appreciation doctrine (Section III.A) and then show that the Strasbourg Court has at the same time begun to establish the contours of a decentralized system of review working under European supervision (Section III.B).

1. The ECtHR: 'The Holocaust on your plate'

Begin with the ECtHR's ruling in *PETA Deutschland v. Germany.*[93] The applicant association—the German branch of the animal rights organization *People for the Ethical Treatment of Animals* ('*PETA*')—planned to start a poster campaign under the head 'The Holocaust on your plate'. The intended campaign, which had been carried out in a similar way in the US, consisted of a number of posters, each of which bore a photograph of concentration camp inmates along with a picture of animals kept in mass stocks, accompanied by a short text. The photographs used were very graphic, showing Holocaust victims at the most vulnerable and degraded: one poster showed a photograph of emaciated, naked concentration camp inmates along with a picture of animals kept in mass stocks; another a photograph of piled up dead bodies alongside a photograph of a pile of slaughtered pigs under the heading 'final humiliation', etc.; others, equally graphic, were presented under the heading 'if animals are concerned, everybody becomes a Nazi'.

The plaintiffs were Holocaust survivors when they were children and one of them had lost her family. They applied, eventually before the Berlin *Regional Court*, for an injunction, submitting that the intended campaign instrumentalized the Holocaust and violated their human dignity as well as the personality rights of dead family members. In its own submission, *PETA* argued that the photographs merely showed disturbing similarities of the treatment of Holocaust victims and animals as fellow creatures but did not intend to debase Holocaust victims and did not trivialize the suffering and had no anti-Semitic background. Due to sensory overload through commercials and advertisements, *PETA* felt it was dependent

[93] ECtHR, *PETA Deutschland v. Germany*, Judgment of 8 November 2012, Application no. 43481/09.

on gaining attention for its cause—which, as it argued, was ethically and morally motivated—in drastic ways.

The Berlin *Regional Court* granted the injunction under the relevant sections of the German Civil Code. The Berlin court considered that the impugned representations constituted expressions of opinion which in principle were protected as free speech under the Basic Law, as there was no indication that the primary aim of the applicant organization was to debase the victims of the Holocaust. Because the expression of opinion related to matters of public interest, it would generally enjoy a higher degree of protection when weighing the competing interests. But the Basic Law puts human dignity at its centre, and the intended campaign had to be interpreted as putting concentration camp inmates and Holocaust victims on the same level as animals. The court reasoned that the decision in this case could not depend on any weighing of competing interests, as the campaign, in its view, violated the plaintiff's human dignity—which under the Basic Law is protected in categorical or absolute terms and hence is considered as 'resistant to balancing' [*abwägungsresistent*].

The German *Bundesverfassungsgericht* confirmed the injunction—but on the basis of a different approach eschewing any reference to human dignity. The *Bundesverfassungsgericht* expressed its doubts as to whether the campaign violated human dignity: the pictures 'merely' implied a view that the suffering inflicted upon the depicted humans and animals was equal. But an injunction was justifiable even without reference to human dignity, as the *Bundesverfassungsgericht* explained. The Berlin *Regional Court* had legitimately based its decision on the assumption that the campaign was banalizing the fate of the victims of the Holocaust and seriously affected the plaintiffs' *personality rights* (*Persōnlichkeitsschutz*) and rights to *personal honour* (*Ehrschutz*). Hence, a balancing—between those rights and the right to free speech—was possible after all. When weighing the competing interests, the plaintiffs' personality rights and rights to personal honour could legitimately trump *PETA*'s right to free speech.

The Strasbourg Court in its own—controversial—ruling argued that the German decisions fell entirely within Germany's specific *margin of appreciation*:

> The impact of an expression of an opinion [. . .] on another person's personality rights [. . .] cannot be detached from the historical and social context in which the expression of opinion takes place [and the Court] observes that a reference to the Holocaust must also be seen in the specific context of the German past [. . .] and [the Court] respects the Government's

> stance that they deem themselves under a special obligation towards the Jews living in Germany.[94]

And the Strasbourg Court added that this assessment 'is not called into question by the fact that courts in other jurisdictions might address similar issues in a different way'.[95]

The ECtHR's reasoning remained controversial, since it seemed to imply that the Court might have agreed to the impunity of *PETA's* campaign in a jurisdiction where the 'historical and social context' was different[96] from the one in Germany. The ECtHR's ruling clearly resonates with the CJEU's ruling in *Omega Spielhallen*, where the outcome did not depend upon all Contracting States sharing the same conception of human dignity and which could be seen as a recognition of 'the possibility—or even perhaps the merit—of value diversity'.[97] But the critics argued that *PETA's* campaign was different insofar as it instrumentalized Holocaust victims.[98] As the concurring—but in substance sharply dissenting—opinion by Judges Zupančič and Spielmann put it,

> the real question here is the relativisation of an unacceptable use of the freedom of expression. [. . .] The [Bundesverfassungsgericht] . . . endorsed the lower German courts' assessment to the effect that the campaign made banal the fate of the Holocaust victims and that the violation of the plaintiffs' personal honour was particularly serious. We, on the other hand, seem to be more 'flexible' and we only maintain that the personality rights (*Persönlichkeitsrechte*) cannot be detached from the social context in which the poster statement has been made and moreover, that the reference to the Holocaust must also be seen in the specific context of the German past.

The concurring (but in substance sharply dissenting) opinion in *PETA* invites the question of whether the ECtHR should instead have stated a general, European-wide, and principled response rather than following the model of *Omega*. Perhaps the Court's majority considered that, contrary to the concurring opinion, a more robust—less restrictive—understanding of freedom of expression *could be legitimate*, but that it was not the ECtHR's role to prevent offense, insult, or social discomfort and to ensure a moral environment of one kind or another.

[94] At para. 49. [95] At para. 49.

[96] Cf. the Concurring Opinion by Judge Zupančič, joined by Judge Spielmann, at para. 9. Cf. also Carole Lyons, 'Just Fatherlands? Judging the Shoah in Strasbourg', in: Dimitry Kochenov, Gráinne de Búrca, and Andrew Williams (eds.), Europe's Justice Deficit? (Oxford: Hart 2015), 383–99, at 398.

[97] Francis Jacobs, The Sovereignty of Law, op. cit., at 108.

[98] Concurring Opinion, at 3–7, 14 f.

The deferential approach taken by the ECtHR in *PETA* may be contrasted with the strong-form judicial intervention by the CJEU in the *Google* case concerning the right to be delisted or 'forgotten'.

2. The CJEU: the right to be delisted

Observe that the ECtHR's *von Hannover* rulings have influenced not only national law but also EU law; arguably, the concept of a decentralized review may also apply here. This section addresses the 'right to be delisted' as a right to control how information about oneself appears online.

Among the questions referred to the CJEU in *Google*[99] was whether the complainant—who was not a public figure—could require *Google* to remove from the list of results, which were displayed following a search made on the basis of his name, links to webpages which had previously and lawfully been published by a newspaper containing true information, on the ground that the information in question is prejudicial to him and no longer relevant. Whenever an internet user entered the complainant's name in the search engine of Google, links would appear to two pages of a regional Spanish newspaper, *La Vanguardia*, both published sixteen years earlier by court order, on which his name appeared in connection with (now long-resolved) insolvency proceedings against him for the recovery of social security debts. The complainant wished these links to be removed so that they would no longer be included in the search results, since the information was prejudicial to him and his business interests and now, as he argued, irrelevant. The Spanish Data Protection Agency, which oversees the dissemination of personal data, upheld his complaint in so far as it was directed against Google Spain and Google Inc., on the basis of its view that the complainant's fundamental rights and human dignity were concerned. Google Spain and Google Inc. subsequently brought actions against the Agency's decision before the referring Spanish High Court.

The case focused on the interpretation of the EU Data Protection Directive 95/46/EC which requires data-processing systems to 'respect [...] fundamental rights and freedoms, notably the right to privacy' as recognized by Art. 8 ECHR and the general principles of EU law.[100] The Grand Chamber, in its response to the Spanish High Court, rejected Google's argument—which, however, had been supported by AG Jääskinen in his Opinion—that Google wasn't a 'processor' but acting as a

[99] CJEU Case C-131/12 (Grand Chamber), *Google Spain SL, Google Inc. v. Agencia Española de Protección de Datos (AEPD), Mario Costeja González.*

[100] Cf. Preamble, rec. 2, 10, 18 to 20, and 25; and Art. 1.

merely neutral intermediary and that therefore its activities could escape the obligations laid down by the Data Protection Directive 95/46/EC altogether. Rather, the Grand Chamber held that search engine operators, by establishing a more or less detailed and structured profile of the data subject,[101] *process* personal data in ways that can be fundamental-rights sensitive. Search engine operators must therefore be considered as 'data controllers' within the meaning of the Directive.

The CJEU's Grand Chamber ruled that the EU Data Protection Directive indeed offered protection to a 'data subject' under the given circumstances:

> even initially lawful processing of accurate data may, in the course of time, become incompatible with the directive where those data are no longer necessary in the light of the purposes for which they were collected or processed. That is so in particular where they appear to be inadequate, irrelevant or no longer relevant, or excessive in relation to those purposes and in the light of the time that has elapsed.[102]

Accordingly, a 'fair balance' had to be struck in particular between the legitimate public interest of internet users potentially interested in having access to information concerning the data subject and the data subject's fundamental rights to privacy under Art. 7 and Art. 8 CFREU:

> In the light of the potential seriousness of that interference, [...] those rights override, as a rule, not only the economic interest of the operator of the search engine but also the interest of the general public in finding that information upon a search relating to the data subject's name.[103]

The Grand Chamber further observed that the meaning of 'fair balance' may

> depend, in specific cases, on the nature of the information in question and its sensitivity for the data subject's private life and on the interest of the public in having that information, an interest which may vary, in particular, according to the role played by the data subject in public life.[104]

So, Google must remove links to webpages that contain personal information unless the public interest in access to that information outweighs the privacy interests of the person concerned. But the ruling was met with fierce opposition.

A first criticism was that the Court got the balance between privacy and free speech wrong in principle: an alleged 'right to be forgotten' opens the

[101] Case C-131/12 (Grand Chamber), *Google Spain SL*, at para. 80. [102] Par. 93.
[103] Par. 81 and 97. [104] Par. 81.

door to private censorship by people wishing 'to photoshop their lives'. With regard to the proper right balance, there emerges an important interpretive difference between US- and European perspectives on the ruling. For example, from a US-perspective, Jeffrey Rosen argued that the right to be forgotten, rather than being a modest expansion of existing data privacy rights, represented 'the biggest threat to free speech on the Internet in the coming decade' and is likely to produce a serious chilling effect on free speech by 'transform[ing] Google . . . into a censor-in-chief for the European Union, rather than a neutral platform'.[105] Moreover, the search engines themselves are spectacularly unsuited to deciding what information is and is not in the public interest and to striking a balance between speech-interests and privacy-interests in individual cases. Thus, in his strongly worded, scathing condemnation of the CJEU's ruling, Robert Post argued that the fact '[t]hat Google is a profit-making corporation no more undermines its role in sustaining this public sphere than it undermined the role of profit-seeking nineteenth-century American newspapers'.[106] According to Post, the Court was severely misguided in seeking to separate the Google link from the *La Vanguardia* website itself. For 'if the *La Vanguardia* website does not violate the right to be forgotten, the Google link ought not be liable'. Members of the public can still find out what happened to the applicant, but they simply 'must pay a much greater price to do so', for example by searching the archives. The ruling's ironic consequence is that it 'does not withdraw personal data from the public sphere; it taxes those who wish to access that data in the public sphere', because the information remains fully available to those wealthy enough to obtain it. 'At the most fundamental level', Post writes, 'what is missing from *Google Spain* is a firm apprehension of the privacy values that the CJEU hopes to realize by the RTBF [right to be forgotten] it has cobbled together'. The ruling's other disturbing consequence is to leave important decisions about privacy in the hands of a private company with strong incentives to err on the side of censorship: '[b]y privatizing the enforcement of the RTBF in Google ... the CJEU has virtually guaranteed that the axiological ambiguity will continue ... But because Google's adjudicative processes remain behind closed doors, because we cannot ascertain what tests Google is actually applying to

[105] Jeffrey Rosen, 'The Right to be Forgotten', 64 Stanford Law Review Online 88 (2012).

[106] Robert Post, 'Data Privacy and Dignitary Privacy: *Google Spain*, the Right to Be Forgotten, and the Construction of the Public Sphere', 67 Duke Law Journal 981 (2018).

what circumstances and in what ways, the actual values that underlie the RTBF created by *Google Spain* remain obscure.'

A second criticism was that a more cautious approach might have recommended itself. As AG Jääskinen had pointed out in his Opinion, the referring Spanish court in its reference had indicated that it had several similar cases pending before it.[107] So, future references from national courts to the CJEU could be expected. The Grand Chamber might accordingly have refrained from issuing a strong statement to the effect that privacy must prevail over free speech 'as a rule' unless the circumstances of individual cases suggest otherwise. Moreover, the Grand Chamber issued its ruling while there was an ongoing legislative process of data protection reform in the EU[108] underway aiming at establishing a single, European-wide law for data protection.[109] The Court might have taken a more cautious approach to allow the political process more time to consider the merits of the issue. In its legislative resolution of 12 March 2004, the European Parliament (EP) clearly recognized that any person should in principle have a 'right to erasure'[110] under the circumstances specified by the new Regulation.

The European Commission, by contrast, welcomed the ruling[111] and pointed out that the scope of the judgment was more limited than the critics suggest: the Court did not rule that the content of the underlying Spanish newspaper archive of the *La Vanguardia* had to be changed in the name of data protection.[112] Those data are still in the public domain and accessible. La Vanguardia published the information by court order in the public interest and should not have to bear the cost of taking down those articles. And the ruling expressly states that the right to be delisted only affects the results retrieved on searches made by the name of the data subject and never suggests that the complete deletion of the page from the indexes of the search engine is required which should therefore remain accessible using any other terms of search.

[107] At para. 7.

[108] Cf. http://ec.europa.eu/justice/newsroom/data-protection/news/120125_en.htm.

[109] Cf. http://europa.eu/rapid/press-release_MEMO-12-41_en.htm?locale=en. Regulation (EU) 2016/679 of the European Parliament and of the Council of 27 April 2016 on the protection of natural persons with regard to the processing of personal data and on the free movement of such data, and repealing Directive 95/46/EC (General Data Protection Regulation) is now, as of May 2018, in force.

[110] Cf. rec. 53 at http://www.europarl.europa.eu/sides/getDoc.do?pubRef=-//EP//TEXT+TA+P7-TA-2014-0212+0+DOC+XML+V0//EN.

[111] CF. Martine Reicherts, the EU Justice Commissioner, at http://europa.eu/rapid/press-release_SPEECH-14-568_en.htm.

[112] CJEU, *Google* ... at para. 88.

Despite the criticisms, one may take the view that the—European—balance which the Court struck was in principle the correct one. When it comes to the effect of standing in the pillory, rightly or wrongly, because of information relating to personal lives being publicized, there's a difference between newspapers, on the one hand—where embarrassing information may eventually lapse into benign obscurity over time once it begins to lose its newsworthiness—and search engines, on the other, where that information remains forever mercilessly present, depriving affected individuals of fate-control and the opportunity to start afresh. Thus, what matters is *what Google*—rather than *La Vanguardia*—has to do, since the personal information, once it is online and copied and replicated over the internet, will take on an unlimited life of its own and forever be instantaneously accessible through search engines at one's fingertips, to the lasting detriment of the lives of those people who find themselves in a position akin to the applicant's and who might, as a consequence of past indiscretions or past wrongs, face a form of social death.[113] The search-results will define one's social identity and also determine the value of one's citizenship. As Eric Posner, in a spirited *defence* of the ruling, has observed, the ruling serves to give people back the privacy that technology has taken away.[114] So the underlying legal-cultural question seems to become whether you trust more the self-correcting capacities of the web itself—a 'domain of actual human meaning'[115]—and corporations as 'neutral platforms', or public regulation.

Yet given the backlash of anti-European sentiment which the ruling provoked, the Court might have been well-advised, on both prudential and foundational grounds, to give political, legislative, and legal debate more time to let a consensus on such a public regulatory framework crystallize.

Consider various elements of the judicial-legislative dialogue. To assist search engines and the national Data Protection Authorities (DPAs) with the task of balancing, the *Art. 29 Data Protection Working Party*[116]—an independent European advisory body on data protection and privacy set

[113] The concept of social death was, in a very different context, formulated by Orlando Patterson in his book *Slavery and Social Death: A Comparative Study* (Harvard UP 1982).

[114] Eric Posner, We All Have the Right to be Forgotten, at http://www.slate.com/articles/news_and_politics/view_from_chicago/2014/05/the_european_right_to_be_forgotten_is_just_what_the_internet_needs.html; cf. also his contributions to the Roundtable on whether the US should adopt the right to be forgotten, at https://www.intelligencesquaredus.org/debates/us-should-adopt-right-be-forgotten-online.

[115] Robert Post, op. cit.

[116] Cf. at http://ec.europa.eu/justice/data-protection/index_en.htm.

up under Art. 29 of the Directive 95/46/EC—subsequently produced a 'factsheet on the [CJEU's] "Right to be forgotten" ruling'[117] and Guidelines on the implementation of the ruling, specifying an operational framework of 'criteria'.[118] Under those Guidelines, the DPAs are bound not only by the tenets of privacy-law doctrine as established by Resolution 1165 (1998) of the Parliamentary Assembly of the Council of Europe (PACE) on the right to privacy—which defines the concept of 'public figure'—but also by the ECtHR Grand Chamber decision *von Hannover v. Germany (no. 2)*. Moreover, the 'right to erasure' is now codified in Art. 17 of the General Data Protection Regulation of 2016 which repeals Directive 95/46/EC. This Regulation cannot be discussed in detail here; suffice it to say that the right to erasure in Art. 17, *inter alia*, in its section 1(a), covers personal data that 'are no longer necessary in relation to the purposes for which they were collected or otherwise processed' unless, as section 3 states, processing remains necessary for a variety of valid reasons such as '(a) ... exercising the right of freedom of expression and information' or (b) compliance with legal obligations or (c) reasons of public health or (d) other public reasons such as scientific or historical research or statistical purposes. The Regulation sets up a complex network of independent national and supranational European supervisory authorities competent to take binding decisions, on the basis of mutual co-ordination and also an EU-wide consistency mechanism (rec. 135)—decisions that may be legally challenged by the 'data subject' affected, either through Art. 263 TFEU before the CJEU or before national courts and the reference procedure under Art. 267 TFEU. Recital 129 states that each measure adopted 'should be appropriate, necessary and proportionate in view of ensuring compliance with this Regulation, taking into account the circumstances of each individual case, respect the right of every person to be heard before any individual measure which would affect him or her adversely is taken'. Thus, in response to changing public sensibilities and new risk-awareness in the public sphere, courts—such as the ECtHR and the CJEU—can begin to identify and specify the concerns about *fair balance* that subsequently lead to legislative innovation. Legislation, too, has a procedural character in that it requires the various actors involved—public and private—to engage in proportionality analysis *outside the courts*

[117] Cf. at http://ec.europa.eu/justice/data-protection/files/factsheets/factsheet_data_protection_en.pdf.

[118] Cf. athttp://ec.europa.eu/justice/data-protection/article-29/documentation/opinion-recommendation/files/2014/wp225_en.pdf.

in the EU multilevel system, with possible effects, as the Regulation spells out, even on third countries. Proportionality analysis in this way diffuses beyond the courts and becomes the *shared discipline* with which actors must engage in order to be, and remain, legitimate interlocutors in the very process of constitutional ordering of a social domain.

The *Google*-ruling and the debate surrounding it throws into relief the question of the analytical distinction between the judicial use of a 'proportionality-' or a 'balancing-' standard of judicial review, on the one hand, and the judicial use of democratic-experimentalist ('proceduralist') techniques, on the other, and provides an opportunity to elaborate both concepts.

Notice, to begin with, that 'proportionality analysis' and 'balancing' can, of course, be applied in a highly judicial-supremacist, centralized manner. The principle of proportionality denotes a multi-stage procedure reviewing courts must observe in assessing the constitutionality of a legislative measure that negatively affects fundamental rights. Commentators disagree about the exact formulation of this procedure and the exact number of stages involved but are agreed that the overall aim of proportionality analysis is to establish whether the legislative goal is sufficiently important to justify certain limitations of a right.[119] That analysis involves, in part, a means-ends test: the reviewing court must determine the purpose of the state act in question and ask whether the state act is suitable (or appropriate) to reach its end. Then, entering the stage of 'necessity analysis', the court must widen the scope of analysis by asking whether the state act under review infringes more on the right than is necessary for the state actor to reach its declared goal—or whether a less intrusive (restrictive) means exists that will likewise reach the state-actor goal. Necessity analysis thus involves a 'least restrictive means' test taking into account the importance of the individual right infringed but still remains within the ambit of means-ends analysis. At the final stage—which according to some commentators can be folded into necessity-analysis[120] but according to others cannot and involves a fresh step[121]—the reviewing

[119] Dieter Grimm, 'Proportionality in Canadian and German Constitutional Jurisprudence', 57(2) University of Toronto Law Journal 383–97 (2007); Alec Stone Sweet and Thomas L. Brunell, 'Trustee Courts and the Judicialization of International Regimes. The Politics of Majoritarian Activism in the European Convention on Human Rights, the European Union, and the World Trade Organization', 1.1 Journal of Law and Courts 61–88 (2013); in the context of private law: Hugh Collins, 'On the (In)compatibility of Human Rights Discourse and Private Law', Hans Micklitz (ed.), Constitutionalization of European Private Law (Oxford: OUP 2014); Duncan Kennedy, 'A Transnational Genealogy of Proportionality in Private Law', Roger Brownsword, Hans-W. Micklitz, Leone Niglia, and Stephen Weatherill (eds.), The Foundations of Private Law (Oxford: Hart 2011), 185–220; Norbert Reich, op. cit., ch. 6 and *passim*.

[120] Stone Sweet, ibid.

[121] Dieter Grimm.

court must strike a 'fair balance' by evaluating, in the light of a context, the relative weight of the objective of the state act, on the one hand, and the weight and magnitude of the fundamental right, on the other. Progression to the final stage of proportionality analysis depends on the law that is challenged having passed each of the previous stages.

In 'horizontal' conflicts concerning civil-society relations between private parties the court must strike a balance between competing values, such as between the right to privacy and free speech. Here, given its open-endedness, the concern about an alleged irrationality of judicial balancing becomes strongest. Those horizontal relationships involve not only a negative constitutional duty to protect fundamental rights vis-à-vis an excessive state but also a positive constitutional duty of the state to protect legitimate interests of the individual vis-à-vis threats derived from private actors or societal forces. Because in horizontal relationships fundamental rights can sometimes be involved on both sides, those threats may themselves be the consequence of an exercise of fundamental rights by one party. Hence the positive constitutional duty can be met only by a reciprocal limitation of one party's constitutional rights so as to protect those of the other party.

Democratic experimentalism brings out the co-operative and institutional dimensions of proportionality analysis and the search for fair balance under conditions of factual and normative uncertainty. Always under pressure from a democratically vigilant public, the parties to the conflict, stakeholders etc. must themselves engage in the discipline of proportionality analysis. But this is not merely a civilizing requirement concerning the *ethical attitude* in which diverse stakeholders should approach a given conflict. Rather, the court will respect the institutional autonomy of stakeholders only if, and as long as, those stakeholders themselves engage in non-hierarchical deliberation and mutual perspective-taking and reason-giving. The stakeholders will typically have a greater 'spherical' knowledge of the context of a conflict and participation enhances empirical legitimacy. With regard to this collaborative reasoning-process, the court will exert a monitoring role and ensure that the deliberative conditions of non-domination—such as the process' openness to participation and the commitment to giving reasons that also others can accept as such—are indeed being met in every round of the discussion. To the extent that the stakeholders do not engage in a practice of reason-giving on the basis of a commitment to mutual-perspective taking, they risk foregoing their autonomy and legitimacy and, ultimately, the loss of fate-control in the form of more immediate judicial intervention. The court in that monitoring process may suggest agendas to be addressed and generalize best-practice and mutually acceptable reasons where they emerge. The process continues in time, often over repeat litigation, and may inform new legislative intervention. Courts enable 'spherical justice', in Ackerman's sense, between and among social spheres, and between those spheres and the public sphere, and mediate between empirical and moral legitimacy. In this way, democratic experimentalism enhances and bolsters the overall rationality and legitimacy of proportionality analysis.

C. Dignitarian constitutionalism: transgender identities and same-sex marriage

The third representative example concerns protections against discrimination on the basis of transgender-identity. The ECtHR here has exerted an *agenda-setting* role by identifying and reinforcing a 'continuing international trend' towards recognition.

In *Goodwin v. United Kingdom*[122]—a landmark case involving the rights of post-operative transsexuals to recognition and to non-discrimination—the Strasbourg Court ruled that the respondent British Government could no longer claim that the matter fell within their domestic margin of appreciation. The applicant, Ms. Goodwin, registered at birth as a male, had undergone gender-reassignment surgery and lived in society as a female. But because the state authorities refused to issue a new National Insurance number, the applicant remained for legal purposes a male. The denial of legal recognition of her gender change subjected Ms. Goodwin to numerous discriminatory and humiliating experiences at work and in her everyday life, forcing her to choose between either revealing her birth certificate or foregoing certain advantages to which she would otherwise be entitled. According to the respondent UK Government, the refusal to issue a new NI number was justified, because the uniqueness—and by implication the immutability—of the NI number is of critical importance in the administration of the national insurance system. But the ECtHR [Grand Chamber] disagreed:

> Nonetheless, the very essence of the Convention is respect for human dignity and human freedom. […] In the twenty first century the right of transsexuals to personal development and to physical and moral security in the full sense enjoyed by others in society cannot be regarded as a matter of controversy requiring the lapse of time to cast clearer light on the issues involved. In short, the unsatisfactory situation in which post-operative transsexuals live

[122] ECtHR, *Christine Goodwin v. United Kingdom*, Judgment 11 July 2002, Application no. 28957/95.

> in an intermediate zone as not quite one gender or the other is no longer sustainable.[123]

In the absence of any 'concrete or substantial hardship or detriment to the public interest' arising from the legal acknowledgment of the post-transition gender of a transsexual person,

> society may be reasonably expected to tolerate a certain inconvenience to enable individuals to live in dignity and worth in accordance with the sexual identity chosen by them at great personal cost.[124]

Because of the dignitarian interest at stake, the Court accordingly attached

> less importance to the lack of evidence of a common European approach to the resolution of the legal and practical problems posed, than to the clear and uncontested evidence of a *continuing international trend* in favour not only of increased social acceptance of transsexuals but of legal recognition of the new sexual identity of post-operative transsexuals.[125] [emphasis added]

So the Court acted both as an agenda-setter and pacemaker as regards UK law. The Court developed a *political conception* of the right to privacy by developing that right into a right to participation and inclusion for marginalized groups where domestic law was found to be deficient.[126]

Observe that the concept of a 'continuing international trend' is key here and of particular interest. This concept straddles the factual and the normative: the Convention both responds to, and influences, changing social values; there is a historically situated constitutional learning-process, of which the Convention is part and which it simultaneously seeks to reinforce.

But, as subsequent case-law illustrates, there also remains deep moral dissensus about the consequences of the step taken in *Goodwin*.

[123] At para. 90. [124] At para. 91. [125] At para. 85.

[126] As Luzius Wildhaber, former president of the ECtHR, points out at http://www.echr.coe.int/NR/rdonlyres/2738F4D8-C03C-4E94-BF6E-CD8E83D9C6DC/0/2004_Johannesburg_Constitutional_Court.pdf (footnotes omitted) with regard to margin of appreciation,

> Without going into details one could roughly summarize the gist of the Court's case-law in this respect by saying that the larger the common ground, in the law and practice of the Contracting States, the narrower the margin of appreciation will be for States that depart from the European consensus, whilst diversity in law and practice pleads in favour of a wider margin. One could hardly find a better illustration of this approach than in the Court's caselaw on transsexualism, which has recently seen some quite interesting developments. In the *Cossey* judgment from 1986 against the United Kingdom, the Court found that the nonrecognition for legal purposes of a post-operative transsexual's new sexual identity did not amount to a violation of Article 8 of the Convention, as the respondent State had not exceeded its margin of appreciation. Concerning the scope of this margin, the Court noted that at that time there was little common ground among the Contracting States in this area and that, generally speaking, the law appeared to be in a transitional stage. Accordingly, this

Consider the Grand Chamber judgment of 2014—the case of *Hämäläinen v. Finland*[127]—concerning same-sex marriage. The Finnish legislation in question provided that official confirmation of a changed gender status required that the person was either not married or that the spouse gave his or her consent. Since in the case at issue the applicant's wife refused to give her consent to the transformation of their marriage into a registered partnership, the applicant's new gender could not be recorded in the population register. The couple clearly preferred to remain married, divorce being against their religious convictions that marriage will last for life. The couple was in a deeply committed and loving relationship: during the couple's history of seventeen years of marriage the assistance and support provided by the applicant's wife had been a crucial element not only for their relationship but also for the applicant's difficult process of transition from male to female. The applicant submitted that the object of her application was not to extend marriage rights to same-sex couples. But the Finnish law placed her in a quandary, forcing her to forego either the right to recognition of her gender identity or the right to maintain her civil status.

The Finnish Government, in its submission, argued that, in its view, the applicant 'rather relied on the social and symbolic significance of marriage'. It pointed out that the impugned Finnish legislation was consistent with a ruling by the German *Bundesverfassungsgericht*, according to which a marriage could be transformed into a registered civil partnership or a legally secured civil partnership *sui generis* while the rights acquired by the couple and the duties imposed on them by the marriage remained intact.[128] Indeed, the German *Bundesverfassungsgericht* had argued in an Order of 27 May 2008:

was an area in which Contracting Parties enjoyed a wide margin of appreciation. This approach was basically confirmed in a number of subsequent cases, all against the United Kingdom. Yet in the recent landmark judgment in the case of *Christine Goodwin v. the United Kingdom*, the Grand Chamber of the Court overturned the case-law on this issue and found a violation of Article 8, relying *inter alia* on the clear and uncontested evidence of a continuing international trend in favour not only of increased social acceptance of transsexuals but of legal recognition of the new sexual identity of post-operative transsexuals. Thus the respondent Government could no longer in the Court's opinion claim that the matter fell within their margin of appreciation, save as regards the appropriate means of achieving recognition of the right claimed by the applicant. In other words, comparative law considerations here had the effect of sizing down the margin of appreciation from the question *whether* to the question *how* gender reassignment was to be legally recognized.

[127] ECtHR, *Hämäläinen v. Finland*, Application no. 37359/09, Judgment of 16 July 2014.

[128] Bundesverfassungsgericht, 1 BvL 10/05, 27 May 2008, para. 49. Cf. the Press Release at https://www.bundesverfassungsgericht.de/SharedDocs/Pressemitteilungen/EN/2008/bvg08-077.html.

> The legislative interest in maintaining the institution of marriage as a union of man and woman must not in principle take a back seat to the interest of a same-sex married couple to uphold their marriage; equally, the legislature cannot unhesitatingly ignore the interests of a married couple to maintain their existing marriage. [. . .]
>
> In the Court's view, it is not disproportionate to require, as a precondition to legal recognition of an acquired gender, that the applicant's marriage be converted into a registered partnership as that is a genuine option which provides legal protection for same-sex couples that is almost identical to that of marriage.[129]

But the applicant in *Hämäläinen v. Finland* considered this compromise to be unacceptable. A comparative legal analysis undertaken by the ECtHR revealed that in those member states where same-sex marriage was not permitted, only three permitted an exception which would allow a married person to gain legal recognition of his or her acquired gender without having to end his or her existing marriage. In twenty-four member states the position was rather unclear, given the lack of specific legal regulations in place. So there was no European consensus.

The Grand Chamber's majority held that there was no violation of the Convention. The majority's conceptual choice of point of departure was that Art. 8 ECHR gave rise to the State's *positive obligation to protect*, and that the complaint had to be analysed from this perspective. This *positive obligation* encompasses the State's obligation to secure to their citizens the right to effective respect for their physical and psychological integrity and may involve the adoption of specific measures to that effect. This conceptual choice was consequential because the Court typically grants States a wider margin of appreciation concerning their positive obligations than their negative ones. The majority agreed with the Finnish Government that the differences between a marriage and a registered partnership are not such as to involve an essential change in the applicant's legal situation;[130] the effects of the conversion of the applicant's marriage into a registered partnership would be minimal or even non-existent as far as the applicant's family life is concerned.[131]

By contrast, the dissenting opinion by Judges Sajó, Keller, and Lemmens argued that Finland's refusal to grant the applicant a new identity card reflecting her acquired gender should be examined as a potential breach of a *negative obligation*, meaning that Finland would only have a very

[129] At para. 87. [130] At para. 83. [131] At para. 85.

narrow margin of appreciation because 'a particularly important facet of [the applicant's] existence or identity [was] at stake'. The dissenters argued that the applicant's quandary was a *genuine dilemma* to which the *Convention itself* must provide a solution instead of delegating the matter to the State's exercise of discretion. Under those circumstances, the applicant could not be seen as having several acceptable options available to her. The lack of a super-majoritarian consensus among States could not be 'the only factor that influences the width of the State's margin of appreciation':

> We submit that the rights and freedoms of others would in no way be affected if the applicant and her wife were permitted to remain married despite the applicant's legal change of gender. Their continued marital relationship would not have detrimental effects for the right of others to marry, or for existing marriages. [. . .]
>
> The only interest in issue is, in plain terms, the public interest in keeping the institution of marriage free of same-sex couples. While we do not purport to deny the legitimacy of the State's interest in protecting the institution of marriage, we do consider that the weight to be afforded to this argument is a different question and one that must be considered separately. In our view, the institution of marriage would not be endangered by a small number of couples who may wish to remain married in a situation such as that of the applicant.[132]

So there was no pressing social need to refuse the applicant the right to remain married after the legal recognition of her acquired gender; a context-specific reasonable accommodation could have been found.

IV. CONCLUSION

This chapter has argued that democratic-experimentalist forms of judicial review can also be appropriate in the domain of core negative liberties and personal rights. The response to the rule-of-law based concern about courts merely following the drift of unfiltered or uncleansed public opinion is that democratic experimentalism can actually strengthen the rule of law. Democratic-experimentalist courts can help bring about a common constitution of discussion by ensuring that opinions are formed on the basis of reasons mutually acceptable to all who are affected by the process of collective democratic will-formation. Courts introduce a further element of normative-discursive complexity into this process,

[132] Dissenting Opinion, at para. 12.

thereby enhancing the reasonableness of deliberative outcomes. Courts beyond the state—such as the ECtHR and the CJEU—strengthen, rather than undermine, the rule of law, understood as the reviewability of decisions of public authorities by independent courts.

But could it also be said that such an approach is contrary to the rule of law and contrary to civility in a democracy? In response, this chapter has argued that even where judicial decisions remain controversial, and mirror (rather than transcend) society's existing normative divisions, *courts beyond the state*—such as the ECtHR and the CJEU—nevertheless can exert a deliberation-enhancing—forum-creative, and sometimes agenda-setting—role. Courts can point to the shared, yet often inchoate, fundamental value commitments in a liberal society and bring those commitments to the fore in public discourse in major disputes over the applied constitutional meaning. Courts enable meaningful engagement between stakeholders as interlocutors and, over time, justificatory ascent. In this way, courts can, sphere-by-sphere, keep deliberation alive and ensure that even the despised and vulnerable are able to remain (or become) *speakers* in the ongoing process of spherical (and ultimately, society-wide) norm-contestation. Initially defensive negative rights—such as freedom of conscience and the right to privacy—are transformed into (also) political rights to participate in dialogue.

Yet courts must at the same time ensure that the vulnerable—people like Ms. Goodwin or the married couple in *Hämäläinen v. Finland*, or headscarf-wearing teachers in public schools in the case-law reported above—do not endlessly remain hostage to interminable debate and infinite adjournment, to the detriment of the substance of their constitutional rights. Courts can achieve this by establishing, even in the domain of personal rights which form part of the classical constitutional essentials, context-sensitive governance or regime-style solutions which provide forms of reasonable accommodation but keep debate open.

Courts beyond the state can actually multiply the sites of dialogue in the multiple spheres of social life and in this sense force reconsideration of constitutional meaning in the various contexts themselves where conflicts arise, ranging from national legislatures to bureaucracies, to lower courts and even in the domain of private-law relationships. They can provide, if you will, a cosmopolitan perspective in the Kantian sense, at least *in statu nascendi*.[133] The dissenting opinion in one of the Strasbourg

[133] Immanuel Kant, Perpetual Peace: A Philosophical Sketch (1795).

Court's free speech cases[134] expressed the idea succinctly: rejecting the view that the national authorities, simply because of their direct contact with the 'vital forces' in their country are *automatically* 'in a better position than the international judge' to make the necessary assessments, the dissenters wrote:

> Whatever these 'vital forces' might be (and they do, in fact include forces which do not stand for human rights), the same direct contact (or vicinity) may have a distortive impact on their judgment. [...] It is for that reason (among others) that the States Parties to the Convention found it necessary to institutionalise an international Court to supervise the myopia of localism. [...] The undeniably better knowledge of local circumstances and sensitivities that militate in favour of the choices of national authorities must not become a fig-leaf for acquiescence in bigotry.[135]

[134] ECtHR [GC], *Mouvement raëlien v. Switzerland*, Application no. 16354/06, Judgment of 13 July 2012.

[135] Joint Dissenting Opinions by Judges Sajó, Lazarova Trajkovska, and Vučinič.

4

Conclusion

Grounded in an analysis of contemporary constitutional transformations in Europe, this book has diagnosed two concurrent, mutually interrelated, and perhaps mutually supportive developments: *first*, a penetration of substantive constitutional norms into private law and the law of civil-society relations more generally; *second*, and concomitantly, a proliferation of weaker-form, 'procedural', or 'dialogic' modalities of judicial review: in domain after domain, there is a spread not only of proportionality-analysis but also of distinctly democratic-experimentalist styles of judicial intervention. At the explanatory level, the book has explored historical-temporal interconnections between both these developments, and suggested that democratic-experimentalist forms of judicial engagement with constitutional law are analytically distinct: they denote a modality of judicial review that allows judges to enforce avowedly open-ended, fundamental, constitutional commitments in a way that institutionalizes—rather than excludes—continuing, social, and democratic determination, through collaboration with other courts, and with legislatures, agencies, stakeholders, private actors, etc., and progressive clarification of what these commitments can and should come to mean in practice.

At the normative level, this book has sought to vindicate these two interconnected developments against two standard objections and critiques. The first critique objects to experimentalist review on democratic grounds as a path to an undemocratic expansion of judicial review or, relatedly, as a path towards a weakening of social protections against economic liberties ('process over substance'). The second critique is rule-of-law based and its objection to democratic experimentalism is that the deliberative turn weakens the basic negative protections of the law by ultimately replacing 'law' by 'policy' or by the transient preferences or opinions of judges.

Engaging with both these critiques, this book has suggested that, counterintuitively, a retreat from judicial supremacy becomes the most promising route towards redeeming fundamental social and personal rights under modern conditions of deep moral dissensus and complexity. But this step would indeed amount to an abdication of judicial role and responsibility (as both critiques fear) unless it goes hand in hand with a moral-practical emphasis on the *proceduralizing*—that is, forum-creative and agenda-setting—role of courts in the process of a progressive clarification of the meaning of a right. Proceduralization emphasizes mutual respect between citizens: for imposing comprehensive judgments about social justice violates the fundamental political-moral duty of democratic civility—of meaningful engagement with (and respect for) people with whom one disagrees. But still, doesn't proceduralization come with a risk of social rights being 'balanced away', in particular in situations of horizontal clashes with economic liberties, as the first critique fears? Engaging with this critique, this book has argued that courts can enhance the inclusiveness of deliberative democracy by requiring explicit attention to reasons by the multiple stakeholders themselves in a given interpretive struggle over constitutional meaning. The role of judicial intervention shifts from directly solving a dispute to supporting the efforts of non-hierarchical deliberation by the stakeholders themselves, often over repeat litigation. Over time, when interpretive answers have crystallized in the light of experience and mutual reason giving, courts can then shift towards stronger forms of judicial intervention that consolidate best practice. In this way, democratic experimentalism opens up the possibility for a gradualistic *constitutionalization* of social rights.

But here the rule-of-law based critique will weigh-in: after all, doesn't this proceduralizing form of *indirect* judicial intervention undermine legality? Doesn't the shift by courts to more procedural forms of judicial intervention amount to a narrative of decline, as Martin Loughlin, a formidable critic of democratic experimentalism, has objected—'a decline in [the] recognition [of rights] as enforceable rights?'[1] If constitutional law expands and if ever more social interests become judicially cognizable as rights-claims, then, so Loughlin claims, '[a]ny strict sense of legality loses its purchase as courts go through a process of examining the public policy justification for interfering with the "right"'. And, as a more far-reaching

[1] Martin Loughlin, 'Political Liberalism or Political Right?', KritV 3, 212–19, at 217 (2015).

consequence, also *politics* is set to lose its purchase: Loughlin is concerned about a colonialization of the lifeworld—a normalization of spontaneous civic politics capable of sustaining a shared sense of collective self-identity and community—through the exponential growth of constitutionalism and of a juridifying, individualistic constitutional-rights discourse: 'Put succinctly, positive constitutionalism's power has grown as its utopian aspects have declined.'[2]

But, in response, the book has argued that democratic experimentalism does not weaken, but may in fact affirm and vindicate the rule of law and legality. The critique's conception of consensus is too limited. The critique assumes that legitimation requires pre-existing consensus. But facts of moral dissensus and problems of interpretation inhere even in the most minimalistic formulations of fundamental rights: legitimacy-endangering moral dissensus extends right into the very core of civil and political rights and into the core of our paradigmatic operative understandings of fair balance. But democratic experimentalism argues that both legality and legitimation do not require a pre-existing actual consensus but a weaker condition is sufficient: a *potential consensus* and the institutionalized practice of deliberation itself can be legitimation-conferring.

Courts provide an important service here. Deliberative proceduralism does not undermine legality. Courts can institutionalize and induce deliberation by acting as instigators and overseers of a non-hierarchical dialogue in which, under conditions of pervasive uncertainty about applied constitutional meaning, conflict parties, state actors, and other stakeholders themselves can reconsider and rethink their initial commitments, internalizing elements of their opponents' antagonistic views and thereby transforming their own. But ongoing deliberation does not mean indefinite postponent of substantive resolution because the underlying proceduralist consensus is robust enough to express a commitment to mutual recognition of participants as stakeholders with legitimate interests. This proceduralist move addresses uncertainty in encouraging joint learning about unforeseen possibilities and limits. It helps legitimize decisionmaking in pluralism by authorizing the participation in the undertakings that concern them and by making a best-practice consensus routinely corrigible. Outcomes are legitimate as long as procedures are sufficiently inclusive to allow citizens whose interpretive views do not prevail in one round of discussion to (re-) initiate scrutiny and revision of shared understandings of the applied meaning of 'fair balance' in the

[2] Martin Loughlin, 'The Constitutional Imagination', 78(1) Modern Law Review 1–25, at 20 (2015).

light of new experience. The rule of law is an always self-substituting element in this iterative process.

The defence of judicial review offered here thus neither amounts to acquiescence in the (seeming) inevitability of current professional habit and institutional inertia—nor to an apostasy from strong democracy. The democratic principle expresses itself in many forms and in various levels of institutional depth. Instead, then, judicial review should be seen as an integral part of a discursively differentiated self-understanding of modern, advanced democracies.

Under conditions of deep uncertainty, which characterize our lives, we may resort to a stance of unilateral self-assertion but we may also address uncertainty in encouraging joint learning about unforeseen possibilities and limits through the mutual exploration of difference. It is this latter choice that *Euroconstitutionalism* epitomizes.

Index